In the Company
of Women

In the Company of Women

Contemporary Female Friendship Films

| Karen Hollinger

University of Minnesota Press

Minneapolis

London

Published by the University of Minnesota Press
111 Third Avenue South, Suite 290
Minneapolis, MN 55401-2520
http://www.upress.umn.edu

Printed in the United States of America on acid-free paper

Library of Congress Cataloging-in-Publication Data

Hollinger, Karen.
    In the company of women : contemporary female friendship films /
Karen Hollinger.
        p.   cm.
    Includes bibliographical references and index.
    ISBN 0-8166-3177-8 (hc : alk. paper). — ISBN 0-8166-3178-6
(pb : alk. paper)
        1. Women in motion pictures. 2. Female friendship in motion
pictures. I. Title.
PN1995.9.W6H66   1998
791.43′652042—dc21   98-2984

The University of Minnesota is an equal-opportunity educator and employer.

10 09 08 07 06 05 04 03 02 01 00 99 98   10 9 8 7 6 5 4 3 2 1

Contents

Acknowledgments

My thanks, first of all, to my mother and aunt for the constancy and generous, loving support that made the writing of this book possible. I would also like to thank Virginia Wright Wexman and Linda Williams, my professors at the University of Illinois, Chicago, for sharing with me their love of film and their insights into cinematic representations of women. Thanks also to Teresa Winterhalter, my colleague and friend, who offered perceptive comments on the manuscript and unfailing encouragement. My appreciation also goes to the readers for the University of Minnesota Press, who provided thoughtful, constructive suggestions for manuscript revision. I am particularly grateful to Chon Noriega for his generous support and advice. Also a note of thanks to my students at Armstrong Atlantic State University, who inspired me with their enthusiastic interest in film and their active engagement in class discussions.

I am grateful to Micah Kleit, Laura Westlund, and Jennifer Moore at the University of Minnesota Press for smoothly guiding the manuscript through production, and to Judy Selhorst for her careful copyediting. Mary Corliss of the Film Stills Archive at the Museum of Modern Art (photos from *The Dark Mirror, Letter to Three Wives, Julia, Girl Friends, The Turning Point, Rich and Famous, Beaches, Steel Magnolias, Desperately Seeking Susan, Housekeeping, Mystic Pizza, Nine to Five, Outrageous Fortune, Thelma & Louise, Mortal Thoughts, Leaving Normal, Personal Best, Desert Hearts, Fried Green Tomatoes,*

The Color Purple, Mi Vida Loca, The Hand That Rocks the Cradle, and *Single White Female*) and the people at Photofest (photos from *Go Fish, Passion Fish,* and *Poison Ivy*) were helpful in locating illustrations. The library staff at Armstrong Atlantic State University and Leigh Ann Williams, our departmental research assistant, facilitated my research. I also appreciate the access I was given to the script collection at the Academy of Motion Picture Arts and Sciences Library in Los Angeles.

Finally, my gratitude and affection go to my husband, Walt, and my sons, Geoff and Mike, for providing encouragement and amusing companionship throughout the composition process.

Introduction: Theoretical and Generic Contexts of Contemporary Female Friendship Films

Genre: The Woman's Film

Mainstream cinema, a term used to describe films that receive commercial theatrical distribution in the United States, has seen a recent wave of films focusing on friendships between women. One need only consider such box office successes as *Julia* (Zinnemann, 1977), *Nine to Five* (Higgins, 1980), *Desperately Seeking Susan* (Seidelman, 1985), *Steel Magnolias* (Ross, 1989), and *Thelma & Louise* (Scott, 1991) to realize the enormous popularity of what appears to be a newly created cycle of films specifically addressed to a female audience. On the one hand, it might be argued that the female friendship film is merely the women's version of the male buddy film that became a staple of mainstream cinema in the 1960s and 1970s. Popular films such as *Butch Cassidy and the Sundance Kid* (Hill, 1969), *Midnight Cowboy* (Schlesinger, 1969), and *The Sting* (Hill, 1973) firmly established the male buddy cycle, which continued to flourish throughout the 1980s and 1990s, represented, for instance, by the extremely successful *Lethal Weapon* series (Donner, 1987, 1989, 1992).[1] In spite of the obvious similarity that both male buddy and female friendship films focus on the relationship between two friends, the male buddy film and the female friendship film are not really very much alike. Whereas the male buddy film typically fits comfortably within the larger confines of the action/adventure genre, the female friendship film is more accurately described as a

1

recently developed subgenre of the woman's film, a multifaceted film genre with a long cinematic history.

The origins of the woman's film lie in the sentimental melodramas of the 1930s and 1940s, and this genre's filmic representatives can be identified by three distinguishing characteristics: they are specifically directed to a female audience, their plots center on the actions and emotions of a female protagonist(s), and they deal with issues of particular interest to women.[2] Although critics often malign older woman's films as "tearjerkers" or "women's weepies," many of them are still quite popular with contemporary female audiences and have provoked lengthy discussion among film scholars. Notable examples of 1930s and 1940s woman's films that still attract substantial attention from critics and viewers alike include *Mildred Pierce* (Curtiz, 1945), *Stella Dallas* (Vidor, 1937), *Gaslight* (Cukor, 1944), *Rebecca* (Hitchcock, 1940), *Back Street* (Stahl, 1932; Stevenson, 1941), and *Dark Victory* (Goulding, 1939). These ancestors of contemporary female friendship films fall into categories that are similar to, yet in many ways very different from, those that distinguish current woman's films. Mary Ann Doane divides woman's films of the 1940s into four groupings: the love story, the plot of which centers on heterosexual romance; the maternal melodrama, which deals with a mother's affections for and tribulations in regard to her children; the paranoid gothic film, in which a recently wed woman fears her husband may be a murderer; and the medical discourse film, in which the protagonist is suffering from a physical or psychological affliction.[3]

These subgeneric divisions of the woman's film were transformed in the 1970s into what some critics have called the new woman's film. This regeneration occurred after woman's films had fallen into a period of hiatus during the 1950s, when family melodramas, aimed much more at both male and female audiences, began to predominate.[4] The new woman's films of the 1970s significantly altered the contours of the genre by dealing with two issues initiated by the growth of the women's movement in this period: the independent woman and female friendship. Films from the 1970s that deal with independent women include *An Unmarried Woman* (Mazursky, 1978) and *Alice Doesn't Live Here Anymore* (Scorsese, 1974), each of which tells the story of a woman's attempt to make it on her own after divorce or the death of her spouse. Female friendship films also proliferated in this decade, notable examples being *Julia, The Turning Point* (Ross, 1977), and *Girl Friends* (Weill, 1978).

In the 1980s, the female friendship film came to dominate the woman's film market. Although other types of woman's films were still evident in this period, they were not produced in numbers even close to those of female friendship films. Films dealing with independent women actually began to die out in the 1980s, or they were converted into more traditional maternal melodramas, creating what might be categorized as the "independent mother film." This development served to modify the more patriarchally challenging aspects of the 1970s independent woman films, which openly championed female independence. The independent mother film modifies the female protagonist's sense of independence by combining it with her devotion to motherhood, a much more traditionally feminine trait. Recent examples of the independent mother film are *Stella* (Erman, 1990), the Bette Midler remake of the 1937 maternal melodrama *Stella Dallas*, *Terms of Endearment* (Brooks, 1983), *The Good Mother* (Nimoy, 1988), and *This Is My Life* (Ephron, 1992). There are also some recent representatives of the paranoid gothic film, which has largely been transformed into the victimized-woman's-revenge film, prominent examples of which include *Sleeping with the Enemy* (Ruben, 1991) and *The Accused* (Kaplan, 1988). The scenario of the abused woman has also become a staple of the made-for-television woman-in-jeopardy film. Television dramas have also adopted plot formulas from earlier medical discourse films involving women's courageous struggles against debilitating illness.

Among the various categories of contemporary woman's films, however, the female friendship film clearly has found the widest audience and the greatest popularity with mainstream production and distribution companies. Interested in the contours and defining characteristics of contemporary female friendship films, which I believe represent an important development in woman's cinema, I will examine in the following pages not only these films' place in the history of mainstream film and in woman's cinema in particular, but also, and most important, their relationship to the female spectators they address.

Theorizing the Contemporary Woman's Film

The nature of contemporary woman's films, of which female friendship films form a substantial component, has been debated by feminist critics, who seem divided in regard to the nature of these films' production, their essential qualities, and their effects on female audiences. Discussions of the films center on two concepts that have been important in film studies since the 1960s but have recently been challenged: the contrasting notions of the progressive and the recuperative text. Some feminist critics welcome the new woman's films cautiously, but with a certain amount of enthusiasm, as progressive forms of popular culture. They see the films as expressing a distinctly female sensibility stemming from the recent influx of women into the production aspect of the film industry and regard them as representing at long last a segment of mainstream cinema that affirms women. Annette Kuhn, for instance, points out that these films offer their female audience the pleasure of identifying with positive female characters as well as with a narrative resolution that constitutes a female victory.[5]

Viewed from this perspective, female friendship films offer not only sympathetic heroines, but ones who have been created by female producers, directors, screenwriters, and stars to serve as role models, validating the self-worth of the female spectator who identifies with them. The heroines of female friendship films also provide images of alternative lifestyles for women based on meaningful social relationships with other women. In so doing, they avoid advocating the submissive behavior that so often characterizes filmic portrayals of women's relationships with men. In other words, the films seem both to challenge male dominance and to provide women with support in thinking through some of the changes stimulated by the women's movement. This positive approach to the female friendship film might lead to the conclusion that even in mainstream cinema, which seems dominated by patriarchal notions, spaces can be found in certain female-oriented film genres where dominant ideas are challenged and shifts in representations of women do occur.

Other critics, however, point to the limitations of the contemporary woman's film's affirmation of feminist ideas and call into question its progressive content. For instance, Lorraine Gamman and Margaret Marshment question whether feminism can really be seen as a significant presence at all in popular culture texts.[6] They see mainstream films as co-opting feminist ideas in order to recuperate them for patriarchy by harnessing them to other discourses that in effect neutralize their progressive potential. The idea of recuperation suggests that radical, oppositional issues—such as ideas concerning sisterhood and female bonding—can be assimilated by the dominant culture so that they lose their critical bite. Viewed from this perspective, female friendship films merely represent this recuperative strategy. They make it appear as if oppositional ideas have caused significant alterations in representational strategies when in fact any changes, if they have occurred at all, are at best superficial.

Certainly, many feminist critics challenge the progressive nature of contemporary woman's films by insisting that any progressive notions they might contain are only reductive appropriations and distortions of feminist ideas. Some are angered by what they see as these films' exploitation of feminism merely to provide fashionable and profitable entertainment. For these critics, the heroines and plots of female friendship films are insufficiently representative of ordinary women's lives, and the problems the films address are rendered in contexts too personal to allow for real engagement with the important issues facing contemporary women. What is most dangerous about the films, according to this critical perspective, is that they appear to deal with women's issues and make it seem as if the problems they raise have been or are in the process of being solved, when in fact they are not.

Consider, for instance, Claudette Charbonneau and Lucy Winer's objections to contemporary woman's films.[7] They argue that by placing women at the center of their narratives, the films seem to present women in a new way, as valuable in their own right rather than merely as accessories to men. However, although they show women working, excelling in their careers, and pursuing friendships with other women, many of these films still follow in the well-worn path of earlier female friendship portrayals. They end by suggesting that women should discount and distrust their relationships with other women and look to men as their true allies. Charbonneau and Winer assert that old prohibitions and prejudices against female friendship resurface in these films in spite of their superficial acceptance of feminism. From this perspective, female friendship films seem particularly insidious, in that they appear on the surface to offer new representations of women and their relationships with each other when in fact they really serve to reaffirm male dominance and the advisability of women's unshakable allegiance to men.

More recently, the notion that one can definitively identify progressive texts and delineate exactly how oppositional ideas are recuperated by mainstream cultural products has been challenged. Critics are beginning to see substantial complexity both in mainstream films themselves and in audience responses. Many observers no longer believe that films offer particular preconstituted meanings to all viewers; instead, they activate varying and contradictory reactions within members of the viewing public. Thus, films can, and often do, trigger responses in different audiences and at different times that range from conservative to progressive. They do so because they contain progressive as well as recuperative elements.

A number of critics argue that contemporary woman's films, dealing as they do with potentially radical feminist ideas, are particularly susceptible to multiple reading possibilities.[8] Those involved in the films' production may view feminism as a potentially volatile subject or as alienating to certain audience members. Because they most likely have no strong idea of their target audience's sympathies toward feminist ideas, or because they fear that these sympathies might be divided, they create films that partake of what Julia Lesage terms "ideologically-implicated ambiguities."[9] They offer both progressive and conservative textual elements to viewers, who are then left largely to construct the readings they prefer.

According to this viewpoint, female friendship films might be best approached neither as progressive challenges to the status quo nor as reactionary props of dominant patriarchal ideology, but rather as complex products of an intricate process of negotiation.[10] This process involves the intersection of competing ideological frameworks held by producers and consumers alike. Because creators and viewers struggle together and in opposition to each other to create meaning from a film text, the intermeshing of these various ideological perspectives can produce a popular cultural product with a very wide address and an openness to varying and even contradictory interpretations. The female friendship film, as an attempt to assimilate into mainstream cultural representations ideas from the women's movement such as female autonomy and sisterhood, seems particularly susceptible to strategies of negotiation. Through a close look at a number of recent female friendship films and their address to their projected female audience, I will examine the complex and multidimensional nature of this negotiation in the chapters that follow. I will discuss the role of female creative personnel in shaping the visions of these films as well as the interpretive possibilities the films open up for their female viewers.

A Typology of Female Friendship Films

In delineating different categories of female friendship films, it is useful to draw on the work of literary critics who have investigated fictional portrayals of female bonding. The insights found in this work can be fruitfully applied to the female friendship film. For instance, Janet Todd suggests that literary female friendship representations break down into five categories: sentimental, manipulative, political, erotic, and social friendships.[11] Variations on these types can be found in contemporary female friendship films.

Sentimental friendships are close, emotionally effusive, dyadic same-sex unions. They are conventionally presented as nurturing and psychologically enriching partnerships that also exhibit a fervent passion that is reminiscent of heterosexual romantic love. Sentimental female friends cry and confide, protest and embrace, and relate so intensely that their friendship acquires many of the signs of a love affair. Although extreme and radical in its expression, sentimental female friendship is frequently quite limited in action. It is often portrayed as stimulating personal psychological growth, but it rarely leads to the promotion of significant social change. Its function is primarily to serve as a temporary respite from the problems women face in their heterosexual romantic encounters.

One can distinguish sentimental from erotic female friendship by the suggestion of a lesbian sexual relationship between the two friends. Although the intensity of the sentimental friendship bond often has homoerotic implications, the sexual potential implicit in the relationship is realized only in erotic female friendships. Erotic female friendship portrayals can take various forms, but by far the most common are the lesbian romance narrative and the coming-out story, in which the female protagonist embarks on a journey that leads to her discovery of her lesbian identity. Although erotic female friendship films often contain at least one scene of explicitly lesbian lovemaking, they sometimes take a more ambiguous form that renders them almost indistinguishable from representations of sentimental female friendship. In this variation, the sexuality of the two friends is left indeterminate. They can be perceived either as very close friends or as lovers.

Works that deal with manipulative female friendship can be deemed anti-female friendship films. The relationship represented parodies the intimate connection that characterizes sentimental female friendship. The manipulative female friend shows the signs of sentimental attachment without its substance. She uses her friend, controls her, and rejoices in this control. The rhetoric and gestures of sentimental female friendship are employed to manipulate the friend for selfish, twisted motives. In these films, an ambitious, intellectually isolated, or socially frustrated woman turns against her female friend, and the relationship between them becomes one of predator and prey.

Political female friendship portrayals involve an alliance that leads to some action against the social system, its institutions, or conventions. These films usually involve low-key female bonding, with little of the emotional intensity characteristic of sentimental or erotic friendship portrayals. The friendship stems not from an emotionally intense sense of connection, but from needs that lead to sociopolitical action. In spite of the emotional force of sentimental female friendship bonds, in terms of political or social action they are most often unable to move beyond unrealized dreams of confronting the institutions of patriarchy. Political friendship portrayals, on the other hand, substitute political engagement for emotion. Freed from the intense intimacy that seems to replace political energy in sentimental friendship, political female friendships are able to move in more socially challenging directions.

Social female friendship portrayals can be seen as the conservative variant of political female friendship. They involve a nurturing tie that does not so much pit women against society as smooth their passage back into it. Through the teaching of female wisdom or the granting of a sympathetic ear, women in these works aid and sustain each other, perhaps by promoting a friend's heterosexual romance or by easing her pain at the loss of her male lover. Although social female friendship does not in any way attack patriarchal society, and even works to facilitate women's integration into the existing social structure, it still challenges articulations of conventional femininity in two ways: by portraying female friendship as an alternative to women's complete dependence on men and by qualifying traditional concepts of feminine passivity.

Like Todd, Paulina Palmer describes two common approaches to female friendship in novels by women: the political and the psychoanalytic.[12] These two orientations also can be found in female friendship films, with the psychoanalytic by far the dominant category. The difference in approaches involves a split between a focus on female friendship as a source of women's political struggle against patriarchy and as an apolitical influence on an individual woman's psychological development. The political approach presents female friendship as a firm basis for the formation of a feminist community, and the goal of the film's female characters is to form a unified identity that will integrate them into feminist collectivity and political action. The psychoanalytic approach, on the other hand, pays little or no attention to the collective, political aspects of relations between women; instead, it concentrates on exploring the personal, psychological nuances of the female friendship bond, highlighting its problematic as well as its positive features.

Combining her analysis with Todd's, Palmer suggests that Todd's sentimental, manipulative, and erotic female friendships fall into the apolitical psychoanalytic category, in contrast to political friendship, which stands apart by virtue of the centrality of the friends' political commitment.[13] I would suggest, although Palmer does not, that social female friendship representations also contain a strong political message, albeit of a conservative nature. As Palmer does point out, this division between personal and political approaches to female bonding reproduces a rift between the personal and political, the private and the public, that is ingrained in Western culture. It also represents, as Palmer further indicates, "the bifurcation of fictional representations of sisterhood and relations between women . . . [that] promotes an unreal divorce between two areas which, as we know from our own lives, are interrelated and interdependent."[14] As feminist thinkers have repeatedly argued, the personal is political, and the societal division between private and public spheres—with women relegated to the private realm of home and family—has served only to isolate and limit female potential. As we shall see, there are political implications to all these films—they are more overt in the categories of political and social female friendship films, but they exist either explicitly or implicitly in all of these works.

The great majority of female friendship films portray sentimental, erotic, or social relationships that fall into the apolitical, psychoanalytic category. They might easily be condemned as mere instruments of patriarchal ideology, inculcating in female spectators a view of women as emotional, irrational, socially conforming creatures who find complete fulfillment in the private sphere of feeling. Many feminist theorists argue, however, that it is important to undertake an investigation of the construction of the female self under patriarchy in order to comprehend women's potential for political action. In order to unite women in a feminist cause, it is essential that one have an understanding of their psychological development, and part of this development involves the influence of popular culture representations of female bonding on women's thinking.

Female Friendship and Women's Development

Feminist psychoanalytic theory provides significant insight into the relationship between women's friendships and the development of female subjectivity by tracing this relationship back to the pre-Oedipal mother-daughter bond. The nature and outcome of female psychological development have been matters of some dispute among psychoanalytic theorists. Freud's theory of female psychology is, by his own admission, "incomplete and fragmentary." In "Femininity," his final essay on female development, he even advises women who "want to know more about femininity [to] enquire from your own experiences of life, or turn to the poets, or wait until science can give you deeper and more coherent information."[15] Indeed, feminist psychoanalysts since Freud have attempted to develop the "science" of psychoanalysis to provide more coherent information about female psychological growth than Freud's theories afford. Their investigations have focused not on the figure of the father in the Oedipal scenario, as Freud's theories do, but on the desire for merging, yet dread of complete engulfment, that connection to the figure of the powerful pre-Oedipal mother involves.

According to Freud's early theory of female Oedipal development, the girl's Oedipus complex is "much simpler" than the boy's and "seldom goes beyond the taking of her mother's place and the adopting of a feminine attitude towards her father."[16] In other words, Freud initially argued that a girl's first and only love object is her father, and her initial attitude toward her mother is one of jealousy and resentment. Later, however, he suggested that female Oedipal development is more complex than his early theory indicated, that the girl's first love object is actually her mother, and that the shift to the father is so difficult that many women never successfully weather the Oedipal transformation. For Freud, a successful change of objects from mother to father occurs as a result of the female version of the castration complex, the girl's recognition of herself, and by implication of all women, including her mother, as castrated. Her resulting desire for a penis (penis envy) and conviction that it can be symbolically obtained by having a child with her father lead her to transfer her love to him and to attempt to take her mother's place in his affections. This Freudian account posits a difficult, but clear and irremediable, break with the mother and a definite switch to the father as love object for the girl.

Recent feminist psychoanalytic thinkers have built on Freud's notion of the pre-Oedipal mother as the first object of childhood affection, but they have rejected penis envy as effectively breaking the initial mother-daughter bond.[17] They stress, instead, the extremely powerful, enduring attraction/repulsion relationship to the mother and the female child's inability to break this bond entirely. Nancy Chodorow, for example, argues that children of both sexes take their mother as their first love object in the pre-Oedipal period. According to Chodorow, there is a crucial difference, however, between a mother's attachment to a female child and her attachment to a male child. A heterosexual mother will become narcissistically attached to a daughter and anaclitically attached to a son. As a result of this narcissistic maternal bond, the female ego develops less rigid boundaries, a less insistent self/other distinction, and the female sense of identity is based on a feeling of similarity with one's mother, whereas the male sense of self is predicated on otherness, on difference from her.[18]

Chodorow also posits a fear of the omnipotent mother from whom both males and females seek to escape. Again, she insists, however, that the son and daughter have different experiences of powerlessness in relation to their mother, because the son has been cathected as sexual other, whereas the daughter has been cathected narcissistically. According to Chodorow, the girl's primary attachment to her mother is never broken; she merely adds a bond with her father to this original involvement. This bonding is triggered not by penis envy, as Freud insists, but by the father's encouragement of the daughter to make him a love object and by the child's desire to flee from the dependence and merging that characterize the primary love relationship with the mother. Chodorow suggests that the girl sees her relationship with her father as a means of attaining autonomy and independence, but adds that this turn to her father always involves a "looking back at her mother," rather than a complete rejection of her. According to Chodorow, "A girl is likely to maintain both her parents as love objects and rivals throughout the Oedipal period."[19]

Chodorow goes on to claim that as a result of this double attachment to both father and mother, heterosexuality fails to gain an exclusive grip on the female psyche. Adult heterosexual relationships fail to meet entirely women's emotional needs. Men, she argues, are always of secondary importance emotionally to women and represent an intervention in the unconscious mother-daughter unity. Whereas a man's attachment to a woman re-creates his unconscious relation to his mother, a woman's relation to a man does not reconnect her to her mother. As a result, according to Chodorow, women look to children to re-create the exclusive symbiotic mother-child bond and to provide the emotional intensity that they truly desire in their relationships.[20]

Chodorow's theories have been criticized on several counts. First of all, they are said to focus too heavily on internal psychic dynamics and not enough on external societal organization as the primary source of women's oppression. Second, Chodorow presents her ideas as universal constructs, when in fact they apply most persuasively to the Western, middle-class, white, heterosexual family. Third, the concept of coparenting that she proposes as a possible solution to developmental problems ignores the fact that even with shared parenting, other societal constructs that denigrate women and idealize men will still be in place. The idea of coparenting represents a questionable solution to long-standing patriarchal structures of male dominance and female subordination. Finally, Chodorow's valorization of feminine nurturance as a means of social transformation seems to encourage a narcissistic discourse of female self-affirmation that blindly champions a monolithic feminine identity and ignores differences among women.[21]

Although these problems are significant, they do not invalidate Chodorow's important recognition of specifically feminine homosocial and homoerotic desires stemming from the close mother-daughter bond. Her theories question Freud's previously unchallenged privileging of the father in the child's identity formation and his positing of a dichotomy in psychic development between objects of desire and objects of identification. Chodorow's work suggests that in the case of female self-formation the two types of objects may be conflated in the figure of the pre-Oedipal mother.

Other theorists have expanded upon Chodorow's work, emphasizing the effect of early female development on women's adult friendships. Jane Flax, for instance, stresses the female child's twin needs for autonomy and relatedness.[22] She suggests that what women want in intimate relationships is both nurturance and independence, and that the genesis of these dual needs can be traced to the mother-daughter bond. According to Flax, the most important tasks in a child's first years of life are separation and individuation from a state of symbiosis with a primary caretaker, usually the child's mother. Separation entails the establishment of a firm sense of differentiation from this maternal figure in terms of the child's physical and mental boundaries. Individuation involves the development of a range of characteristics, skills, and personality traits that are uniquely one's own. In order for this process to proceed smoothly, the mother must be emotionally available to the child in a constant, reasonably conflict-free way in the initial symbiotic state. When differentiation and separation begin to take effect, however, she must willingly sacrifice mother-child symbiosis to allow the child to take pleasure in her or his new skills and developing capacities as a separate person.[23]

As Flax points out, there are several reasons this developmental process is more difficult for daughters than for sons. First, in the symbiotic state mothers tend to identify very closely with their daughters, without a definitive sense of physical boundaries between them. The mother-daughter bond also may reactivate unresolved conflicts from the mother's own infantile developmental process, and the homophobic and patriarchal nature of our society tends to make women value and feel more comfortable with feelings of closeness to a son than with such feelings for a daughter.[24] As a result, it is difficult for a mother to be emotionally available to a female child during the differentiation/individuation process.

According to Flax, the effect of this situation on female development can be devastating. As differentiation/individuation progresses, the female child may feel a lack of support from her mother for the breaking of the symbiotic bond between them. At the final stage of individuation, rapprochement, a male child can turn from his seemingly omnipotent and all-engulfing mother to identification with his father as a way to form an autonomous ego. A girl cannot use this means of building her sense of power and autonomy. Also, a boy is rewarded for the renunciation of his infantile wishes by the promise of another mother figure in an adult heterosexual partner.[25] A girl is simply left to see her needs for nurturance and autonomy continuously collide. As a result, she never attains complete individuation and separation from her mother.

Flax outlines the effects of this developmental scenario on adult female friendships in ways that are only suggested by Chodorow. Flax asserts that women can heal the pain suffered during their psychic development through adult relationships with other women that offer both nurturance and independence. As a result, female friendship is an extremely important aspect of women's lives, with the potential to heal or reactivate early psychic wounds. Women's friendships involve an intensity and depth not found in their relationships with men. When female friendship succeeds in providing nurturance and autonomy, it can be a life-enhancing experience, but when it fails to nurture a woman's sense of self, it can create feelings of profound rage, hurt, and betrayal that stem from the intensity of the mother-daughter bond.[26]

According to Flax, adult female friendships inherit from the mother-daughter relationship an importance and intensity in women's lives, as well as all the problems inherent in a reactivation of childhood experiences. The euphoria and commonality that characterize the symbiotic state of mother-daughter fusion are revisited, but also stimulated are fears of engulfment by an all-powerful mother whose nurturance can be perceived as contingent upon the child's relinquishment of autonomy. The "paradox within female development" can lead to the paradox of female friendship: "an overidentification with the mother" and a need for her nurturance "can mask a deep rage toward her, and by extension toward all women," especially those who in any way act to thwart one's wishes for autonomy.[27]

Many women feel uncomfortable with the idea of a strong connection between female friendship and childhood mother-daughter bonding. They see the connection as reducing women's adult relationships to the level of infantile regression and thus reflecting the patriarchal denigration of female relationships. Some lesbian theorists have found particularly offensive the pathologizing of lesbian relationships as recreations of the infantile mother-daughter bond or as enactments of incestuous desire. Yet it seems vital to be able to analyze female relationships from a psychoanalytic perspective as suitably displaced mother-daughter unions, just as male heterosexual relationships are often studied as displaced desire for the lost mother. There is no reason these analyses of women's relationships should be any more pathologizing or invalidating than connections made between boys' Oedipal desires and their later adult love relationships.

Fictional Portrayals of Female Friendship and the Mother-Daughter Bond

Drawing on the conception of female friendship as a reactivation of childhood mother-daughter bonding, Elizabeth Abel and Judith Kegan Gardiner have developed typologies of relational behavior patterns that they believe characterize the female friendship situation and have applied these typologies to fictional female friendship portrayals.[28] Abel argues that fictional representations of relationships between women, like real-life female friendships, offer readers a fluid, nonhierarchical empathic bond that has a significant affinity with the therapeutic analytic situation. Female friendship, like psychoanalytic therapy, "generate[s] understanding through intimacy and the collaborative construction of meaning from experience."[29]

According to Abel, the relationship between these two modes of interaction, female friendship and therapy, clarifies the particular dynamics of fictional representations of female friendship. Fictional female friends adopt roles similar to those of analyst and patient. By trying to know and understand her female friend, a woman comes to know herself, and through this self-knowledge she can begin to understand not only her friend's situation, but her own. In other words, identification in female friendship is a means of mutual recognition and interpretation. It becomes "a self-reflexive enterprise as each psyche gains definition through relation to the other."[30]

This interpretive process requires the projection of the self onto the other and a consequent reshaping of one's own identity. Abel calls this a "mirroring relationship," because it involves a blurring of ego boundaries between two female alter egos that refines and clarifies both friends' self-images. According to Abel, this mirroring situation allows literary portrayals of women's relationships ultimately to extend beyond the specific concerns of female friendship. The friendship's intimacy dramatizes the importance of imaginative empathic identification to psychological and moral growth.[31] Friendship becomes a vehicle of self-knowledge, a uniquely valuable relationship attainable only with another version of the self.

Gardiner takes Abel's ideas a step further, proposing that the concept of self-definition through female friendship extends out from the characters in a novel to the relationship between text and reader. For Gardiner, fictional portrayals of female friendship promise that women's identities can be fully formed through "a continuing process of give-and-take that recreates both self and other in a supportive collective or community of women."[32] This promise is not confined to the characters in the work alone. The reader is invited to join in this self-creation by interacting with the text and its characters in order to attain greater self-understanding.

Using terminology drawn from self-psychology, Gardiner proposes different types of therapeutic narcissistic transference relationships that can be replicated in the female friendship bond: mirroring, idealizing, and twinship transferences. All of these transference relationships replicate early bonds between parent and child. The mirroring transference involves the parent empathically reflecting the child's displays of achievement while at the same time "non-traumatically deflat[ing] her or his archaic illusions of grandiose power."[33] This transference relationship leads the child to positive self-esteem and realistic goals and ambitions. The idealizing transference situation can take two possible forms: the admiring child may imitate and attempt to merge with an idealized parental figure, or a rebellious child may flee from parental ideals only to find him- or herself formed by the very ideals he or she rebels against. The final transference situation, the twinship transference, differs from the other two in that it is not formed with a parental figure; instead, it provides a way for the child to escape the parental bond through a relationship with an alter ego who provides needed confirmation of a shared commonality.[34]

The implications of Gardiner's theories are significant for an examination of a woman-oriented film cycle such as the female friendship film because they point to the major effects that films of this type can have on women's lives and to the importance of studying the films' intended effects on their female audience. The different types of transference relationships that Gardiner describes are applicable to female friendship portrayals in film as well as in literature. A filmic female friend can become a mirror, ideal, or twin for another character, and the empathic, nonjudgmental support for self-development found in female friendship can be portrayed as instrumental in structuring the deepest layers of female personality. If the female bonding that takes place on the screen in a female friendship film reaches out to involve the female viewer in the transference situations enacted by the film's characters, the effects of the film in reshaping and reinforcing the identities of its female viewers may be profound.

Female Friendship Films and Female Spectatorship

The theorization of mainstream film's effects on its female spectators has had a long and contested history. To trace this history is to turn, first of all, to a groundbreaking 1975 article by Laura Mulvey that actually denies the existence of any implied female spectator in mainstream film at all. In "Visual Pleasure and Narrative Cinema," Mulvey articulates her now famous, or infamous, pronouncement that in Hollywood cinema the gaze is male.[35] She argues for the deep-rooted nature of patriarchal ways of viewing narrative films and for the intimate connections among the male gaze, the patriarchal unconscious, and spectatorial pleasure. For Mulvey, the spectator position offered by Hollywood cinema is masculine, with female characters positioned merely as objects of male desire. From the perspective of male characters with whom the spectator is encouraged to identify, the sight of the female body evokes castration anxiety. To counteract this evocation, two means are employed: fetishistic scopophilia, or disavowal of castration by the substitution of a fetishized female object for the feared object; and sadistic voyeurism, or the investigation of the feared female object in order to reenact the original trauma, reassert control (usually by punishment), and thereby disavow castration.[36]

Mulvey's article has been extremely influential in two ways: it not only raised the crucial questions of pleasure, spectatorship, and gender identity in mainstream cinema, it also drew these terms together into a relational whole. In addition, Mulvey's ideas posed a significant challenge to a feminist theorization of female spectatorship. Her monolithic conception of the workings of the Hollywood system seems to condemn its female spectator to a position of silence, masochism, and absorption within male fantasy.

Where could feminist critics go from here, and who, in fact, was this female spectator that Mulvey introduced, then denied, and that feminist critics have since been trying to theorize? As ideas about female spectatorship continued to be formulated, it became increasingly clear that the female spectator being discussed was not the actual viewer sitting in the audience (the empirical spectator), but the textually created spectator, what in literary studies would be called the implied reader. As Mary Ann Doane explains: "I have never thought of the female spectator as synonymous with the woman sitting in front of the screen, munching her popcorn. . . . It is a concept which is totally foreign to the epistemological framework of the new ethnographic analysis of audiences. . . . The female spectator is a concept, not a person."[37] Or as Giuliana Bruno suggests, the female spectator is "an effect of discourse, a position, a hypothetical site of address of the filmic discourse."[38] After Mulvey foregrounded the existence of this spectator, or for Mulvey really her virtual nonexistence, feminist critics attempted to theorize the textual construction of this female spectator more thoroughly.

This project was first undertaken by Mulvey herself in an essay titled "Afterthoughts on 'Visual Pleasure and Narrative Cinema' Inspired by *Duel in the Sun.*"[39] Rethinking the idea of Hollywood cinema as a monolithic apparatus uniformly producing male subject positions and excluding female ones, Mulvey proposes, instead, a theory of female spectatorship that involves an oscillation between masculine and feminine poles of spectator positioning. Based on the Freudian theory of the girl's movement through a masculine phallic phase to the acceptance of a feminine sexual identity, Mulvey's argument posits a greater tendency for female spectators to adopt bisexual identifications. The female spectator is said to oscillate between identification with the female image and identification with the male figure of active looking and desire. In other words, active female spectatorship involves masculinization, and although the female audience may be "restless in its transvestite clothes,"[40] as Mulvey suggests, it really has no alternative but passive identification with its own cinematic objectification, with what Mulvey terms "to-be-looked-at-ness."[41]

Teresa de Lauretis transformed the concept of female spectatorship from oscillation to double identification, simultaneous alignment with an active masculine gaze and figure of narrative movement and with a passive feminine image and figure of narrative closure.[42] This double identification, however, does not make mainstream cinema any less patriarchal than it is in Mulvey's formulation, because de Lauretis still insists that visual as well as narrative pleasure in Hollywood film is male. The traditional Hollywood film narrative, according to de Lauretis, reactivates the male Oedipal scenario, which produces spectatorial pleasure through the working out of male desire. This Oedipal drama offers a situation in which the male spectator "creates and recreates *himself* out of an abstract or purely symbolic other."[43] In order for this drama to take place, this other must itself be created. As de Lauretis proposes, filmic narratives act not only to resolve male Oedipal anxieties but also to work out the female Oedipal drama in a way beneficial to patriarchy. "In other words, women *must either* consent *or* be seduced into consenting to femininity . . . for women's consent may not be gotten easily, but is finally gotten, and has been for a long time, as much by rape and economic coercion as by the more subtle and lasting effects of ideology, representation, and identification."[44]

Mary Ann Doane argues not for oscillation or double identification, but for overidentification. According to Doane, mainstream film offers a female spectator position that allows women only one alternative: a narcissistic overidentification with the image of their like projected on the screen. As Doane sees it, "The female look demands a becoming," and as a result does not possess the distance that characterizes the voyeuristic male gaze: "For the female spectator, there is a certain over-presence of the image—she is the image."[45] This lost distance, Doane argues, might be recoverable if women as presented in film were perceived differently. Drawing on Joan Riviere's concept of femininity as masquerade, Doane advocates a perception of cinematic femaleness as "excess." This filmic "flaunting" of femininity could be used to achieve the distance lacking in dominant cinematic constructions and might allow for the "denial of the production of femininity as closeness, as presence-to-itself, as precisely imagistic."[46]

Finally, Linda Williams suggests that certain female-oriented genres attempt to create a multiply identified female spectator. According to Williams, many woman's films engage their female audience by appealing to the multiplicity of psychological and social particularities that characterize women's subcultural experience under patriarchy. They have "reading positions structured into their texts that demand a female reading competence" based on women's traditional social roles as wives, mothers, daughters, housekeepers, and caretakers.[47] The many and contradictory roles that women are expected to play in patriarchical society prepare them for the multiple identification that female-oriented genres demand. Williams believes that female spectators view woman's films dialectically from a variety of different, even contradictory, subject positions, and that as a result they come to identify with contradiction itself rather than with a single character's controlling viewpoint. The female spectator is able to "alternate between a number of conflicting points of view, none of which can be satisfactorily reconciled."[48]

Some critics have called into question the very idea of gendered spectatorship as a useful concept in film studies. Gaylin Studlar, for instance, as early as 1988 offered a masochistic model of spectatorship that involves a nongendered spectatorial desire to fuse and be dominated rather than to control and dominate.[49] More recent models of spectatorship by Miriam Hansen and David Rodowick have moved toward a notion of bisexual vacillation between masculine and feminine positions taken up by spectators regardless of actual gender, and Elizabeth Cowie argues for a flexibility of spectator positioning in film viewing based on the similarity between film and fantasy.[50] Cowie proposes that film, like fantasy, offers multiple subject positions of cross-gender identification that are available to viewers of both sexes. These models pose a significant problem for feminist criticism. If spectatorship is really a free-floating, autonomous smorgasbord of offered identifications, then sexual difference may not even be an issue of determining significance in the cinematic viewing experience.

Certainly, many aspects of the spectator-text relationship can be theorized without reference to the spectator's gender. Murray Smith, for instance, proposes that a structure of sympathy operates within a text to guide all viewers, regardless of gender, in their engagement with its characters. This structure of sympathy includes three distinct elements: recognition, alignment, and allegiance. Recognition involves the various ways in which a text allows its viewer to recognize its characters by perceiving "a set of textual elements, in film typically cohering around the image of a body, as an individuated and continuous human agent."[51] Alignment situates the spectator in regard to characters and includes two interlocking functions: spatiotemporal attachment (the spectators' connection to a certain character or characters whose actions seem to lead the way through the narrative) and subjective access (the degree of knowledge the spectator has about what a character is thinking and feeling). Finally, allegiance involves the text's creation of its own moral system, which influences the spectator's evaluation of a character's moral status.[52]

Smith proposes that this structure of sympathy is supplemented by an interconnected structure of empathy. Sympathetic reactions to characters involve what Smith calls "acentral imagining," understanding the character and situation represented and reacting emotionally to the thought of that character in that situation. Empathy, on the other hand, he defines as "central imagining," actually adopting the point of view and mental state of a character.[53] According to Smith, empathic responses are brought about by one of two functions: emotional simulation or motor and affective mimicry. Emotional simulation involves imaginatively projecting oneself into a character's situation and hypothesizing the emotions that character is experiencing. Smith believes this most commonly occurs when the audience is given limited information about a narrative situation and therefore must adopt a character's point of view in order to predict resulting behavior. Whereas emotional simulation is voluntary, motor and affective mimicry is not. It relies on the spectator's reflexive simulation of the emotions perceived as experienced by a character through facial and bodily cues.[54]

These non-gender-specific influences on spectatorial response are undoubtedly important for the analysis of textual methods of audience engagement, but they should not be regarded as completely invalidating the idea of gendered spectatorship. The very fact that certain types of films and stars attract gender-specific audiences suggests that gender cannot be ignored in an evaluation of a film's appeal to its viewers. Certainly, in a film cycle such as the female friendship film, where the address is specifically to a female audience, the issue of gendered spectatorship seems unquestionably pertinent. In fact, a female-oriented genre would appear to be a privileged site for the interrogation and application of just such a concept.

Another related area where the idea of gendered spectatorship seems pertinent is in the determination of the relationship between female viewing behavior and the attractions of female stars. Jackie Stacey recently conducted an ethnographic study of British female viewers' responses to Hollywood stars of the 1940s and 1950s, and her theoretical conclusions offer additional ways to approach the female spectator-text relationship and its construction in female-oriented film cycles. Whereas many psychoanalytic theorists insist that identification, and specifically cinematic identification, can only reinforce already existing spectator identities, Stacey suggests that spectator-star relationships can also change these identities. The responses of Stacey's female interviewees show that while watching films, female spectators are involved in a constant process of transformation. Their film viewing experiences facilitate the combination of their existing identities with desired self-images associated with admired female stars.[55] A similar process can take place in female friendship films, as women viewers are encouraged to alter their identities in accord with the identity transformations enacted by the films' female characters.

Stacey's most significant proposal is her theorization of relationships between female spectators and female stars as forms of intimacy between women that involve identification and desire simultaneously. Stacey sees in these relationships no direct articulation of homosexual object choice, yet she still perceives a distinctly homoerotic element. This aspect, she believes, is more than the expression of identification devoid of erotic pleasure or desire. For Stacey, the intensity and intimacy found in the relationship between female spectator and female star involves much more than the spectator's mere desire to become the star. Articulated in this intense, intimate bond is a "homoerotic pleasure in which the boundary between self and ideal produces an endless source of fascination."[56]

The female friendship film would seem to offer exactly this sort of homoerotic pleasure as "an endless source of fascination" to its female viewers. If the relationships between female spectators and female stars are any indication of female spectatorial involvement with female-oriented film cycles, and I would suggest that they are, it would seem that female friendship films may involve a complex process of spectatorial involvement. What occurs is the continual negotiation of self (spectator) and ideal (characters) involving the mediation of similarity and difference across multiple registers of cinematic desire and identification. Following Stacey's ideas, the particular appeal of female-oriented film cycles such as the female friendship film would seem to involve a blurring of identification and desire, what one might call the eroticization of identification.

If identification and desire are often conflated in the female friendship film, causing a female-specific pleasure from the spectatorial experience of eroticized identification, a question then arises as to how one can even speak of a category of erotic female friendship films. How might these films be distinguished from other categories of female friendship portrayals that also have homoerotic implications? Teresa de Lauretis's theories of lesbian spectatorship seem particularly useful in regard to this issue. De Lauretis offers strong objections to Stacey's ideas.[57] She insists that in likening female friendship portrayals to lesbian representations, Stacey is confusing desire with narcissistic identification,[58] but Stacey argues that rather than confusing the two, she is instead seeking the eroticization of identification. She is not saying that identification and desire are the same, but that "female identification contains forms of desire which include, though not exclusively, homoerotic pleasure."[59]

De Lauretis's objections to Stacey's ideas seem to stem from her fear that they will lead to a dangerous conflation of female bonding and lesbianism. According to de Lauretis, the drawing together of female bonding and lesbianism, which she believes to be two distinctly different types of female relationships, can result in the radical difference of lesbianism being swept "under the rug of sisterhood, female friendship, and the now popular theme of 'the mother-daughter bond.'"[60] In contradistinction to Stacey's arguments, de Lauretis proposes that female friendship portrayals can be clearly distinguished from lesbian representations because the former entail only identification, whereas lesbian portrayals involve desire between women. By studying lesbian films in comparison with other female friendship portrayals, it is possible to examine the validity of de Lauretis's and Stacey's theories. Later in this volume, I will address the issue of whether there is, in fact, a radical difference between female friendship and lesbian representations, and exactly what that difference, if it does exist, involves.

The Idealization of Female Friendship

Just as de Lauretis believes Stacey's eroticization of female friendship can obscure its differences from lesbianism, other critics argue that female friendship's connection with mother-daughter relationships can lead to its overidealization. Jane Flax, for instance, finds "the maternal turn so prevalent within recent feminist theorizing increasingly disturbing and suspicious."[61] According to Flax, the recurrent valorization of maternity and female relatedness serves, rather than challenges, the cause of patriarchy by obscuring other issues that feminists should be investigating. A particularly important concern she feels has been ignored is the existence of such negative feelings as rage, jealousy, and envy in relationships between women. Flax believes the idealization of female relationships encourages women to focus their energies on cultivating what are often portrayed unproblematically as the virtuous attributes of relatedness and connection. Gains for patriarchy from this type of thinking include heterosexuality's protection and reinforcement through the conflation of the terms *woman* and *mother*, the desexualization of female nature, the reinforcement of cultural prohibitions against female individuality and aggressiveness, the denial of the mother's sexuality, and indifference to racial and class differences in women's relationships.[62]

Similarly, Pat O'Connor argues in her sociological review of contemporary British women's friendships for a less idealized conception of female relationships. She suggests that there is more to be gained from demythologizing female friendship than there is from treating it as an unambiguous source of joy, positive mental health, and progressive social change.[63] Her study indicates that women's real-life relationships are, in fact, complex constructs involving conflict, anxiety, and personal pain, as well as psychological and social rewards. O'Connor strongly criticizes the tendency of some feminist critics to celebrate female relationships unequivocally as a means to progressive social change. She believes that cultural feminists such as Janice Raymond and Lillian Faderman fail to analyze the complexity of both female friendships and lesbian relationships because they are preoccupied with presenting them as ways to cure the world. Raymond, for instance, glorifies what she terms "Gyn/Affection" as creating a "culture of female friendship—a culture that has vitality, elan, and power of its own."[64] As O'Connor points out, this celebratory assessment is based on little systematic analysis and much essentialist thinking about women's naturally positive characteristics stifled under patriarchy.[65]

The idealization of women's relationships often involves their comparison to male friendships. Relationships between men are criticized for relying primarily on shared interests and activities rather than generating the intimacy, empathic communication, and mutual helpfulness that are said to characterize female interactions.[66] A high degree of intimacy is often seen as a very desirable aspect of the exalted female bond, yet, as O'Connor points out, this intimacy can actually be a double-edged sword. Although it may work to provide women with needed ego support, it can also reinforce their social disempowerment. Intimate self-disclosure and endless confiding may represent what O'Connor calls "palliative coping."[67] By confiding her problems to a female friend, a woman can improve her mental state purely on the level of feeling, and this emotional uplift may serve as a substitute for attempting to change an unpleasant situation. Thus, the privatizing and depoliticizing effects of close dyadic female friendships may actually have negative repercussions on women's lives. As entirely personal relationships separate from the outside world, they can reinforce women's traditional confinement to a privatized feminine space and discourage their venturing out into the public sphere.

O'Connor's study not only demonstrates the complexity of female friendship, it also suggests that relationships with other women hold a place of particular significance in many women's lives. This aspect of her study seems particularly useful in thinking about the appeal of female friendship films. Many women, according to O'Connor, feel the need for friendships with other women so intensely that they mentally create an idealized female friendship that in reality does not exist. The women believe this friendship involves a high level of what O'Connor calls "felt attachment," which includes a deep feeling of specialness, solidarity, and confiding, a history of shared experiences, the security of promised practical help, and the assurance of complete acceptance. O'Connor discovered, however, that the actual friendships described by her informants in this way really involved few, if any, of these qualities. The women simply mentally constructed a female friendship that fulfilled their emotional needs. This was particularly true of women who did not have the time and/or resources needed to bring about the actual existence of this type of idealized relationship.[68] As I will demonstrate in the following chapters, many female friendship films can serve this same function. They offer prepackaged mental constructs of idealized female friendships that women can use as fantasy substitutes for real-life relationships.

According to O'Connor, the most politically and socially progressive type of female relationship is the group friendship. Women's coming together in groups for fun, companionship, and shared enjoyment can be seen as socially challenging in a number of ways: such friendships undermine the ideology of romantic love by showing that women can enjoy themselves without male companionship; challenge men's control of public social meeting places; undermine "the equation of femininity with maternity, domesticity, and the private area"; dispute "the culturally legitimated tendency for women to base their identities on such 'caring' relationships"; and subvert the exclusivity of the marriage bond by allowing for the public demonstration of solidarity among women.[69] As I will show, contemporary female friendship films initially concentrated on intimate, dyadic relationships, but as the cycle developed, that situation changed dramatically. Group friendship portrayals have come to dominate the genre, but these representations are not nearly as socially progressive as O'Connor's work with real women's friendships would suggest. The extremely conservative messages of most group female friendship films indicate that the films may actually represent a particularly insidious form of social control. Their underlying ideological project seems to involve channeling potentially progressive elements of group female friendship into more benign conformist forms.

Whether they depict dyadic or group relationships or propagate socially conservative or progressive messages, female friendship films clearly represent complex cinematic structures that can have significant influence on the lives of their female viewers. They can be personally and socially liberating for women or can work to entrench them all the more in powerlessness, personal misery, and deference to male authority. Because these films have the potential to affect their female audience so strongly, it is particularly important that we analyze closely both their modes of production and the responses they attempt to elicit from their female viewers. It is to this analysis that we now turn.

1 | Woman's Film Precedents

Theorizing the Woman's Film and Its Audience

The predecessors of contemporary female friendship films are the woman's films of the 1930s and 1940s. Both generations of woman's cinema attempt to examine "women's issues," but the plots of 1930s and 1940s woman's films make it clear that the issues filmmakers deemed important to women in that time period involved romance and domesticity, not female friendship. The relationship of woman's films to their female viewers is, in fact, a matter of some dispute among film scholars. The films have been analyzed most extensively by three critics: Molly Haskell, Mary Ann Doane, and Jeanine Basinger. Haskell devotes one chapter to the woman's film in her larger study, *From Reverence to Rape: The Treatment of Women in the Movies*. Published in 1974, this work represents the first feminist attempt to counter the dismissal of the woman's film by male critics, yet Haskell offers a very mixed appraisal. She laments the "low caste among highbrows" and the "untouchable" reputation woman's films have had and suggests that the amount of critical opprobrium launched against the genre reflects not the films' inherent lack of quality, but the widespread social belief that their subject matter, "women, and therefore women's emotional problems, [is] of minor significance."[1]

Haskell admits, nevertheless, that the majority of 1930s and 1940s woman's films offer their female viewers masochistic scenarios of female victimization. As Haskell describes the films, they "embrace the audience as victims, through the common myths of rejection and self-sacrifice and martyrdom as purveyed by the mass media" and create a world of masochistic feminine self-pity in which women reconcile themselves to their misery rather than rebel against it. Yet Haskell also argues that these masochistic woman's films represent only the lowest common denominator of the genre. Not all woman's films remain at this level. The ones Haskell champions deal with extraordinary women who are, according to Haskell, emancipated "aristocrats of their sex" or with ordinary women who become extraordinary by rejecting their initial status as victims and overcoming pain and hardship in order to control their own fates.[2]

For Haskell, then, woman's films can be either socially conservative or progressive. Many simply provide women with the opportunity to spend endless "wet, wasted afternoons" resigning themselves to the patriarchal status quo and crying over their sad lot.[3] Others offer their female viewers some sense of accomplishment and pride by celebrating the exceptional woman who transcends the traditional role of the female victim. According to Haskell, all of these films are worthy of study, not because of their inherent merit, although she does believe a number of them represent considerable artistic accomplishments, but because they are "the closest thing to an expression of the collective drives, conscious and unconscious, of American women."[4] In Haskell's opinion, these drives involve a complicated mixture of conscious adherence and unconscious resistance to the established patriarchal order, especially in terms of its treatment of women.

Haskell's appraisal of the woman's film was followed in 1987 by Mary Ann Doane's book-length study *The Desire to Desire: The Woman's Film of the 1940s*.[5] Doane's approach is very different from Haskell's. Haskell employs an analytic technique that has been called the "images of women" approach.[6] She compares cinematic portrayals of female characters with real women's lives in order to determine the portrayals' accuracy and relevance. Doane, on the other hand, has been heavily influenced by developments in 1960s and 1970s film theory. She utilizes concepts of spectator positioning, gaze structure, and subject formation gleaned from apparatus theory and cine-psychoanalysis to look not just at the images of women presented in films, but at how these images are constructed by the filmic apparatus and how spectators are positioned to read them in certain ways. Accepting Mulvey's argument that the spectator in Hollywood cinema is posited as male, Doane investigates 1940s woman's films as examples of what happens on those rare occasions when Hollywood attempts to address specifically a female spectator.

Doane's resulting appraisal is extraordinarily negative and condemning. Although she recognizes that, because of their address to a female audience, woman's films most often postulate a female gaze, she insists that this gaze is offered to the female spectator only to be used against her. Doane sees the films as inevitably placing their female viewers in "a masochistic position defined as 'the (impossible) place of a purely passive desire'" and as offering spectatorial pleasure that is too often indissociable from pain, suffering, and aggression turned against not only female characters but the female spectator herself.[7] In the final analysis, according to Doane, the woman's film not only offers its female spectator masochistic scenarios of women's victimization but encourages her to accept a masochistic spectatorial position by denying her any other possibility. Again following Mulvey's theorization of female spectatorship as oscillation between male and female poles of spectatorial positioning, Doane suggests that the woman's film de-eroticizes the gaze to accommodate an address to a female spectator, and in the process de-eroticizes the female image, essentially denying women "the space of a reading" by eliminating the feminine pole of spectator positioning.[8] In attempting to address a female audience, it manages only to alienate the female spectator from its de-eroticized female character and to implicate her all the more fully in a male perspective that victimizes or pathologizes her screen representative.

In conclusion, Doane suggests that feminist critics are often drawn to genres directed to a female audience because they want to find there something that belongs to women and "escapes the patriarchal stronghold." As a result, she says, they approach these texts redemptively, reevaluating as positive characteristics that would commonly be seen as negative or neutral in significance. Their evaluation often involves championing traditionally feminine qualities as hierarchically superior to male values and attributes. This sort of essentialism Doane rejects as postulating a too narrow definition of femininity that simply identifies it with a limited set of positively reevaluated feminine characteristics. Doane objects as well to another type of redemptive textual analysis that emphasizes not how a film positions its spectator but how real female viewers use mass culture texts for their own purposes, producing more positive and empowering readings for themselves than the texts seem to encourage. Doane condemns this approach as reading viewers rather than texts.[9]

In her evaluation of the woman's film, Doane herself definitely looks at texts and not viewers. What she finds is absolutely nothing that "escapes the patriarchal stronghold" and belongs to women. This is not to say that Doane sees these films as unrelated to women's culture or to individual women viewers. She suggests that the films follow a mass cultural tradition termed *respeaking*. Popular culture texts are said to respeak the real socially rooted needs, desires, and identities of the social groups that produce and consume them. In this process of respeaking, an "echo of our actual or virtual collective speaking" is heard, but something gets lost in the translation, and that something makes the message very different from what it echoes.[10] For Doane, the woman's film represents just such an echo of women's experiences.

Jeanine Basinger, the most recent analyst of the woman's film, responds very differently to her subject, arguing that woman's films are double-voiced or, as she puts it, "two-faced, providing [female] viewers with escape, freedom, release, and then telling them that they shouldn't want such things; they won't work; they're all wrong."[11] Basinger's approach is clearly influenced by the recent wave of audience studies that has swept over film research and that Doane condemns. Like other audience-oriented critics, Basinger suggests that real women viewers use films in ways that empower them in spite of the messages that scholarly close reading might suggest are inherent in the texts. Basinger claims that beneath the conservative stance that woman's films seem on the surface to take, the texts offer women a sense of temporary liberation. For a brief time at least, female viewers can escape into romantic love, sexual awareness, a luxurious lifestyle, or the temporary rejection of traditionally feminine roles.[12]

Representation of Female Friendship in the 1930s and 1940s

Of the three woman's film analysts mentioned above, only Basinger devotes a significant section of her book, although only one chapter of twelve, to the films' portrayals of relationships among women. Examining a wide range of woman's films from the 1930s through the 1950s, she concludes that their representations of female relationships fall into two categories: female double films and life choices films.

Double films present two women, one good and one bad, who embody oppositions or contradictions within female nature. As Lucy Fischer points out in her study of these films, the good woman's traits are aligned with conventional femininity (passivity, sweetness, emotionality, asexuality), and the bad one's personality is associated with masculinity (assertiveness, acerbity, intelligence, eroticism).[13] Often the two women in such films are identical twins or sisters who are both played by the same actress. Two of the most prominent 1940s female double films, *A Stolen Life* (Bernhardt, 1946) and *The Dark Mirror* (Siodmak, 1946), feature Bette Davis and Olivia de Havilland, respectively, both major female stars of the period, playing dual roles as identical twins. The plot of the female double film centers on a conflict between the two women that is eventually resolved in a simplistic but morally uplifting manner, with the good woman triumphant and the bad one defeated or destroyed.

Fischer claims that this good/bad girl split unequivocally reflects patriarchal assumptions about women.[14] The text of the double film situates its audience's moral allegiance firmly on the side of the good woman by associating her with qualities not only connected with traditional femininity but also with what is posited as morally right. The evil sister is presented as rejecting the traditional feminine role and acting in ways deemed morally reprehensible. She is, for instance, typically treacherous, deceptive, and jealous. This division between good and bad femininity is not formed only along moral lines but in terms of gender identification as well. The traditional Freudian picture of women, based as it is on patriarchal preconceptions, portrays female nature as engaged in a lifelong struggle between opposing masculine and feminine forces. This battle stems from what Freud saw as the inadequate resolution of the female Oedipal crisis, resulting in a constant battle in the female psyche to repress clitoral (masculine) phallic sexuality in favor of vaginal (feminine) eroticism. According to Fischer, female double films are a reworking of exactly these issues—issues that reflect not real female development but male fantasies of female nature. These fantasies picture women as assuming a "proper" feminine role by repressing both phallic sexuality and attachment to other women. This repression is reenacted in the good twin's rejection of her "more masculine" sister as evil.[15]

Fischer's conception of double films as projecting upon female nature a false bifurcation between battling masculine and feminine forces differs considerably from Basinger's ideas about the films. Basinger sees double films as sites of limited but real liberation for their female audience. Through temporary identification with the bad girl, the female viewer, according to Basinger, is able to engage with a version of female radicalism.[16] The difference between Fischer's and Basinger's perspectives is crucial to a determination of the effects these films attempt to cultivate in their female audience. For Fischer, the films have a distinct ideological project—they identify the female psyche with evil, jealousy, and an underlying masculinity that could always erupt as a threat to the male. This message is really not aimed at women at all, and it certainly does not investigate legitimate female developmental problems. Rather, it rearticulates and controls male fears of femininity stemming from a childhood relationship with a seemingly all-powerful, threatening "phallic mother." This is an ideological project deeply imbricated in patriarchal social constructs. For Basinger, in contrast, the films become benign cultural products that speak in many languages and say different things to different viewers. They offer liberation for those who want to escape and confirmation of social taboos for those who want to be reassured of the righteousness of their conformity. They really have no coherent ideological project at all; instead, they just try to appeal to everybody.

The Female Double Film: *The Dark Mirror*

In order to weigh the validity of Fischer's and Basinger's approaches, we can look at *The Dark Mirror*, a female double film that both authors cite as supporting their views. *The Dark Mirror* falls into the category of films that Mary Ann Doane has labeled "medical discourse" films. The plots of such films typically involve a male doctor's investigation of the female protagonist's diseased physical or mental state through the use of medical science or psychoanalysis. In *The Dark Mirror*, Olivia de Havilland plays the dual roles of twin sisters, one of whom is insane and has committed a murder. While investigating the crime, the police come to realize that they are dealing with identical twins whose visual appearance does not allow them to be distinguished from one another. The murderess has convinced her sister of her innocence and has persuaded her to refuse to cooperate with the police, who are unable to make an arrest because they cannot determine which sister was at the scene of the crime on the appointed evening. The innocent sister has an alibi, but she will not reveal whether it was she or her sister who was at that location.

In the female double film The Dark Mirror *(Siodmak, 1946), Olivia de Havilland plays the dual role of identical twin sisters, one good and one evil, personifying the film's bifurcated view of female nature.*

Because visual appearance alone cannot provide adequate information for an assessment of the female characters' true natures, a psychiatrist, Dr. Elliott (Lew Ayres), is called upon to determine by the use of psychological testing which twin is good and which is evil. He subjects Terry, the evil twin, to a lie detector test that reveals the reason for her murderous nature. The markings on the lie detector tape indicate her extreme agitation at the very mention of her sister's name, and her stories about her relationship with her sister Ruth suggest that she is extremely jealous of Ruth's attractiveness to men. Dr. Elliott comes to believe that this insane jealousy is the root cause of Terry's mental illness.

The doctor's psychological testing probes the duplicitous female image and divides the evil from the good. In accord with Fischer's ideas, the film can be said to portray female nature as a battleground not only between good and evil but also between masculinity and femininity. Terry is clearly portrayed as the "masculine" twin. She is more assertive and controlling than her more demure, retiring sister, and she is also branded as evil. The information that Dr. Elliott obtains from his psychological testing allows him to break Terry's "masculine" control over her more "femininely" submissive sister. As a result of his investigation, the police are able to trick Terry into confessing to the crime and to her animosity toward her sister. She is quickly arrested and taken off to a psychiatric hospital, and the female image is purged of its evil dimension and realigned with goodness in the person of the angelic Ruth. Dr. Elliott, who has fallen in love with Ruth, pronounces his final validation of the purified image of femininity that she represents. He asks her why she is so much more beautiful than her sister. The film ends not with her reply but with the image of the beautiful star, Olivia de Havilland, in close-up as she smiles at the doctor and into the camera. Her image is shown to fit perfectly with Dr. Elliott's verbal description.

The Dark Mirror works very hard to place its female viewer in a prescribed spectatorial position. Its various textual elements combine to serve a common thematic purpose, the eradication of the duplicitous female image, and the female spectator is encouraged to do the same in regard to the text, to reach the conclusion the film advocates, a conclusion that argues that proper femininity is passive, self-sacrificing, masochistic, safely asexual, totally devoted to men, and therefore beautiful. The film seems unequivocally a portrayal of the triumph of the culturally acceptable "good" woman, the only woman left on the screen at the film's end and the woman who is shown to represent a purified female nature essentially compatible with patriarchal society. This designated "good" heroine is also finally realigned with her "proper" position in patriarchal society as an object of male desire, and the designated "bad" villainess is entirely eliminated from social consideration.

The film does encounter problems in working toward this resolution, but this does not suggest that it offers the female spectator in the character of Terry the type of outlet for liberating rebellion that Basinger envisions. Terry is shown to be a totally reprehensible and extremely deranged individual capable of murdering her own sister out of jealous rivalry. To identify with Terry's pathologically aggressive femininity, a female spectator must read the film "against the grain" and wrench apart its ideological project. This can be done; audience studies have shown repeatedly that viewers sometimes perform radically "against the grain" readings in order to derive pleasure from films that do not offer them pleasure otherwise. This does not mean, however, that the film "offers" this subject position to the spectator, as Basinger suggests; it means, rather, that a resisting spectator (and I think audience studies

are showing that there are many more of them than critics have sus-
pected) can tear a film apart to read it against its textually constructed
meaning.

Woman's films perhaps are particularly susceptible to these oppositional readings by female viewers because they often attempt, as Fischer suggests, to superimpose a patriarchical view of female character
and development on actual female nature and offer male fantasies of
femininity as female realities. As a result, they are plagued by textual
contradictions that they just cannot satisfactorily resolve. This does not
mean, however, that they work as Basinger suggests to offer liberation
as well as conservative support of the patriarchal status quo. It means
that they offer the conservative perspective and inadvertently open
themselves up to alternative readings. For instance, *The Dark Mirror*
clearly is not fully convincing in accounting for the division between
good and evil it sees hidden behind an ambiguous female image. At the
film's conclusion, when Dr. Elliott affirms Ruth's goodness by declaring
her more beautiful than her sister, her final close-up, as suggested above,
seems intended to confirm this evaluation. Yet based on what the spectator sees, Ruth is, in fact, no more beautiful than Terry, given that the
same actress is playing both roles and looks equally attractive in both
incarnations. The film's final close-up, calling attention to this fact, indicates that the "doubleness" of female nature is perhaps not so easily
purged. As Fischer suggests, the female double film, by employing a single actress to play both the good sister and the bad, emphasizes "that
the *same* woman can be regarded in contradictory ways, depending on
the perspective from which she is viewed."[17]

Dr. Elliott attempts to explain away this duality by attributing
Terry's tendencies toward evil to an innate jealousy in woman's nature.
He proposes that all women are jealous of each other but manage to
overcome this sentiment by blaming others' successes on unequal circumstances. Twins have fewer circumstances to blame, so they can more
easily develop an insane jealousy of each other. This explanation seems
to hold female nature itself responsible for Terry's tendencies toward
evil, but it fails to explain why Ruth did not fall into the same pattern as
her sister. Dr. Elliott simply proposes that she miraculously managed to
avoid these tendencies, just as her image at the film's end is amazingly
more beautiful than that of her identical twin sister. By this dubious rea-
soning, the film avoids considering the possibility that the evil it finds in
women may be attributable to social structures that adversely affect

them rather than to innate female tendencies. Although the film may avoid considering this possibility, the gap opened up by its refusal to do so allows for a resisting spectator to consider this possible explanation and much more in regard to the film's projection of patriarchal male fantasies onto its female characters. Still, this is not a position offered by the text per se; instead, it represents an interpretation that the spectator can construct only by closely analyzing the film's ideological flaws.

Group Friendship Films in the 1930s and 1940s

Basinger argues that group friendship films of the period offer even less potential liberation to their female audience than do female double films.[18] Films portraying group friendships typically revolve around three or more friends who represent different female life choices. In films of the 1930s and 1940s, these choices center on the conflict between marriage and career or the conflict between love and money. Inevitably, as Basinger points out, marriage and love win, and women are repeatedly informed that their role in life is to dedicate themselves to husband and family. Basinger sees little liberation in these films, yet it is unclear from her argument why they should really be much different from any of the other woman's films that she discusses. A female viewer could always stretch the text, as Basinger suggests she might with the double films, and identify with the career woman or the woman who is out for money rather than with the one who ends up choosing a husband and family.

Consider, for instance, Joseph L. Mankiewicz's *A Letter to Three Wives*, a 1949 film that focuses on the group friendship among four women. Addie Ross (Celeste Holm), the film's disembodied first-person voice-over narrator, tells the story of her attempt to steal one of her friends' husbands. After leaving her hometown one morning, she sends her three best friends a single letter announcing her intention to extricate one of their husbands from his marriage, but she does not say which one. She times the letter to arrive just as the women are leaving to chaperon a children's picnic and cannot contact their spouses. Each woman is left to speculate about the possible reasons her husband might be the one who has run off with Addie. Thus, the film comes to center not on the women's friendship, but on their relationships with their men, a characteristic not uncommon in female friendship films of this time period.

Group female friendship films in the 1940s concentrated more on women's relationships with men than on their friendships with each other. In A Letter to Three Wives *(Mankiewicz, 1949), the three wives (played by, from left to right, Linda Darnell, Ann Sothern, and Jeanne Crain) begin to contemplate the nature of their marriages after they receive a letter from their friend Addie, who claims to have run off with one of their husbands.*

The film's narrational perspective is extremely confused. Addie is the narrator, and she seems a very powerful one, as well as a figure of intended audience engagement. Her introductory voice-over commentary, in fact, immediately sets up a connection between her perspective and the viewer's: "To begin with, all the incidents and characters in this story might be fictitious, and any resemblance to you or me might be purely coincidental." Addie is also a seemingly omniscient, omnipresent vocal presence throughout the film. She seems so far above her surroundings that she is contemptuous of them, and the spectator might be inclined at first to identify with her contempt for the wives, their small-town lives, and their unfulfilling marriages. Addie ridicules not only the provincial environment she has rejected but also the silliness of the women she feels she has defeated.

In spite of this initial attempt to cultivate audience attachment to Addie, the film moves quickly away from her perspective, encouraging instead strong spectatorial engagement with the plights of the three wives. In fact, the film's ideological project appears to be a validation of the three wives' decisions to dedicate themselves more fully to their husbands and a condemnation of Addie as a contemptible woman who not only ridicules her friends behind their backs but even tries to ruin their marriages. Yet Addie's narration casts an ironic light on the wives' renewed dedication to their men that cannot be entirely dismissed. Addie is portrayed as an independent and powerful female figure, an object of male admiration and female jealousy. The men see her as a woman of taste, class, and beauty, and the women ask themselves, "Why is it that whatever we talk about we always end up talking about Addie Ross?" Addie comments sarcastically in voice-over, "Maybe it's because if you girls didn't talk about me, you wouldn't talk at all."

Whenever Addie is discussed in the film, she is portrayed not so much as a figure of evil and cruelty, but as an ideal of female beauty and independence. These discussions, combined with the film's refusal to present her visually, enhance her position as the ultimate threat to her friends. The men talk about her as a woman who had the courage to give her husband the "heave-ho." She is said to dress in a fashion that provokes male admiration and female envy. When she sends a present to one of the husbands for his birthday, it is the perfect gift, a rare recording of a classical piece that he loves, and when she sends champagne to her friends' table at a dance, it is, of course, of the finest vintage. Because the spectator never sees Addie to judge her appearance or demeanor, her status as an object of male admiration and female envy is never impaired.

Yet in the final analysis, *A Letter to Three Wives* is not really about Addie or about her friendship with the three wives. What it comes to focus on and what we see recounted in flashback for the great majority of screen time is the three women thinking back over their marriages. Each of them remembers incidents with her husband that lead her to believe that she may have neglected him and that he may be the one who has run off with Addie. The female viewer's allegiance may initially be split between engagement with Addie's cynical, ironic condemnation of the wives and the wives' perspectives, which in the course of the narrative involve a growing recognition of their devotion to their husbands and the importance of their marriages. This ambivalent reading is gradually discouraged, however, as the text develops its structure of sympathy. The plot of the film unequivocally comes to validate the wives' decisions to dedicate themselves completely to their marriages. Addie's ironic voice-over narration may call this dedication into question for some resisting spectators, but most viewers will follow textual cues and become completely sympathetic to the wives' perspectives, pitying them as Addie's victims and championing their newfound appreciation of the importance of their marital relationships.

Finally, at the film's end Addie's defeat is complete. She cannot extricate even one of the men from his marriage, and in the concluding sequence she is reduced to an ineffectual ghostly presence at the three wives' final victory celebration. At a dinner party attended by all three reunited couples, a champagne glass is overturned on the table where the three wives sit triumphantly with their husbands. We then hear Addie's final ironic voice-over comment, "Heigh-ho, goodnight everybody!" Addie has the last word, showing her disdain for the three wives and their dedication to their marriages, but the three wives have their men, and the film firmly proposes that the men are what really count.

In portraying group female friendship, *A Letter to Three Wives* utilizes a number of negative cultural stereotypes that characterize women's relationships as involving envy, gossip, duplicity, betrayal, and deadly competition for men.[19] The independent nonconformity of Addie's character does leave an opening for a resisting reading that sympathizes with her rejection of the devoted wives' boring provincial lifestyle, but this reading is not supported by the film's structure of spectatorial engagement as a whole. Instead, the film seems to employ possible female fascination with Addie's character as a "fantasy bribe" of sorts, to use Fredric Jameson's terminology, to draw the female spectator into the text, only to turn this fascination against her.[20] In this way, the effect of Addie's final condemnation as an evil, manipulative woman who will stop at nothing to get a man is heightened.

Men—Not Female Friendship

Essentially, then, at the center of *A Letter to Three Wives,* a film ostensibly about four female friends, are three husbands. In fact, most of the women's films of the 1930s and 1940s that deal with female bonding end up centering on male-female relationships and reaffirming the female protagonists' dedication to men. They also tend to use female relationships as a way to denigrate not only women's friendships but their career ambitions as well. For instance, in *A Woman's Secret* (Ray, 1949) the heroine, Marian Washburn (Maureen O'Hara), is a famous singer who due to an illness has permanently lost her singing voice. In order to fulfill her career ambitions through another woman, she determines to act as patroness to a talented younger singer, Susan Cauldwell (Gloria Grahame), but Susan turns out to be totally selfish and allows Marian to take responsibility for a shooting accident that was really her fault. Marian finds her true self only by severing her connection to her protégée, repudiating completely the last remnants of her career ambitions, and accepting the marriage proposal of her dedicated male lover, who has stood by her throughout her ordeal.

Similarly, *Mildred Pierce* (Curtiz, 1945) and *All About Eve* (Mankiewicz, 1950) project the evil consequences of their heroines' career ambitions on younger women whom they befriend and with whom they overidentify. Mildred (Joan Crawford) is totally devoted to her daughter Veda (Ann Blyth), even to the extent of taking responsibility for Veda's murder of Mildred's second husband. Veda's total selfishness and insensitivity to the needs of others is a projection of what the film portrays as the ultimate consequences of Mildred's unbridled female ambition, and Mildred's overidentification with her daughter signifies her recognition of Veda's character as merely the logical outcome of her own quest for female independence. In *All About Eve,* the situation is similar. Margo Channing (Bette Davis), a celebrated Broadway actress, takes as her protégée Eve Harrington (Anne Baxter), a young admirer and would-be star. Eve turns out to be a manipulative, overly ambitious woman who advances her own career at Margo's expense. The resulting conflict pits the two women against each other and leads Margo to recognize that her true fulfillment lies not in her career but in her relationship with Bill (Gary Merrill), the man who supports her throughout the struggle.

Like *All About Eve* and *A Woman's Secret,* many films of this period begin by focusing on relationships between women, but as they develop their major struggles turn out to involve a female protagonist and her male love interest. For instance, in *The Gay Sisters* (Rapper, 1942), the title of which might suggest a focus on the relationship between the heroine and her two female siblings, the plot actually revolves around Fiona Gaylord's (Barbara Stanwyck's) stormy romance with Charles Barclay (George Brent) as they engage in an extended court battle, first for her estate and then for custody of their son. In this film, as in so many woman's films of the period, relationships between women serve merely as a backdrop for a central male-female interaction that provides the real source of the film's narrative engagement.

Concluding Comments

The relationship between earlier woman's films and the contemporary female friendship film, first of all, raises the question of the films' disputed address to female viewers. As we have seen, woman's film analysts disagree strongly about the nature of the films' audience appeal. Whereas Molly Haskell asserts that the woman's film is a mixture of both progressive and regressive representatives, Mary Ann Doane condemns the entire genre for leading women to adopt a male spectatorial position that pathologizes and victimizes female characters. Jeanine Basinger, in contrast, argues for the films' creation of a double-voiced discourse that offers women temporary liberation under a surface structure that supports the patriarchal status quo. These diverging views of the woman's film's relationship to its female audience indicate that this issue is far from settled. They also suggest that there is a pressing need for the investigation of individual female-oriented film cycles, such as the female friendship film, to examine in some depth the types of relationships they attempt to create with their female viewers.

My analyses of selected woman's films of the 1930s and 1940s that deal with female friendship suggest that these films offer their female audience much less liberatory potential than Basinger suggests. In order to construct a progressive reading, a resisting viewer must dismantle the films' ideological projects by reading the texts against the grain, looking for gaps and flaws in their narrative logic. To a non-resisting spectator, both female double and group friendship films of the 1930s and 1940s offer patriarchally inspired views of female friendship as a conflict between "good" passive and "bad" aggressive femininity. They also subordinate women's friendships to their attachments to men and family; stereotypically represent female friendship as involving jealousy, envy, and competition for men; and even use the portrayal of female relationships as a means to denigrate women's career ambitions. What emerges most strongly as a crucial aspect of these early representations of female friendship is that their focus is not really on female friendship at all, but rather on women's relationships with men. The primary legacy of these films seems to be a typically patriarchal championing of female devotion to husband and family. In the remainder of this volume, I will demonstrate how contemporary female friendship films respond to this inheritance.

2 | The Sentimental Female Friendship Film

The films that initiated the contemporary female friendship film cycle cluster around the period of the late 1970s and early 1980s and represent various approaches to the topic of female relationships, ranging from the more to the less politically challenging. The most prominent type of film in this period is by far the dyadic sentimental female friendship film, which can be seen as potentially the least politically challenging representative of the cycle. The four groundbreaking female friendship films—*Julia* (Zinnemann, 1977), *The Turning Point* (Ross, 1977), *Girl Friends* (Weill, 1978), and *Rich and Famous* (Cukor, 1981)—all concentrate heavily on the intense feelings and personal dynamics within highly charged emotional relationships between two female friends. Yet these films also move beyond the personal to make statements of significant, if limited, political and social importance for women. As the decade of the 1980s continued, the sentimental female friendship film flourished and even moved to new heights of sentimentality. Two films, *Beaches* (Marshall, 1988) and *Steel Magnolias* (Ross, 1989), stand as paradigmatic examples of the sentimental female friendship film's movement to high sentimentality in the late 1980s.

With the notable exception of *Girl Friends,* a film written and directed outside the Hollywood system by independent filmmaker Claudia Weill, these initiating sentimental female friendship films are also very much Hollywood products. They were made either under the watchful eyes of established male studio-era directors such as George

Cukor and Fred Zinnemann or by such emerging directorial talents as Herbert Ross and Garry Marshall, both of whom went on to establish long and successful careers as purveyors of popular Hollywood entertainment. Thus, the beginnings of the female friendship film hardly seem associated with radical ideas or significant innovation. For the most part, female friendship films were introduced into mainstream cinema not by female filmmakers with new and different conceptions of how women should be presented on the screen, but by male establishment figures brokering "feminist" ideas cautiously into the mainstream by drawing on their extensive studio experience and subscribing wholeheartedly to established Hollywood norms.

Julia

Initiating the Contemporary Female Friendship Film on a Sentimental Note

The initiating contemporary female friendship film is the 1977 Hollywood feature *Julia*. Directed by Fred Zinnemann, the film was clearly intended as a major studio effort. Zinnemann had a solid reputation as an established studio director known for fashioning such quality products as *High Noon* (1952), From *Here to Eternity* (1953), *Oklahoma!* (1955), and *A Man for All Seasons* (1966). *Julia* was adapted by a male screenwriter, Alvin Sargent, from a story in *Pentimento,* the memoir of the respected playwright Lillian Hellman, and starred two prominent actresses of the period, Jane Fonda and Vanessa Redgrave. The film's central focus is on the intense friendship between Lillian (Fonda), a struggling writer, and Julia (Redgrave), a dedicated anti-Nazi political activist.

In many ways, *Julia* exemplifies the major characteristics of traditional sentimental female friendship portrayals. The relationship between Julia and Lillian is presented as intensely personal and intimate, existing primarily on the level of feeling, and their shared intimacy is much exalted and greatly admired. Their friendship is emotionally effusive, with their deep attachment expressed through frequent physical displays of affection, intimate confiding, and the exchange of longing looks suffused with deep significance. Janet Todd argues that these qualities render sentimental female friendship portrayals politically ineffective, because they are presented as influencing only the personal lives of the women involved rather than leading them to action within the public sphere.[1] Because sentimental female friendship is traditionally portrayed

In Julia *(Zinnemann, 1977), when they meet again after many years of separation, Lillian (Jane Fonda, left) and Julia (Vanessa Redgrave) exchange the affectionate gazes that characterize sentimental female friendship films.*

solely in terms of physical affection and intimate self-disclosure, the friends remain confined to the private realm of personal relationships, and women's social situation of disempowerment in public life is thereby reinforced.

Julia alters this traditional sentimental female friendship portrayal by merging personal, emotional intimacy with political activism. The film suggests that Lillian's close relationship with Julia leads her to undertake a dangerous antifascist mission. It is Lillian's devotion to her friend that convinces her to transport money into the Third Reich to help free political prisoners. This attempted combination of sentimental with political female friendship seems a progressive innovation in female friendship portrayals. Feminist critics such as Carolyn Heilbrun, for instance, have lamented the fact that male friendships in literature have so often been presented as leading to greater participation in the outside world, whereas portrayals of female friendships have confined them entirely to the domestic sphere.[2] *Julia*, however, attempts to show a sentimental female friendship that encourages women's participation in the public arena of political and social activism.

The film's politically challenging characteristics are not confined to its heroines' antifascist activities, but also involve their dedication to their respective careers. Neither woman is presented as conventionally domestic: Julia is totally devoted to her intellectual life and ideological commitments, and Lillian is seen working relentlessly to develop her literary talents. It may be difficult to appreciate fully now, when it is more common to see working women represented on the screen, the innovative quality of this presentation in 1977, when cinematic images of women at work outside the home were much less frequent.

In spite of these progressive aspects, *Julia* has definite limitations as a politically challenging film. First of all, its combination of sentimental and political female friendship is problematic. Although the film does imply that female bonding leads women to join together to fight an oppressive social structure, the exact motivation for Lillian's dedication to the antifascist cause remains unclear. Her political activism is confined to a single instance of courageous behavior, guided entirely by the instructions of Julia and by the help of other members of the underground resistance organization to which Julia belongs. There is no indication that this isolated act of heroism leads Lillian to continued activism or really that it involves any political commitment whatsoever on her part. The film, in fact, suggests that Lillian's decision is made entirely for personal reasons, to prove to Julia that she can live up to her heroic ideals, and the political implications of her decision seem almost incidental. Thus, the sentimental aspects of *Julia*'s female friendship portrayal, which emphasize the importance of the emotional bond between the two friends, interfere with the force of the film's political message.

The overriding sentimentality of the film's portrayal of female friendship is particularly apparent when the film is compared with its source, Lillian Hellman's memoir *Pentimento*. Hellman's account of her relationship with Julia constitutes only a small segment of the work, which includes a number of portraits of people who were important to Hellman, as well as sections on her experiences in the theater. As part of this larger multidimensional whole, Lillian's relationship with Julia has neither the appearance of centrality in Lillian's life nor the sentimental force that it has in the film. The effusive displays of emotional attachment and physical affection found in the film are also largely absent from the memoir, where the relationship seems much more one of intellectual and political influence than one of sentimental affection.

Whereas Hellman's memoir is straightforwardly an antifascist political statement and a clear endorsement of women's involvement in the public sphere, the film's political effectiveness is more limited. The political goal for which Julia and Lillian work is rendered safe by its historical displacement into the past. Few audience members in 1977 would be opposed to a courageous woman working against the Nazis in the 1930s. Although dedication to the antifascist resistance movement can be interpreted as symbolically representing opposition to any oppressive political system, including patriarchy, this interpretation is far from mandated by the film's structure of spectatorial engagement. Setting the female characters' politically subversive behavior in the historical context of Nazi Germany minimizes the possibility that audiences will apply the implications of the women's actions to contemporary times.

The film also minimizes the political implications of Julia's and Lillian's dedication to their work in the public sphere. Because both women are presented as extraordinary in their commitment to public life, the average female viewer might be led to feel distanced from them and to believe that only the rare and unusual woman would attempt to go beyond home and family to seek political, intellectual, or artistic achievement. The casting of Fonda and Redgrave, two highly regarded actresses known at the time for their political involvement, only serves to heighten the characters' positioning as exceptional and rare. Also significant is the manner in which the women's work experiences are presented.

Although Julia seems to be a very dynamic woman, passionately committed to learning and to putting her ideas into political action, the film never shows her in the context of her day-to-day political activities.[3] Instead, we are regaled with images of her youthful idealism and adolescent friendship with Lillian. Not only is the adult Julia mostly off-screen, but the fact that the story is narrated by Lillian further distances the viewer from Julia's character, who is rarely seen doing anything—political or otherwise. What we do get are Lillian's repeated assertions that Julia is remarkable and accomplishes remarkable things. Whereas the viewer is only told of Julia's brilliant, courageous, and self-sacrificing political activism, her physical mutilation and eventual brutal murder are visually presented.[4] What the spectator is allowed to see are not Julia's accomplishments, but her severe punishment for her entrance into public life.

Lillian's work is shown in somewhat greater detail than Julia's, but this detail amounts almost exclusively to clichéd depictions of her work habits. As she writes, she compulsively smokes and drinks, repeatedly tears pages out of her typewriter, and frustratedly kicks a wastepaper basket filled with crumpled sheets of paper. As Joan Mellen suggests, such trite scenes make it hard to take Lillian's work seriously.[5] Also, Lillian's literary talents are shown to depend heavily on the sustained tutelage of her male companion, the famous mystery writer Dashiell Hammett (Jason Robards). Her status as an independent artist is seriously compromised by her constant reliance on him for guidance and support. In fact, male interference becomes a major problem in *Julia*'s rendering of female friendship.

Male Interference

The film's portrayal of Dashiell Hammett is an addition to the narrative that is not drawn from Hellman's memoir account of Julia, which contains no mention of her relationship with Hammett whatsoever. In some ways, the character of Dash stands in opposition to earlier portrayals of male love interests in literary works dealing with sentimental female friendship. Traditionally, the male lovers of sentimental female friends are strongly opposed to the women's relationship, which they see as a threat to the exclusivity of the romantic heterosexual bond, and sociologists have found that this view still frequently characterizes modern male attitudes toward female friendship.[6] By violating this tradition, the portrayal of Dash in *Julia* seems to advance a more tolerant male attitude toward women's relationships.

In spite of Dash's characterization as understanding and supportive, some critics have found his role in the film troubling. Joan Mellen, for instance, argues that Dash's listless, disillusioned personality seems to confirm antifeminist assertions that attachment to a strong intellectual woman emasculates a man and reduces him to a position of passive weakness. She also proposes that the film's failure to portray the sexual dimension of the Hellman-Hammett relationship implies that intellectual achievement and sexuality are mutually exclusive for women.[7] Annette Kuhn suggests further that Lillian's relationship with Dash encloses, relativizes, and reduces the importance of her friendship with Julia.[8] I would argue, however, that Lillian's relationships with Dash and Julia seem instead to interconnect closely in terms of the effects they have on Lillian.

As the film progresses, it follows earlier literary models of sentimental female friendship in portraying the women's relationship as a means of psychological empowerment for one or both of the participants. In *Julia* it is Lillian who gains psychologically, but her psychological empowerment comes not solely from her friendship with Julia, but also from her relationship with Dash. In fact, the two relationships are constantly juxtaposed, with both Julia and Dash acting as mentors to Lillian. The film can be seen from a psychoanalytic perspective as positioning Julia and Dash as parental figures who create an ideal developmental environment for the more childlike Lillian. Both characters offer Lillian guidance toward greater maturity by creating a nurturing environment that supports the development of her creativity and sense of social responsibility without jeopardizing her autonomy. In fact, Lillian's relationships with Dash and Julia closely approximate the childhood idealizing transference situation in which a parental figure (or a substitute when the relationship resurfaces in an individual's adult life) serves as a source of strength and value to the child, who seeks to absorb into her or his personality the positive qualities attributed to this ideal figure. Julia is Lillian's ideal of courage and beauty, and Dash represents artistic talent and integrity.

Lillian's psychological development is charted through her voice-over narration, a cinematic device frequently employed to illustrate a character's growing sense of personal identity. In the opening moments of the film, Lillian tells us in voice-over of the influence these two formative relationships had on her life. We see the distant image of an older woman sitting in a rowboat fishing and reflecting on her past:

> Old paint on canvas as it ages sometimes becomes transparent, and when that happens it is possible in some pictures to see the original lines. . . . That is called pentimento. The painter repented, changed his mind. . . . I'm old now and I want to remember what was there for me once, and what is there for me now.

Through the act of storytelling, Lillian is trying to understand how these two important influences shaped her life and helped form her identity. Indeed, as the story progresses it becomes clear that Lillian's relationships with Julia and Dash made her a stronger, more creative person, yet at the film's conclusion the influence that her voice-over celebrates as most important to her is of a different nature. We return at the film's end to the opening narrating situation of the older Lillian in a rowboat contemplating the tale she has just told. She concludes: "I've gone on for a good many years since. Sometimes fine, not always. But he [Dash] was right. I am stubborn. I haven't forgotten either of them." Lillian's reflections seem to suggest that it is the memory of these two idealized mentors that has sustained her through both the good and the bad times of her life.

This final voice-over message reduces the film's political impact significantly and places it much more in the category of the social, rather than political, female friendship film. Lillian's attachment to Julia, like her relationship with Dash, has led her to fit more comfortably into her existing social milieu, rather than to work to change it. These relationships have offered Lillian a refuge from the outside world and solace for her bruised psyche. What seems to be suggested at the film's conclusion is that female friendship, properly combined with heterosexual romance, does not so much challenge the status quo as offer temporary relief from the strain of living in a world that unfortunately cannot be altered.

Engaging the Female Spectator

Julia's potential effect on its female spectator is difficult to calculate because the film works both to challenge and to support the existing social structure. Although it is critical of patriarchy in a number of ways, its progressive potential is recuperated by the combination of this critique with more conservative elements. One such element is the film's highly idealized presentation of women's friendship as involving perfect trust, acceptance, and understanding. While this type of relationship offers the female spectator an affirmation of female solidarity, it also supports an unrealistic conception of women's relationships that cannot serve as a practical model for real-life friendships. Based primarily on a close adolescent bond, the friendship between Lillian and Julia exemplifies a mental construct of female friendship that in adulthood involves almost exclusively idealization from a distance.

This idealized portrayal can have a negative effect on the female viewer, encouraging her unrealistically to expect this type of bond in her everyday life or to use this idealized cinematic friendship as a substitute for real relationships. The film after all offers women viewers the same security and satisfaction that the mental construct of an idealized friendship would. It provides the dream of a perfect union of two people who relate to each other without even a hint of disagreement or misunderstanding. The cinematic realization of this dream can actually prevent women from forming real female friendships by encouraging them to live in fantasy friendships, either real or cinematic, rather than attempt to construct actual, day-to-day bonds with other women.

Julia not only idealizes Lillian and Julia's relationship, but reflects at the same time negative patriarchal notions of female friendship and its connection to lesbianism. Several critics have commented on the film's curious attempts first to associate Lillian and Julia's friendship with lesbianism, and then to disavow this connection. Initially, the relationship has obvious erotic overtones. Even given the tendency for sentimental female friendships to be portrayed as intensely emotional, the emotional charge between Lillian and Julia seems particularly strong. When together, the women are always situated in close proximity and are demonstrably affectionate. They also frequently are shown in close-up exchanging affectionate looks. The gaze between them seems highly coded for eroticism, especially in comparison to that exchanged between Lillian and Dash, who rarely are seen close to each other or even exchanging glances. Lillian's gaze at Julia, on the other hand, is long, lingering, and loving.

This eroticism is repudiated, or perhaps protested too much, by a scene situated three-quarters of the way into the film. Lillian is shown having a drink with an intoxicated male acquaintance who tells her, "The whole world knows about you and Julia. . . . If anyone understands the sex urge of the adolescent girl, it's me." In the course of their conversation, the man not only implies that a lesbian relationship existed between Lillian and Julia at least in their adolescent years, but also compares that relationship to his incestuous attachment to his sister. Lillian responds violently to these insinuations by hitting the man and overturning the table at which they are seated.

Several critics read this scene as homophobic in its implications. Claudette Charbonneau and Lucy Winer go so far as to suggest that it represents an instance of gratuitous antilesbianism, unconnected to the film's plot, and serving only to reinforce the notion that verbal attacks on homosexuals need no justification. They accuse Zinnemann of exploiting titillating hints of lesbianism to add an erotic charge to his film, then repudiating these hints, and chastising the audience for entertaining the very insinuations that the director deliberately cultivated. They also argue that what makes the scene "doubly pernicious" is that it is connected to an otherwise particularly feminist moment. When Lillian attacks her accuser, she is presented as a woman unafraid to make clear her displeasure and ready to express her anger openly to a man who has offended her, yet Zinnemann puts this representation of feminist rage "to the service of a basically anti-feminist cause, to the service of creating fear and distrust between women."[9] Mellen sees the incident as additionally homophobic because it associates lesbianism with incest and, as she sees it, invites the viewer to share Lillian's horror at the possibility of her lesbian attraction to Julia.[10]

This scene can be interpreted, however, as much more ambiguous in its implications than these critics allow. As Kuhn points out, the episode can actually be read in two contradictory ways: Lillian's response can be seen as homophobic, in that she seems to perceive the man's accusation of lesbianism as a slur on the purity of her ideal relationship with Julia, or her outrage can be interpreted instead as a defense of lesbianism against its comparison with incest.[11] In either case, the scene's spectatorial effect remains uncertain. It can work to grant its audience the kind of "discursive consent" that Teresa de Lauretis sees operating in many mainstream female friendship portrayals.[12] Viewers are authorized to enjoy safely the erotic implications of the suggested attraction between Lillian and Julia because these implications are finally disavowed by Lillian's seeming rejection of lesbianism. On the other hand, spectators can interpret Lillian's excessive protest as substantiating the validity of the accusation. They can read the scene as confirming what they may have assumed all along. Thus, the film's positioning of its female spectator in regard to the erotic aspects of its central female relationship remains ambiguous.

This ambiguity is not found in *Pentimento*, where Hellman is much more forthright about the erotic implications of her attachment to Julia:

> In those years, and the years after Julia's death, I have had plenty of time to think about the love I had for her, too strong and too complicated to be defined as only the sexual yearnings of one girl for another. And yet certainly that was there. I don't know, I never cared, and it is now an aimless guessing game.

Zinnemann, on the other hand, seems to have tried to have it both ways: to benefit from creating an erotic charge between the two women and thereby draw viewers into the emotional intensity of their interchanges, but at the same time avoid alienating any part of his audience that might be offended by suggestions of lesbianism. This ambivalence leaves his direction open to the accusation that he exploited the lesbian overtones of the women's relationship for reasons of sexual titillation and then later dishonestly and ungenerously renounced them, deliberately attempting to cultivate a homophobic response in his viewers.

The issue of *Julia*'s possible lesbian subtext is only one of a number of ways in which the film ambiguously positions its female spectator. *Julia* also attempts to engage its female viewer by implicating her strongly in the film's central female friendship portrayal. As noted above, the relationship between Lillian and Julia is similar to the therapeutic idealizing transference situation. Lillian finds a new identity through her relationship with Julia, with whom she identifies as an ideal. The film incorporates the viewer into its textual structure in much the same idealizing way. Lillian's voice-over narration leads the film to focalize on her perspective, and she becomes the major figure of audience engagement. As a result, the female spectator is encouraged to share her admiration and desire for Julia. She is also invited to idealize, admire, and desire Lillian—in terms of both Hellman's literary skills and Jane Fonda's attractive physical appearance. In other words, the female spectator is encouraged to establish an idealizing transference relationship with the two women and their friendship similar to the one that Lillian forms with Julia. Then, the viewer is invited to follow Lillian's lead in using this idealization as a way to form a new identity.

What identity is the spectator offered? Here, the film's ambiguity again takes hold, and a number of possible subjectivities are proffered. A viewer can, for instance, find inspiration in Julia's courageous political work and Lillian's successful antifascist mission. One can also find either support for or a homophobic attack on lesbianism in the film's presentation of the erotic aspects of the women's relationship. The ending of the film offers yet another possibility, in that Lillian describes the contentment that her relationships with Julia and Dash have brought her. This concluding statement can have a palliative effect on the female viewer, leading her to seek solace from the outside world in personal relationships rather than enter into the public sphere and engage in political action. In other words, the film can be read for its political or personal significance or for both. Its potential effects are multiple, and the reading each audience member chooses is substantially determined by his or her own views.

The type of female spectatorial engagement encouraged by the text is also similar to that described by Jackie Stacey in regard to women viewers' fascinations with female stars.[13] *Julia* offers a spectatorial subject position that involves both identification with its female characters as ideals and desire for them as erotic objects. In accord with Stacey's theories, the film blurs the distinction between desire and identification in the feminine fascinations it offers. In *Julia*, as in a number of other female friendship films, identification and desire work together to draw the spectator into the text through the representation of a simulated transference situation that encourages spectatorial identity formation.

The identity that the film advocates, however, is so ambiguously presented that it creates a polysemy or openness to different audiences and different, even contradictory, reading positions. This openness reflects the negotiational strategies that characterize the production and consumption of Hollywood films as they try to attract the widest possible viewership while still appealing to specific target audiences. As we shall see as we look at the next film, this ambivalence is much more operative in *Julia*, a big-budget Hollywood product created with substantial male input, than it is in another major breakthrough film in the contemporary female friendship cycle. The low-budget independent film *Girl Friends*, written and directed by a relatively unknown female director, uses its female friendship portrayal to fashion a much more unambiguous critique of women's social situation under patriarchy than *Julia* is able to offer.

Girl Friends

A Naturalistic Rather Than a Sentimental Female Friendship Film

Claudia Weill's independent feature film *Girl Friends* found its way into mainstream distribution just a year after *Julia*, but its production history is very different from that of the earlier film. *Girl Friends* was begun in 1975 as a short produced with a grant from the American Film Institute. When Weill, an artist and still photographer who had previously only made short documentaries and experimental films, received positive critical feedback, she expanded the film and began reshooting, but she was still unable to get Hollywood financing. After the film was completed and gained critical acclaim on the film festival circuit, it was given limited commercial distribution by Warner Bros. As an independent feature written and directed by a woman, *Girl Friends* has the distinction of being one of the few films with a distinctly female, even feminist, perspective seen by mainstream audiences in the late 1970s.[14]

Like *Julia*, *Girl Friends* portrays what at first glance might appear to be a sentimental dyadic female friendship. We enter *in medias res* into a close relationship between two female roommates: Susan (Melanie Mayron), a photographer, and Anne (Anita Skinner), a writer. From the film's opening scenes, however, Weill minimizes the possibilities of a sentimental interpretation. There are no effusive displays of emotional attachment or attempts to portray the women as partaking of an idealized intimacy. Sacrificing emotional effect, Weill draws her viewers in by emphasizing verisimilitude rather than sentimentality. She creates a naturalistic sense of felt life by utilizing a low-budget, high-contrast film stock that gives the film a grainy pseudodocumentary quality, a shooting style that is notable for its simplicity and lack of flourish, an accumulation of surface detail, a nonglamorous actress in the lead role, and an episodic structure. In contrast to *Julia*, *Girl Friends* takes the portrayal of sentimental female friendship from the level of the idealized fantasy construct into the realm of naturalistic representation, creating the illusion of an eyewitness account.

Because of its increased verisimilitude and decreased emotional effect, *Girl Friends* avoids the problems that *Julia* encounters in moving from the private realm of personal emotional attachment into the public sphere of social criticism. *Girl Friends* develops very clearly and persuasively feminist themes concerning societal attitudes toward women's roles in marriage, women's friendships with each other, and women's careers. Its naturalistic mode of representation allows it to avoid dwelling on the private emotions experienced by the friends and to move quickly from personal experience to sociopolitical statement.

Critiquing Women's Social Position

In offering a critique of women's social positioning in friendship relationships, careers, and marriage, *Girl Friends* presents a substantial revision of earlier female friendship films that follow a life choices formula. As we have seen in regard to 1930s and 1940s woman's films, life choices films typically present a group of women choosing to follow different directions, with the most common choice being between love and career. In *Girl Friends*, Susan and Anne are shown choosing different life paths: Anne decides to marry Martin (Bob Balaban) and to start a family, while Susan remains single and pursues her career as a photographer.

The film may seem at first merely to reverse the traditional life choices formula, which typically presents marriage as the appropriate choice for women. Its attitude toward contemporary marriage and its effects on women is in many ways highly critical. Although Anne marries Martin convinced that she wants him to take care of her, she quickly comes to feel stifled in the relationship. When Susan visits the couple shortly after their wedding, Anne confides to her that she is planning to go back to school to take writing courses because she is feeling isolated, would like to be around other people, and needs some feedback on her writing. The problems Anne finds in combining her ambitions as a writer with marriage are exacerbated when she becomes pregnant. The demands of motherhood clearly seem to interfere with her work. After the baby is born, we see her trying to type, but she is repeatedly interrupted by Martin and their child.

Although *Girl Friends* is critical of married life, it does not simplistically contrast Anne's marital difficulties with Susan's success and happiness as a single career woman. Juxtaposed with Anne's problems are Susan's as she attempts to further her career in New York. In contrast to the traditional life choices formula, *Girl Friends* argues not that the single life and a career represent the true path to female fulfillment, but that both the choices of marriage and the single life are difficult ones for women. The film actually offers a careful analysis of both Susan's and Anne's life choices. Societal expectations of women in both marriage and the single life are shown to create difficulties that women must work to overcome. Anne struggles with the confinement of married life, while Susan confronts the loneliness and frustrations of the single career woman. What the film laments most is that they allow their divergent life paths to interfere with their friendship, a relationship that seems to have the potential to support them in their struggles in a way that their relationships with men cannot.

Although *Girl Friends* attempts to show the crucial importance of female friendship in women's lives, it does not idealize female bonding; instead, it portrays realistically a troubled relationship that is hindered by both women's internalization of societal conceptions of appropriate female behavior. The friendship between Susan and Anne resembles not the idealized transference situation found in *Julia,* but a twinship transference in which both women find in each other reassurance and support for their similar career goals. Susan discusses her photographs with Anne, and Anne asks Susan for advice about her writing. Unfortunately, they allow Anne's marriage to destroy the commonality of their bond.

Girl Friends argues effectively against the patriarchal notion that

Marriage's interference with female friendship is visually symbolized in this scene from Girl Friends *(Weill, 1978). Anne (Anita Skinner, left) and Susan (Melanie Mayron) argue as Anne's husband, Martin (Bob Balaban), and her child stand between the two women.*

female friendship should be regarded merely as a temporary bond terminated by marriage. By portraying these two types of relationships as essentially similar, the film reverses traditional portrayals of female friendship as plagued by jealousy and competition for men. In *Girl Friends*, Susan and Anne do not compete for Martin; instead, Susan and Martin are in competition for Anne. Female friendship emerges as such a crucial aspect of women's lives that it is just as important as their heterosexual relationships.

While the film critiques societal attitudes toward women's social roles and implies that change is needed, it offers no solutions to these problems. Its conclusion suggests the ongoing nature of, or perhaps a fatalistic resignation to, women's struggles against patriarchal norms. Critics have noted the film's lack of closure: Anne has had an abortion, temporarily left Martin, and fled to a country retreat, where Susan joins her. The two women talk, drink, and enjoy each other's company until suddenly a voice is heard offscreen, and Anne, now quite drunk, announces to Susan with amusement that it must be Martin. The film ends with a close-up of Susan's face as she reacts to the interruption with displeasure.

Although this ending may appear ambiguous, the avenues it opens up for multiple reading possibilities are actually quite limited. The possibilities of interpretation all lead to a single conception of women's lives as characterized by continued struggle. Neither woman's problems are resolved in any way. Susan has had a showing of her photographs in a small art gallery, but the future of her career remains uncertain. Anne's abortion and separation from Martin can signify her repudiation of that relationship or represent merely a small act of independence that in no way suggests her rejection of her marriage or her husband. Even the ending's significance in regard to the women's friendship points to future problems, symbolically rendered by the intrusion of Martin's voice into Susan and Anne's idyllic country retreat and the triangulation of desire that is implied to exist among them. The two women's attempts to fulfill their career goals, establish successful relationships with men, and maintain their friendship seem equally plagued by difficulties that can be overcome only by future struggle.

Annette Kuhn has proposed that the lack of closure in *Girl Friends* stems from the film's inability to make its "buddy structure" conform to the requirements of classical Hollywood cinema. She suggests that the characteristics of the classical Hollywood ending demand that the film conclude in one of two possible ways: the establishment of happy heterosexual relationships for both women or the formation of a lesbian bond between them.[15] These two possibilities represent only one real alternative, however. In the classical Hollywood text, the key to adequate and satisfying closure is romance. The ending of *Girl Friends* violates Hollywood norms because it implies that romantic love does not provide the answer for its female characters and that an answer to their problems may not even be possible in a society that puts such a high premium on romance. What Anne and Susan need are successful careers, happy heterosexual relationships, and female friendship. The fact that the film does not close on this note indicates that Weill did not perceive the combination of these three possibilities to be a viable option for women in a society that envisions true female fulfillment only in romantic love.

Girl Friends and the Female Spectator

The irresolution that characterizes the conclusion of *Girl Friends* has a significant effect on the film's relationship to its female spectator. As noted above, the openness of *Girl Friends* is very different from that in

Julia, where the film's resolution makes available to its audience conservative as well as progressive reading possibilities. The openness of *Girl Friends* serves a very different purpose. The film's lack of final resolution seems designed to leave the spectator in a questioning state. It conveys a sense of the social contradictions that make it difficult for women to combine heterosexual love with career success and female friendship. As a result, *Girl Friends,* unlike *Julia,* is less open to conservative recuperation. Its ending seeks to leave its audience with a feeling of unresolved tension that cannot be easily brushed aside.

Girl Friends also differs from *Julia* in that the female spectator is drawn into the film not by an idealization of the friendship bond, but by the verisimilitude of its portrayal. The twinship transference relationship formed between Susan and Anne is extended out to the female viewer, who is encouraged to form a similar bond of twinship with the two characters. The film's naturalistic style encourages the female spectator to recognize similarities between her life and the lives of the women represented on the screen. Its detailed presentation of the characters' daily experiences contributes to the female spectator's implication into a feeling of commonality with them that is not found in the idealized friendship portrayal in *Julia.* The casting of Melanie Mayron in the lead role of Susan also contributes strongly to the viewer's feeling of commonality with her character. Mayron is not a glamorous film star like Jane Fonda in *Julia.* Her average physical appearance allows her to be seen as a representative of the common rather than the exceptional woman; thus, her role as the film's protagonist offers affirmation to the female spectator who does not meet the Hollywood ideal of beauty.

The film also works to engage the female spectator with its female characters in a twinship bond by presenting a balanced view of women's friendship. Susan's relationship with Anne is shown to contain both good and bad aspects. While it is obviously important to both of them, it is also plagued by their internalization of societal norms that work against its continuation. The spectator is drawn into the women's relationship not as an idealized mental construct but as a reflection of the imperfect nature of real-life female bonding in a society that does not encourage the maintenance of women's friendships.

The imperfect nature of female friendship is replicated in the imperfectly resolved nature of the narrative itself. As noted above, *Girl Friends,* unlike *Julia,* does not offer its audience the satisfaction of emotional closure; instead, it presents the issues it raises as unresolved and seemingly unresolvable in the existing social structure. Whereas *Julia* leaves its audience feeling satisfied that Lillian has found solace in remembering her beloved female friend and male lover, the spectator that *Girl Friends* seems to envision is left thinking about the problems of women in contemporary society. She is encouraged to feel as troubled as Susan is at the end of the film. Her final close-up as she hears Martin's offscreen voice again coming between her and Anne is an emblematic expression not only of Susan's but also of what the film projects as the female viewer's frustration and dissatisfaction with things as they are.

New versus Old "New Woman's Films"

Both *Julia* and *Girl Friends,* in spite of their limitations, still merit the designation "new woman's films" of the 1970s because they initiated important alterations in the cinematic representation of female friendship reflective of the changing social roles of contemporary women. Not all 1970s new woman's films were as responsive to women's evolving historical situation. Two other female friendship films of the late 1970s and early 1980s, *The Turning Point* and *Rich and Famous,* take a more regressive approach to their subject. Like *Girl Friends,* they adopt the old life choices formula found in group friendship films of the 1930s and 1940s to investigate women's relationships in the context of their career ambitions. Unlike Weill's independent film, however, which represents a significant reworking of this formula, these Hollywood products transform the life choices scenario only in that they apply it to contemporary dyadic friendships. In fact, they maintain so many of the reactionary aspects of earlier woman's films that they represent throwbacks to previous negative portrayals of female friendship rather than progressive rethinkings of outdated ideas.

The Turning Point
The Life Choices Film Revisited

The Turning Point, a big-budget Hollywood feature set in the glamorous world of professional ballet, was released in 1977, the same year as *Julia.* The characters who make up the film's central dyadic female friendship are again, as in *Julia,* played by major female stars. Shirley MacLaine portrays Deedee, a wife and mother who twenty years earlier gave up her ballet career for marriage, and Anne Bancroft plays

Although Deedee (Shirley MacLaine, left) and Emma (Anne Bancroft) seem to be reestablishing a close sentimental female friendship in The Turning Point *(Ross, 1977), it is never made clear exactly what the positive aspects of this friendship are. Whenever they talk to each other, they end up arguing, until their continuing antagonism finally erupts in a spectacular catfight.*

Emma, a successful but aging star of the American Ballet Company. Female involvement in the project, however, was confined to acting talent; screenwriting and directing responsibilities were placed completely in male hands. The film was written by Arthur Laurents and directed by Herbert Ross, who were also its coproducers.

Although *The Turning Point* is divided between its elaborately staged and photographed ballet sequences and its dramatic plot, the film's portrait of women's friendship clearly serves as its narrative center. This friendship involves a complicated mixture of elements drawn from sentimental, manipulative, and social female friendship portrayals. In the tradition of sentimental female friendship, Deedee and Emma's relationship is initially exalted, even idealized, for its intimate and emotionally intense qualities. The film opens with Deedee and her family preparing to attend a performance of the American Ballet Company as it stops in their hometown as part of a national tour. After the performance, we learn that Deedee and her husband Wayne (Tom Skerritt) were both once members of the company. When they go backstage to congratulate old friends still involved with the ballet troupe, Deedee has an emotional reunion with Emma. Although the two women seem to be reestablishing a close sentimental female friendship, it is never made clear exactly what the positive aspects of this friendship are. Their current relationship, as well as the descriptions they give of their earlier one, seems to involve only jealousy and resentment. Whenever they talk to each other, they end up arguing, until their continuing antagonism finally erupts in a spectacular catfight as the two women storm through the halls and out into the foyer of the ballet theater where Emma has just performed.

Although initially appearing to represent a sentimental bond, Deedee and Emma's relationship quickly moves into the realms first of manipulative and then of social female friendship. Under the surface warmth of the relationship lies a secret animosity. For twenty years, Deedee has resented Emma's career accomplishments. The women's conversations gradually reveal the exact situation that led Deedee to forsake the ballet for marriage. Having found herself pregnant with Wayne's child, she went to Emma for advice. Just at that moment, the two women were in competition for the lead role in an important new ballet. As Deedee remembers the incident, Emma advised her to give up her career and marry Wayne. Deedee took Emma's advice and since has come to question her decision. Because her marriage to Wayne eliminated her from competition for the upcoming ballet, Deedee is convinced that her best friend betrayed her by deliberately advising her to abandon her career in order to further her own.

As the film progresses and the women engage in continued discussions of the past, manipulation is transformed into social female friendship. The film's life choices plot comes to dominate, propagating the reactionary message that marriage and career are mutually exclusive alternatives for women. This perspective is modified by the suggestion that twenty years ago, when Deedee made her decision to marry Wayne, this was undoubtedly the case, but that things have changed. To illustrate this point, a subplot is introduced involving Deedee and Wayne's daughter, Emilia (Leslie Browne). Emilia, like her mother, is a talented dancer, and she is asked to join the ballet company and go to New York. Throughout the film, it is repeatedly suggested that, unlike Deedee and Emma, Emilia will find satisfaction in both her career and her romantic life. The film even concludes with

Emma telling Deedee that Emilia will "have it all," as the young ballerina dances triumphantly across the stage.

Emilia's endeavors, as the representative of a new generation, to find fulfillment in both her career and her romantic life do not, however, serve as the film's primary narrative focus. *The Turning Point* is much more concerned with Deedee's problems than with her daughter's, and these problems are worked out through her stormy relationship with Emma. The verbal sparring between the two rivalrous friends develops inexplicably into a nurturing relationship in which Emma helps Deedee realize that she could have been successful in the ballet world if she had really wanted to be, that she freely chose marriage over a career, and that she is happy with her decision. The film suggests further that Deedee can find additional fulfillment by living vicariously through her daughter's career success. Emma, on the other hand, as an artist past her prime who sees her own career disintegrating, can only watch Emilia's rising success with feelings of growing envy and despair.

What *The Turning Point* finally does is rehash tired clichés concerning the advantages for women of choosing family over career. It suggests that the woman who sacrifices her career for love finds greater fulfillment in the end, that a mother can live vicariously through her child, and that marriage lasts, whereas career success is fleeting. Deedee learns through her friendship with Emma to accommodate herself all the more comfortably to the traditional female role of wife and mother. At the same time, Emma's life, reduced to shambles by the demise of her career and the fact that she does not have a man to turn to for romantic fulfillment, serves as a grim reminder of the emptiness that the film suggests awaits a woman who chooses career over love.

The Turning Point and Its Female Spectator

The possible effects of *The Turning Point* on its female viewers are more complex than is immediately apparent. In addition to its reactionary textual qualities, the film also contains a number of progressive elements. Its beautifully choreographed ballet sequences celebrating Emilia's artistic talent and career success affirm women's self-worth and accomplishment. In addition, the film challenges traditional images of female passivity by portraying Deedee and Emma as strong, forceful women. At the same time, however, these shifts in traditional portrayals of women are harnessed to discourses that neutralize their progressive potential.

The female spectator's engagement with *The Turning Point*'s central female friendship actually carries her through a sequence of diverse subject positions. Initially, spatiotemporal attachment and subjective access draw the viewer into a twinship relationship with Deedee, the down-to-earth wife and mother, in contrast to Emma's more remotely glamorous star persona. Deedee's envy of her friend's success as well as the poise and gracefulness of Emma's manner eventually pull the female spectator into an idealizing relationship with Emma as a distant, unattainable, but desired ideal. This idealization is broken, however, when Emma's disintegrating career and unhappy personal life are gradually revealed. The viewer is finally drawn into a mirroring transference relationship with Deedee as Emma nurtures her into an acceptance of her marriage as the source of true and lasting fulfillment.

By carrying the female spectator through this sequence of subject positions, the film seems to provide her with the opportunity to compare the possible satisfactions offered by career with those of family life. This comparison is presented, however, only to reaccommodate her all the more to the traditional female domestic role as the position in life that brings women the greatest happiness. In spite of the surface praise the film gives to female career success, *The Turning Point* uses its portrayal of female friendship very much as earlier woman's films did, to advocate only one truly satisfying life choice for women—traditional domesticity.

Rich and Famous

Looking to the Past for Models of Female Friendship

Like *The Turning Point, Rich and Famous* begins as a sentimental portrayal of a dyadic female friendship. The story involves two former friends who are reunited after many years when Liz (Jacqueline Bisset), a promising young novelist, comes to Los Angeles for a speaking engagement and stays at the home of Merry (Candice Bergen), her old college roommate, who is now married to a Hollywood screenwriter. As in *The Turning Point,* this long-distance friendship, which seems to have existed since the characters' college days only as a mental construct for both women, is exalted and idealized. The two friends have not seen each other for years, but when they meet again they are suddenly intimate companions. As Lucy Fischer suggests, because we never see their college friendship, it is impossible to feel the strength of their bond; indeed, it is difficult even to imagine what brought these two very different women together or what interests they might share.[16] The film simply expects its audience to believe that these two women are confidantes and helpmates even though we are provided with no explanation for their closeness.

Like *The Turning Point, Rich and Famous* resurrects the old life choices formula found in earlier woman's films and updates it to apply to a contemporary dyadic female friendship. Again, the life choices plot is used to transform the film from a sentimental into a social female friendship portrayal that advocates women's acceptance of the status quo and their traditional role within it. The film's plot relies heavily on establishing a series of contrasts between the two friends: the troubled career woman versus the happy housewife, the serious writer versus the popular author, and finally the miserable single woman versus the failed wife and mother. It brings its female characters into the public sphere of work and career success only to show how empty and meaningless this success is without a man. Like *The Turning Point, Rich and Famous* looks back to the woman's films of the 1930s and 1940s, and like these earlier films, it uses female friendship not to demonstrate the importance of women's relationships with other women, but instead to show the crucial importance of their bonds with men.

The film's attempt to reach into the past to find models for its portrayal of female friendship is evident in the character of both its director and its literary source. The last film of the elderly George Cukor, a major woman's film director of the 1930s and 1940s, *Rich and Famous* was adapted by screenwriter Gerald Ayres from the 1940 stage play *Old Acquaintance*, by John van Druten.[17] The reactionary nature of Cukor's film is most apparent when it is compared with the original play, which is actually more progressive in its treatment of women than is the 1981 screen adaptation.

A Progressive 1940 Play into a Regressive 1981 Film

Whereas *Rich and Famous* bases its female friendship on its central characters' unexplained attachment to each other, *Old Acquaintance* makes the foundation of their friendship very clear. In the play, the women's bond is based primarily on their shared writing careers. Although Milly (renamed Merry in the film) writes popular fiction and Kit (Liz in the film) is a more serious writer, they critique each other's novels. This connection between two female authors who work in different fictional forms but can still come together to discuss their writing is totally missing from the contemporary film. The film, in fact, repeatedly minimizes the satisfaction that Liz and Merry find in their work, concentrating instead on their authorial rivalry and their failed love lives.

A comparison of the endings of the film and play demonstrates the differences in their themes. In the play, Milly blames Kit unfairly for the dissolution of Milly's marriage and for her troubled relationship with her daughter. The two women engage in a heated argument that ends with Kit grabbing Milly's shoulders and shaking her. The film turns this argument into an extended catfight similar to the one in *The Turning Point,* with the women abusing each other both verbally and physically. As Lucy Fischer points out, the way the women fight, attacking one another's sexuality by calling each other "cunts" and resorting to physical violence, seems to represent a "male fantasy of female confrontation and reflects male modes of hostility." Fischer also suggests that the film's use of the catfight is a way of humiliating its female characters, who are positioned "for the pleasure of the masculine viewer, like female mud wrestlers."[18]

In both play and film, the two women resolve their differences in the final scene, but this resolution is presented quite differently in the two works. In the play, Milly comes to see Kit and apologizes, adding, "We needn't talk about what's happened. We can talk about your book. I'd like to go right through it with you."[19] The play clearly suggests that the core of the women's bond and the source of greatest satisfaction in both their lives is to be found in their work. The film, on the other hand, presents both women's careers as ultimately unfulfilling, responsible for their psychological problems, and the cause of their trouble with men. Merry, who initially appears to be a contented, well-adjusted housewife, is transformed into a harridan when she achieves success as a writer. Similarly, Liz's writing career has left her tormented by writer's block, alcoholism, and psychosexual problems. The film, in fact, seems to dwell excessively on Liz's sexual hang-ups, portraying her stereotypically as "the sick career woman."[20] In several scenes she confesses to experiencing sexual frigidity as a result of her writer's block, to writing better after she has been "emotionally mauled" by a man, and to seeking out anonymous sexual encounters. Liz's problems are further illustrated as the film progresses and she becomes involved with a much younger man, breaks off their relationship when he asks her to marry him, and then deeply regrets her decision.

In the concluding scene of Rich and Famous *(Cukor, 1981), Liz (Jacqueline Bisset, left) and Merry (Candice Bergen) lament the loss of their men and drink a toast to the duration of their friendship.*

Because the film associates Liz's status as a career woman with psychological illness, it cannot conclude with the play's affirmation of female literary talent. Career success for both women is, instead, shown to result only in regret and depression. On New Year's Eve, Liz goes off to her country cottage to lament the loss of her young lover, and Merry, who has just won the National Writer's Award, dejectedly leaves her victory party to join Liz. She too is despondent because she has just learned of her ex-husband's plans to remarry. After she arrives at Liz's cottage, the two women sit together before the fireplace, and Liz suddenly announces, "We're terrific. We've accomplished one hell of a lot in one lifetime. We deserve a rest." She then proposes that they sail around the Greek isles together and "only sleep with guys who can't pronounce our names."

This denouement has the despondent Liz encouraging the disillusioned Merry to share her psychosexual hang-ups and join in the dubious pleasures of anonymous sex. Liz seems to regard the women's literary accomplishments as meaningless in comparison with their need for the sexual satisfaction that only men can offer. As Merry nods in agreement, Liz confesses that she always thought that she wanted men to find something "mysterious and seductive" in her work, but now she realizes that what she really wanted was for them to find "the poetry in [her] body." Finding no men around, the two women turn to each other only as a last resort. At the stroke of midnight, Liz asks Merry to kiss her, and Merry responds homophobically, "After all these years are you going to tell me that there's something strange about you?" Liz counters desperately, "It's New Year's Eve. I want the press of human flesh, and you're the only flesh around. Kiss me."

There is something very strange about both of these women and about the film's attempted "happy ending," but it has nothing to do with lesbianism. What is strange is the film's regressive portrayal of female friendship. The pathetic fate reserved for these two remarkably successful women writers offers a grim warning to the film's female viewers that the only hope a woman has for happiness lies in abandoning her career ambitions in order to devote herself completely to the task of finding a man who can provide her with the sexual fulfillment she really needs. As Lucy Fischer suggests, the film's ending is fitting given its misogyny and "transvestite projection of male fantasies onto women." Liz and Merry's projected future together "screwing around on a worldwide tour" is the "perfect scenario for a macho 'buddy movie,'" which indeed in many ways *Rich and Famous* really is.[21]

Rich and Famous is, in fact, remarkably similar to *The Turning Point* in terms of the relationship it attempts to create with its female audience. Both films encourage women viewers to idealize the female characters. The female spectator is allowed to enter the glamorous world of the highly successful career woman, the realm of the "rich and famous," but then this idealization is turned against her when career success is shown in the end to bring a woman nothing but misery and depression. The conclusion of *The Turning Point* tells the female viewer that only a husband and family can provide a woman with lasting fulfillment. The end of *Rich and Famous* asks the audience to share Liz's more "liberated" conviction that only a sexual relationship with a man offers a woman real satisfaction. In both films, as in 1930s and 1940s woman's films, men, not female friendship, emerge as the central concern.

The Movement to High Sentimentality in the 1980s

As we have seen, sentimental female friendship films, beginning with *Julia* and *Girl Friends* in the late 1970s, initially opened themselves up to the possibility of progressive readings. The two other major female friendship films of the period, *The Turning Point* and *Rich and Famous,* on the other hand, utilized the life choices formula of earlier woman's films to propagate a conservative social message. As the sentimental female friendship film developed in the 1980s, both of these directions remained open to it. The films could accentuate the politically challenging reading possibilities that characterized their more political predecessors or devote themselves instead to the conservative messages found in social female friendship films. Following the course set by *The Turning Point* and *Rich and Famous,* sentimental female friendship films in the late 1980s adopted the conservative option and disassociated themselves entirely from politically challenging messages. They became in their thematic content unequivocally social rather than political female friendship films.

Two popular films of the late 1980s, *Beaches* and *Steel Magnolias,* carry the sentimental female friendship film to the level of high sentimentality. The films' sentimentality, however, does not stem from an increase in the sentimental qualities associated with the women's relationships that are portrayed. Like earlier sentimental female friendship portrayals, these films present relationships between women that involve a certain amount of intimate self-disclosure, but this intimacy is not the films' primary focus, nor is its emotional potential particularly exploited. The high sentimentality associated with these films comes instead from the alignment of female friendship with plot conventions of older woman's films. For example, Caryn James suggests that many films addressed to a female audience in the late 1980s, including *Beaches* and *Steel Magnolias,* are "retrograde" and "shamelessly manipulative." She describes *Beaches* specifically as an "updated weepie . . . true not only to its 'pulp fiction' source, but even truer to the old tearjerker tradition of 'woman's films.'"[22] This tearjerker tradition can be more specifically identified as evolving from two categories of 1930s and 1940s woman's films: the maternal melodrama and the medical discourse film.

Whereas some medical discourse films, such as *The Dark Mirror,* focus on a male doctor's attempts to cure a mentally or physically diseased female patient, others focus on the tragic but courageous life of a female protagonist stricken by a debilitating and often fatal illness. These films outline the heroine's pathetic but ultimately triumphant life as she confronts and wins a moral victory over her physical infirmity and sometimes even over her own death. Paradigmatic of this category of medical discourse film is the 1939 Bette Davis star vehicle that initiated the medical discourse film cycle, *Dark Victory* (Goulding). In this quintessential tearjerker, a spoiled socialite is stricken with a deadly brain tumor. She finds love with her brilliant neurosurgeon, but despite his efforts to save her, their happiness is cut short when she eventually succumbs to her illness in the film's tear-drenched final scene.

In contrast to the medical discourse film, the maternal melodrama achieves its intense emotional effect somewhat differently. It focuses on a mother's threatened or real separation from her child and foregrounds the pathos of maternal self-sacrifice and suffering. Within this category of woman's film, the paradigmatic example, among many others, is *Stella Dallas* (King, 1925; Vidor, 1937). It tells the heartbreaking story of a struggling working-class single mother who gives up her daughter to her wealthy ex-husband and his new wife in order to provide the girl with a chance for a better future.

These two types of woman's films are similar, however, in that they strongly incarnate the "weepie" aspects of the genre and their liberal employment of emotional shock tactics to achieve their desired tear-inducing effect is often ridiculed by critics as crassly manipulative. For instance, Mary Ann Doane condemns both types of films for luring their female audience into an "overinvestment in and overidentification with the story and its characters." Doane describes the films' "violent sentimentalism" as having a "pathetic effect" on the female spectator, who, by being led to identify with female suffering, loss, and victimization, is made to assume a passive, masochistic subject position.[23] In contemporary sentimental female friendship films such as *Beaches* and *Steel Magnolias,* the association of women's friendship with this "pathetic effect" is used in a way that appears indeed to reach new heights of audience manipulation. It also seems to prevent the films from being read in politically challenging ways and to facilitate the transmission of a very conservative social message.

Beaches

Who's Responsible?

Released in 1988, *Beaches* was directed by Garry Marshall, a very successful television producer turned film director who is known for his popular entertainment savvy rather than for his artistic accomplishments. Marshall's popular triumphs include not only the highly

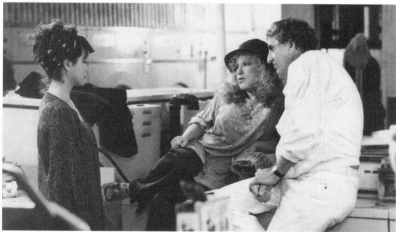

Director Garry Marshall with his stars, Bette Midler and Barbara Hershey, on the set of Beaches *(1988).*

successful film *Pretty Woman* (1990) but also the long-running television sitcoms *The Dick Van Dyke Show, Happy Days,* and *Laverne & Shirley,* all of which, in spite of their glaring shortcomings as works of art, tapped into the popular culture sensibilities of their audience in a way that made them extremely lucrative ventures for their creator.

Beaches, although ultimately under Marshall's directorial control, also was the product of considerable female input. It was coproduced by its star Bette Midler, Bonnie Bruckheimer-Martell, and Margaret

Jennings South as the first project of Midler's newly established production company. The screenplay, written by Mary Agnes Donoghue, is based on Iris Rainer Dart's novel of the same name. Female involvement in a Hollywood project, however, does not by any means assure a progressive text. Its effect can be severely limited by the heavy hand of a dominating male director, the strong force of Hollywood filmmaking conventions, and even the expression by female writers and directors of internalized patriarchal ideas.

In a 1993 interview, Donoghue described her experiences in writing the screenplay for *Beaches,* placing responsibility for the film's heavy sentimentality squarely on Marshall's shoulders. Without detailing the differences between her original script and the final film, she argued that her screenplay "wasn't that sentimental" and that she was even temporarily fired for refusing to write "this terrible stuff" that Marshall insisted she include. Even after she was allowed to return to the project, Marshall still insisted on making significant changes in her work. Donoghue described his impact as follows:

> But it's amazing how much a director can change a script. You don't need to alter the words for the whole thing to be destroyed. If I had made the movie my way, it would have been a little more honest, a little tougher. And maybe then it wouldn't have been as successful.[24]

Although Marshall, as a popularly oriented director, may have been anxious to exploit the sentimental aspects of his material, he cannot be blamed entirely for the film's emotional overload. The literary source for *Beaches,* Dart's novel, contains all of the film's sentimentality and more. The changes made from novel to film indicate little alteration in the story's sentimentality, yet they do suggest that the import of the novel's sentimental plot was substantially altered in its conversion to the screen—by whose hand, Marshall's or Donoghue's or both, remains unclear.

From Novel to Film

The novel and film versions of *Beaches* are very similar in their heavy reliance on the tear-inducing effects of the medical discourse and maternal melodrama plot formulas. Both works recount the story of the lifelong friendship between two women who first meet as young girls on an Atlantic City beach: C.C. Bloom (Bette Midler), Cee Cee in the novel; and Hillary Whitney Essex (Barbara Hershey), Roberta (Bertie)

White Baron in the novel. The two women develop a close friendship, first as pen pals and later as roommates, sharing their life experiences as they move through a number of crises, from career setbacks and successes, romances, marriages, and divorces to the final death of one of the friends. In both works, Hillary/Bertie suffers a slow, emotionally devastating death at a young age from a lingering illness. Her death means that she must leave her young daughter, whom she decides to place in C.C./Cee Cee's care. Both plots also involve the career-driven C.C./Cee Cee's transformation into a more maternal and caring person as she nurses her dying friend and assumes responsibility for her daughter.

The two works begin to diverge in terms of their representation of this transformation. First of all, the novel accentuates the fact that Cee Cee and Bertie have followed very different life paths. Cee Cee is a plain but talented singer who devotes herself completely to her career and becomes a major star. Bertie, on the other hand, is a very beautiful, intelligent young woman who decides instead of pursuing a career to dedicate herself to being a traditional homemaker. The novel suggests that neither life choice brings the woman who has chosen it perfect fulfillment, yet Cee Cee does find a significant amount of satisfaction in her career, whereas Bertie on her deathbed looks back on her life and can describe it only as "brief but boring."[25] In fact, Bertie's death and her decision to give her child to Cee Cee can be read as symbolically enacting the demise of the traditional homemaker, who passes on her legacy of maternal nurturance to a new type of woman, represented by the more assertive, more career-oriented Cee Cee.

The film, in what is possibly a misguided attempt to render Bertie a more progressive character, portrays Hillary, her filmic counterpart, as a successful lawyer. As a result of this crucial change, Hillary loses her symbolic significance. In her illness, she becomes only a pathetic victim of random misfortune, and her death no longer can be interpreted as a symbolic portrayal of the contemporary woman's progression from unfulfilled homemaker to independent working mother. As a result of this change in Hillary's character, C.C.'s final transformation is also altered. In the novel, as noted above, Bertie recognizes on her deathbed that her life as a wife and mother has not brought her true happiness, and this admission shapes the reader's perception of Cee Cee's decision to assume responsibility for Bertie's daughter's care. In spite of Cee Cee's assumption of the maternal role, the novel's ending does not read as a validation of motherhood as the ultimate goal for every woman. After all, Bertie admits that it did not bring her true happiness. Instead, the novel's conclusion signifies a recognition that motherhood represents one source of fulfillment among others and that it can be combined successfully with a woman's career ambitions.

Whereas the novel suggests that both career and motherhood are necessary in order for a woman to find real fulfillment, the film denigrates women's career ambitions and champions motherhood as every woman's ultimate goal. In the novel, Cee Cee persuades Bertie to place her daughter in her care by pointing out that her career success allows her to offer the child significant advantages in life. The film, on the other hand, connects Hillary's motivation for placing her daughter in C.C.'s care with her belief that through C.C. she can live on in her daughter's memory. C.C. is thus reduced at the film's conclusion to a mere conduit through which her memories of the deceased Hillary can be conveyed to Hillary's daughter. These changes entirely eliminate the novel's symbolic enactment of changing female social roles and replace it with the pathetic story of a dying mother's attempt to use her friend to stay alive in the mind of her child.

Beaches and the Female Spectator

Like other female friendship films, *Beaches* attempts to engage its female spectator by associating its female friendship portrayal with a psychoanalytic transference situation. Significantly, the transference relationship found in the film differs from the one found in the novel. The novel's female characters are united by a bond of complementarity that leads them to admire qualities in each other that they feel they themselves lack. Cee Cee envies Bertie's good looks and caring personality, and Bertie admires Cee Cee's driving ambition and assertiveness. An idealizing transference is formed between them that is complemented by a mirroring transference in which Bertie fosters in Cee Cee more giving, nurturing qualities. In return, Cee Cee offers Bertie practical support by caring for her during her final illness and for Bertie's child after her death. In the film, the idealizing transference situation is completely eliminated. Rather than admiring each other, the two women are engaged in constant competition and rivalry. The only transference situation portrayed in the film is a mirroring one. By allowing C.C. to care for her and for her child, Hillary, like Bertie in the novel, nurtures her friend into an acceptance of the mothering, caregiving aspects of her personality.

The female spectator who enters the film by engaging with Hillary and C.C.'s friendship is encouraged to follow C.C. as she is mirrored into accepting a maternal role. Although C.C.'s career success is never openly condemned, the film's failure to idealize her lifestyle, as the novel does, makes it less likely that the female spectator will construct the type of reading that the book fosters. Whereas the novel stresses the importance of both career and motherhood in a woman's life, the film's final focus is strongly on the fulfillment found in the maternal role. This strong concluding emphasis on motherhood draws the spectator all the more forcefully into the "pathetic effect" created by the film's medical discourse and maternal melodrama plot structures. The novel aligns its female spectator primarily with Cee Cee as a successful career woman and finally as a working mother. The film, on the other hand, by eventually reducing C.C. to a mere vessel through which Hillary can stay alive in her child's mind, encourages greater spectatorial engagement with Hillary. As a result, the traditional themes of the medical discourse film and the maternal melodrama, played out most fully in terms of Hillary's character, assume greater centrality, and the female spectator is led to align herself with the image of woman as passive victim, triumphant only through suffering.

The masochistic female spectatorial position thus created is antithetical to the development of more progressive themes related to female bonding and women's career success. Because the plot structures associated with the medical discourse film and the maternal melodrama stress so strongly women's positioning as passive victims, they cannot easily be combined with portrayals of women as active agents capable of career success and personal independence. Instead, the pathetic emotional effect they elicit and the masochistic subject position they create overwhelm more progressive elements and deny them textual prominence.

Beaches also has a significant appeal to a female audience because Marshall has created a slick piece of popular entertainment that resolves irresolvable contradictions and combines very different trajectories for women's lives. The film presents the story of a woman's career success that ends in motherhood, of female bonding that replicates heterosexual marriage even to the extent of the two women coparenting a child, and of a female friendship that validates heterosexuality and motherhood. C.C. and Hillary's bond is presented as so strong that it comes to resemble heterosexual love, which, in spite of the film's glorification of female friendship, is still posited as the model by which all other relationships are judged. Deceptively, the film masks its thematic concerns under the intense emotional effect of its high sentimentality. Beneath the tears it so effectively elicits from its female audience, *Beaches* is hiding a very conservative social message.

Steel Magnolias
Southern Sentimentality

Like *Beaches, Steel Magnolias* relies upon traditional woman's film plot conventions associated with the maternal melodrama and the medical discourse film. It is based on real-life female experiences that are filtered through the perspectives of a male screenwriter and director. The film was directed by Herbert Ross, who, as we have seen, previously rendered *The Turning Point* a conservative throwback to earlier woman's films, and the screenplay was written by Robert Harling, who adapted it from his stage play of the same name. The story is based on a personal tragedy in Harling's family. Like the character Shelby in play and film, Harling's diabetic sister died as a result of kidney failure precipitated by complications following a pregnancy.

Steel Magnolias is not only the story of a young woman's tragic death but also of her mother's terrible loss and of the support her mother receives from her female friends. Both play and film take place in a small Louisiana town, where a group of women gather at Truvy's beauty salon. Harling takes pains to have this network of female friends represent a cross section of the local female community, at least in terms of age and class, if not of race. In addition to the middle-class Shelby (Julia Roberts) and her mother M'Lynn (Sally Field), the group includes two wealthy older women, Clairee (Olympia Dukakis), the widow of the town's deceased ex-mayor, and Ouiser (Shirley MacLaine), the local curmudgeon; Truvy (Dolly Parton), a working-class beautician; and Truvy's assistant Annelle (Daryl Hannah), a destitute young woman whom Truvy has hired literally off the street.

The high sentimentality of the film comes not from the friendship among these women, whose interchanges remain largely comedic, but from the emotional impact of Shelby's death and her mother's overwhelming sense of loss. Intertwined throughout both play and film are the progression of Shelby's illness and her mother's desperate attempts

The stars of Steel Magnolias *(Ross, 1989) pose in a publicity still for the film. Back row, from left to right, Dolly Parton, Sally Field, and Daryl Hannah; front row, from left to right, Shirley MacLaine, Olympia Dukakis, and Julia Roberts.*

to deal with it. These "tearjerker" plot elements, although also prominent in the play, are accentuated by the film's attempts to open up Harling's very stagy single-set drama to multiple settings. The play takes place entirely in Truvy's beauty salon. As a result, its emphasis falls primarily on the comedic interactions among the group of female friends and the positive influence they have on each other's lives. Although Shelby's death and her mother's almost unbearable sorrow still represent the dramatic center of the play, its restricted setting places Shelby's emotionally charged death scene offstage. In the film, in contrast, the audience not only witnesses Shelby's death but also hears M'Lynn's subsequent account of this highly emotional event again when she discusses it with her friends. As a result, the film's bathetic evocation of a tragically severed mother-daughter bond overwhelms its emphasis on female friendship.

A Contemporary "Female World of Love and Ritual"

Lisa Tyler argues persuasively that the presentation of female friendship in *Steel Magnolias* very much resembles what historian Carol Smith-Rosenberg has identified as the most prominent form of nineteenth-century female bonding. According to Smith-Rosenberg, nineteenth-century women, segregated from their husbands and male children by rigid gender-role differentiation, formed what she terms a "female world of love and ritual."[26] These female homosocial groups, centered on the nexus of an extremely strong mother-daughter bond, cooperatively managed domestic duties, passed on essential female knowledge, and provided the emotional support that women could not find in their relationships with men. In fact, according to Smith-Rosenberg, the primary emotional relationships that nineteenth-century women experienced in their lives were most often with their close female friends rather than with their emotionally and intellectually distant husbands.

The women of *Steel Magnolias* seem to have carried this nineteenth-century female world of love and ritual into twentieth-century provincial southern society. As Tyler points out, both play and film take place in what can be seen as "women's territory." The play never leaves the all-female setting of Truvy's beauty salon, and the film does so only to enter into women-centered and -organized ritualistic events: a daughter's wedding, a church festival, a Christmas party, a wedding shower, a child's birthday party, a mother's deathbed vigil, and an Easter egg hunt. Within this woman-centered milieu, the female friends share a separate subculture based on traditional female topics of discussion: local gossip, recipes, clothes, and hairstyles. This isolated female subcultural experience is segregated from the surrounding male-dominated society. Men are completely absent from the play and are only marginally present as "shadowy, half-drawn characters" in the film.[27] When they are mentioned or portrayed, it is as strange, exotic, even idiotic creatures who shoot guns and explode firecrackers to scare birds from trees, spend all of their time in bed watching television, or devote themselves compulsively to hunting.

Tyler regards both play and film as positive celebrations of a twentieth-century variant of the female homosocial bonding that Smith-Rosenberg identifies as a strictly nineteenth-century phenomenon, but what Tyler ignores is the fact that what can be seen as mildly subversive in the nineteenth century is not necessarily progressive in the twentieth century. The friendship groups that Smith-Rosenberg identifies represent attempts by nineteenth-century women to form compensatory subcultural friendship networks. In the face of the restrictive social structure of nineteenth-century America, such friendship groups offered a mild form of female resistance to overwhelming male dominance. Harling's conception of contemporary group female friendship, on the other hand, divests it of its subversive potential and places it entirely in the service of the patriarchal status quo.

The bonding experienced by the group of women portrayed in *Steel Magnolias* is presented as their response to a "natural" inclination to remain separate from men, rather than as a reaction to their exclusion from a male-dominated society. They appear to gravitate instinctively to discussions of local gossip, recipes, hairstyles, and clothes. Because they are, after all, "*steel* magnolias," they also appear, in what is clearly Harling's appeal to female narcissism, quite "naturally" to be stronger than men. This strength is demonstrated not in their accomplishments in the public sphere, from which they seem inclined to remain contentedly divorced, but in their ability to withstand the pain, suffering, and sacrifice that is represented as inevitably a part of their chosen female domestic sphere.

What *Steel Magnolias* ultimately celebrates is female bonding as an extension and support of the "natural" female role of motherhood. Like Smith-Rosenberg's description of nineteenth-century female homosocial networks, the film's group of twentieth-century female friends is centered on an intense mother-daughter relationship. Tyler even proposes that M'Lynn's attachment to Shelby, as "a primal dyad between mother and daughter, not intruded upon by father or siblings, could fairly be called 'a family romance.'"[28] Shelby's decision to risk death to give birth to a child presents motherhood as such a natural and crucial aspect of a woman's life that this young woman is all too willing to die in order to experience it, and M'Lynn's moving ode to the joy within sadness

In Steel Magnolias, *female friendship is reduced to serving merely as a support for women's dedication to motherhood. Here, Ouiser (Shirley MacLaine, left) comforts M'Lynn (Sally Field) at M'Lynn's daughter's funeral.*

that motherhood has brought her represents the emotional high point of both play and film.

After Shelby's death, M'Lynn comes to Truvy's beauty salon in desperate need of her friends' emotional support. She laments her daughter's death and confesses that she finds the pain of losing her almost unbearable. As she describes the feelings she experienced while watching vigilantly at Shelby's deathbed, she offers a picture of motherhood as the ultimate experience in a woman's life:

> I just sat there . . . holding Shelby's hand while the sounds got softer and the beeps got farther apart until all was quiet. . . . I realized as a woman how lucky I was. I was there when this wonderful person drifted into my world and I was there when she drifted out. It was the most precious moment of my life thus far.

Because motherhood is presented as women's true source of fulfillment, female friendship is granted importance only as a way for women to find the support they need to fulfill their maternal role. One might call *Steel Magnolias* a maternal melodrama masquerading as a female friendship film. It uses friendships among women merely as support for what it presents as women's "natural" maternal role.

In the tradition of the maternal melodrama, this role is portrayed as bringing a woman her greatest joy as well as almost unbearable suffering, and both of these effects are presented as inevitable and unalterable. There is no questioning of Shelby's decision to risk death in order to have a child, no suggestion that her overwhelming, and ultimately self-destructive, desire for motherhood might be socially constructed and not the result of her "natural" maternal instincts. In fact, even M'Lynn, who initially offers the greatest opposition to Shelby's determination to have a child, finally after Shelby's death expresses in her ode to motherhood her implicit approval of her daughter's self-sacrificial actions and thereby repudiates her earlier criticism. The film identifies motherhood so strongly with suffering and self-sacrifice that at its conclusion it can fully support the social validation of motherhood at any cost to the mother.

Steel Magnolias never even begins to ask whether there might be something wrong with a society that so strongly validates self-sacrificial motherhood that a young woman would feel the need to endanger her own life in order to give birth to a child. It never questions Shelby's decision because it never questions woman's traditional social roles under patriarchy; instead, it celebrates these roles as natural and positive even if a woman must kill herself to fit into them. It glorifies women's suffering and self-sacrifice in the service of the female procreative role and champions female friendship as a way for women to console each other in their pain.

Engaging the Female Spectator in a "Female World of Love and Ritual"

Steel Magnolias attempts to engage its female audience in two primary ways: by encouraging spectatorial identification with its portrayal of a group female friendship and through the bathetic effects of its maternal melodrama and medical discourse plot conventions. The two strategies of engagement, however, are intimately related. The female viewer is invited to identify with the twinship transference relationship that unites the film's female friends as well as with the passionate mother-daughter bond at its center. She is drawn into their strong homosocial union by the intensity of this mother-daughter bond, the emphasis on shared female subcultural experiences, and the suggestion of women's alienation from male culture. Important as well is the film's appeal to female narcissism through the celebration of a "natural" femininity identified with woman's traditional social roles. As is typical of the maternal melodrama and the medical discourse film, these roles are aligned with a masochistic subject position that presents women as happy and fulfilled in their suffering and loss. The strongly bathetic effect produced by these plot structures also encourages spectatorial overidentification with and overinvolvement in a scenario of female victimization.

In the final analysis, *Steel Magnolias* offers its female spectator a subject position very affirmative of the patriarchal status quo. By identifying with the film's female friends, the female viewer is encouraged to accept happily her traditional role as wife and mother as appropriate and fulfilling and to support other women's dedication to this role even unto death. Although the film is based on real-life female experiences, the interpretation of the significance of these experiences is filtered through a male fantasy construct that envisions women as finding complete fulfillment in the traditional roles that patriarchy has assigned them. It is a fantasy that acts to naturalize these roles in order to assure women's willing acceptance of their given situation in life. Any questioning of this given situation is presented as decidedly unnatural.

Like *Beaches, Steel Magnolias* also offers its female audience the reconciliation of social contradictions in contemporary women's lives that are in reality irreconcilable. As its title suggests, its female characters are as delicate as magnolias but as tough as steel. They are pathetic victims but strong survivors, sad but fulfilled. In addition, these contradictory characteristics are naturalized to prevent their ever being challenged. The film's "steel magnolias" are confined to their traditionally feminine roles as if encased in steel, the steel bars of a male fantasy that insists on seeing women as happy in their misery.

Concluding Comments

The development of the sentimental female friendship film throughout the period of the late 1970s and 1980s takes two primary directions. First of all, the films demonstrate a movement to heightened sentimentality. It is a sentimentality, however, that results not so much from the sentimentalization of the female friendship bond itself as from its association with plot formulas drawn from such earlier woman's film precedents as the maternal melodrama, the life choices film, and the medical discourse film. This increased sentimentality masks a second prominent characteristic of these films. As the decade of the 1980s wore on, sentimental female friendship films began to reject the possibilities demonstrated in earlier representatives of the cycle in the late 1970s, films such as *Julia* and *Girl Friends*. No longer was the sentimental female friendship film used for progressive political purposes, to challenge the patriarchal status quo, or to critique women's limited roles within it. As the sentimental female friendship film developed, its impact became increasingly emotional and its political message increasingly conservative.

3 | The Female Friendship Film and Women's Development

Whereas the sentimental female friendship film relies primarily on emotional effect to engage female viewers, other female friendship films released throughout the period of the 1980s cultivate viewer involvement by focusing on women's relationships as they relate to female maturation and psychological development. These filmic investigations of female maturation parallel work being done by psychologists, who single out adolescence as a time of particular significance in regard to the formation of a woman's sense of self. As Nona P. Lyons points out, traditionally, psychological studies examined the adolescent's movement to adulthood in terms of male experience, and female development as a distinctly different process was largely ignored.[1] Psychologists describe male adolescent maturation as a linear progression from dependence to autonomy, involving the rejection of familial relatedness in the process of creating an autonomous sense of self. Recent studies of adolescent girls, however, demonstrate that female psychological development involves not a rejection of relatedness for autonomy but an attempt to merge these two aspects of one's personality. For the adolescent girl, autonomy is often seen as a way to improve relationships with others—to establish more mature connections that involve a sense of attachment combined with a recognition of the other as an autonomous individual.[2]

These conceptions of adolescent female development are reflected in a number of films from the period of the middle to the late 1980s. Films such as *Desperately Seeking Susan* (Seidelman, 1985), *Housekeeping*

(Forsyth, 1987), and *Mystic Pizza* (Petrie, 1988) all focus on the connection between women's psychological maturation and their relationships with other women. This association of female friendship with women's development provides another avenue through which female friendship films engage their female spectators, allowing the films to reach a wider audience. As we shall see, both *Desperately Seeking Susan* and *Mystic Pizza* seem carefully calculated to court the youth market, a target audience that Hollywood in the 1980s was particularly eager to attract.

Desperately Seeking Susan
A Female Friendship Film with Youth Appeal

Desperately Seeking Susan is the only Hollywood female friendship film of the 1980s that was directed by a woman. Director Susan Seidelman even proposes that her control of the production allowed her to give the film a distinctly female point of view that would have been diffused by more male involvement.[3] Not only was the film directed by a woman, but its screenplay was written by Leora Barish, and it was produced by Sarah Pillsbury and Midge Sanford for Orion Pictures, whose vice president at the time, Barbara Boyle, was influential in bringing about the film's production.

Barish's female-oriented screenplay had circulated in Hollywood for five years before finally being sold as a package to Orion once Seidelman and actress Rosanna Arquette became attached to the project.[4] The key to the film's sudden salability was not its appeal to female audiences so much as the youth appeal that both Seidelman as director and Arquette as star brought to the production. As Seidelman has described the situation: "Before I got involved with it, a lot of names were thrown around [for the lead role], but they were of a different age group, like Mary Steenburgen. I wanted to make the casting younger. I think my graphic style has a young, energetic quality to it. Rosanna is young and energetic."[5] The film's youth orientation was solidified by the casting of Madonna in the second lead. Seidelman was again influential in this casting decision and in working with Madonna to shape her role. According to Seidelman, she had to overcome studio objections in order to cast Madonna, who at the time was a relative unknown, over some two hundred other actresses who tested for the part.[6] During the filming, Madonna's song "Borderline" went to the top of the music charts. Suddenly, Madonna was a major star, and the film's youth appeal increased appreciably.

Seidelman's involvement in the project also led to significant alterations in Barish's original screenplay, the story of Roberta (Arquette), a young suburban housewife who becomes obsessed with the life of Susan (Madonna), an unconventional female drifter. In both versions, Roberta suffers amnesia after a fall and comes to believe she is Susan. After having temporarily adopted Susan's more liberated lifestyle, Roberta realizes when she recovers her memory that she prefers the greater freedom she has found as Susan to her previous way of life. Barish has attributed to Seidelman a major influence in reshaping the screenplay into the final film: "Susan Seidelman has a vision of her own, . . . and she interpreted it [the screenplay] differently. . . . I can't watch the movie without a dissonance between what I imagined and what has emerged." Although Barish seems to express some regret at the extent of Seidelman's changes, when asked if she approved of the final film, she commended Seidelman for maintaining her original theme and added, "If it has a strengthening effect, an opening-up effect on people, then I like it."[7]

Seidelman, on the other hand, sees her contributions to the film as much more limited and relegated primarily to updating a five-year-old screenplay "that wasn't really contemporary" and establishing an appropriate tone that could make the comedy in Barish's screenplay work. Seidelman has described her involvement in the project as follows: "When I first read the script, I felt a device like amnesia, which Roberta experiences, could be really dumb. . . . I tried to create a tone for the movie that would make something like that work. Not too serious, but not too cartoonish either."[8] Whatever the extent of Seidelman's influence, *Desperately Seeking Susan,* the only Hollywood female friendship film of the 1980s written, produced, and directed by women, represents a major Hollywood studio release made with substantial female input. The film demonstrates that although such input can be significant, it does not automatically guarantee a progressive film.

But Is It Really a Female Friendship Film?

Seidelman's direction of *Desperately Seeking Susan* had one measurable effect that cannot be disputed. Seidelman took the female friendship film to a younger audience than Barish's screenplay or earlier female friendship films had attempted to attract. One might even question whether the film falls into the female friendship category at all. After all, Roberta never even meets Susan face-to-face until near the film's conclusion, and their relationship lacks many of the outstanding qualities of sentimental female friendship, including emotionally intense personal involvement, nurturance, and intimacy between the two women. Yet Roberta's fascination, even obsession, with Susan clearly represents a psychologically empowering idealizing transference situation that triggers in Roberta a significant rebirth, a transformation of character very similar to what occurs in other female friendship films. Seidelman has even attributed her interest in the project to having "liked the idea of a woman becoming obsessed with another woman. We've seen enough movies about guys growing up, and it's about time to see the other side."[9]

The film also resembles other female friendship films in its use of two staples of the cycle: the life choices formula and the good/bad girl scenario. Roberta and Susan represent two very distinct female lifestyles: Roberta is a self-effacing, subservient, sexually repressed suburban housewife in an unfulfilling marriage to a self-centered hot tub salesman who is cheating on her with another woman. Susan, on the other hand, is a free-spirited drifter and con woman, single, promiscuous, and irresponsible, who moves from city to city and man to man. Roberta watches Susan from afar and begins to identify with her more liberated, self-sufficient femininity. She comes to idealize Susan, whose life serves as an example not only of liberation but also of romance and excitement. Roberta's temporary assumption of Susan's identity as a result of her amnesia allows her to merge with her ideal and experience a psychological rebirth. She finds a new identity by introjecting the positive qualities she finds in Susan into her own personality.

Revising Earlier Woman's Film Formulas

In many ways, *Desperately Seeking Susan* consciously revises conventions associated with earlier woman's films. For instance, Susan Morrison suggests that the film rewrites Alfred Hitchcock's classic rendering of female development in *Rebecca* (1940). Morrison notes that at the beginning of her journey to a new identity, Roberta is shown watching a scene from *Rebecca* on television. In this scene, the protagonist's husband, Maxim, laments his young wife's acquisition of a newfound maturity: "Gone forever, that funny young lost look I loved. It won't ever come back. I killed that when I told you about Rebecca." Morrison sees this scene as the beginning of *Desperately Seeking Susan*'s revision of the earlier film's story of an immature heroine's journey to adulthood.[10]

Exhibiting similar attitudes and attire, Rosanna Arquette (left) and Madonna exhibit the wanna-be phenomenon in a publicity still for Desperately Seeking Susan *(Seidelman, 1985).*

As I have argued elsewhere, *Rebecca* can be read as a female Oedipal drama that traces its childlike heroine's struggle to overcome her debilitating obsession with Rebecca, her husband's deceased first wife.[11] The figure of Rebecca represents the liberated, independent femininity that the film insists must be repudiated for a woman to enter successfully into a heterosexual love relationship and to fulfill her appropriate role in patriarchal marriage. In contrast to *Rebecca, Desperately Seeking*

Susan structures its heroine's Oedipal trajectory around her obsession with another woman as a positive, rather than a negative, image of female independence and freedom. Unlike Rebecca, Susan is presented as a model of competent, fulfilling, independent femininity that Roberta seeks to emulate rather than reject. By merging with the liberating aspects of Susan's personality, Roberta is able to attain a mature female identity and find personal fulfillment outside the bounds of patriarchal marriage. Unlike the heroine of *Rebecca,* who reaches maturity only by learning to despise another woman, Roberta grows up because she comes to like and admire one.

As Lisa Lewis suggests, *Desperately Seeking Susan* enacts cinematically the admiration many teenage girls feel for popular female rock stars, such as Madonna. Lewis terms this attraction the "wanna-be phenomenon" and sees it enacted in the film by Roberta, who, like a rock star's fans, voyeuristically observes and vicariously participates in Susan's more exciting life from afar.[12] She eventually begins to imitate the dress and look of her idol and to adopt aspects of Susan's personality that she previously had been too inhibited to express. As a result, Roberta develops a more complex and mature personality, gaining the confidence to reject the past, act upon her own desires, and choose a new path to self-fulfillment.

Desperately Seeking Susan's revision of earlier woman's film formulas also includes a deconstruction of the good/bad girl split so often found in female double films.[13] Roberta is the good girl associated with feminine sweetness, passivity, asexuality, and devotion to men, and Susan is the bad girl, assertive, sexually promiscuous, and self-involved. The plot structure of the traditional female double film, as shown in the discussion of *The Dark Mirror* in chapter 1, has the good girl, as the symbolic representation of socially approved femininity, triumph over her evil counterpart, the symbol of a subversive femaleness that challenges the patriarchal status quo. *Desperately Seeking Susan,* however, violates this traditional pattern by mocking rather than validating the good girl posture.[14] It resolves the contrast between its two female characters not by having the good girl triumph over and eventually destroy her bad double, but by merging the two women into a new female self that represents an active, autonomous femininity dedicated not to pleasing men but to pleasing oneself.

Finding an Ending

Desperately Seeking Susan's revision of older woman's film formulas affirms contemporary female viewers in a number of ways. The film supports women's sense of self-worth, personal development, and autonomy while critiquing male dominance, patriarchal marriage, and women's attempts to find self-definition entirely within the confines of conventional domesticity. In addition to these progressive elements, however, the film, like so many other female friendship films, also contains a number of recuperative aspects that limit its ability to provide useful avenues for thinking through important changes in women's contemporary social roles.

Screenwriter Leora Barish has identified her major problem in writing the script as a difficulty in finding an appropriate conclusion for Roberta's quest for self-identity. According to Barish, Roberta's process of self-liberation was "relatively easy to establish, . . . [but] what Roberta changes into was hard to find. I could only lead her to the point of an adventure, but not articulate what it was."[15] This problem of finding an appropriate conclusion for Roberta's quest is evident in the final film as well. In fact, a comparison of the film's conclusion to the ending of Barish's original screenplay indicates that her initial ideas for the outcome of Roberta's quest for self-identity and fulfillment were altered significantly in the process of the film's production.[16]

Both film and screenplay end on a note of victory and empowerment for their female characters, but the nature of this empowerment is different in the two versions. In Barish's original screenplay, Roberta discovers in the course of her adventures an interest in paleontology. Unlike the final film, the screenplay's plot does not center on the attempts of criminals to recover valuable stolen earrings that Susan has in her possession; instead, it involves Roberta and Susan's discovery of a rare fossilized bone. The reward they receive for this discovery allows them to go off together to study fossils in the desert, leaving their respective boyfriends behind. Clearly, the screenplay's ending emphasizes career interests and female bonding, not heterosexual romance.

The film's conclusion is quite different, and there is evidence that the changes that were made were studio mandated.[17] In the final version, Roberta's interest in paleontology and the women's discovery of a rare fossil are dropped in favor of slapstick comedy sequences involving

Roberta's job as a female assistant to an amateur magician. During one of the performances of the magic act, the film climaxes in an extended chase sequence that concludes with Roberta finally meeting Susan and rescuing her from capture by the criminal who is pursuing her. Although the new ending still involves Roberta's acquisition of a career and demonstrates the salvific quality of female bonding, her position as a magician's assistant can hardly be taken as seriously as the original script's conception of her as a would-be paleontologist.

Both film and screenplay end with a coda. As noted above, in the screenplay Susan and Roberta leave their male lovers behind. The script's final scene shows the two men peering at a photograph of their girlfriends, who are seen sitting together on a camel about to ride off into the desert. The men wonder whether they should set out in pursuit of the women, and the screenplay ends. The film's ending is entirely altered. Roberta's lover, Des (Aidan Quinn), who works as a film projectionist, is interrupted in his projection booth by Roberta, who comes to tell him that she has left her husband. As they kiss, Roberta and Des disturb the running of the film in the projector, and the exposed film begins to burn. An immediate cut to the theater audience watching the film that Des has been projecting reveals that it includes Susan, who is resting her head on the shoulder of her lover, Jim (Robert Joy).

This ending performs a recuperative function not found in Barish's screenplay by repositioning the film's transgressive female characters neatly within the patriarchal confines of heterosexual romance. Concluding in this way, the film loses much of the subversive potential found in the screenplay's celebration of women's career ambitions and female bonding, but Seidelman adds one final shot that calls this studio-mandated ending into question. As Susan puts her head on Jim's shoulder, the film that we are watching seems to burn like the film that Des was projecting when he and Roberta kissed. The film's conclusion on a note of heterosexual romance, with both women kissing their boyfriends, is then replaced by a final image of female bonding as Roberta and Susan are shown receiving a reward check for apprehending the criminal. Susan grabs Roberta's hand and raises both their clenched fists into the air in a victory salute. The camera pulls back and the scene becomes a picture on the front page of a newspaper whose headline reads, "What a pair!"

This final shot can be read as an ironic comment on the film's concluding focus on heterosexual romance. While Seidelman shows the ending that the studio wanted, reinscribing her female characters into traditional heterosexual love relationships, this ending is presented as cinematic illusion. When the film burns, what is revealed behind this illusionistic heterosexual romantic resolution is the reality of female bonding and personal fulfillment, themes that are expressed more directly in Barish's earlier screenplay. While Seidelman made concessions to studio demands by imposing on Barish's script a more conventional romantic ending, by adding the final shot of the two women together she managed to subvert that ending and remain faithful to the major theme of self-development through female bonding that characterizes Barish's screenplay.

Why would Barish's original ending, with its focus on two women going off together, provoke the studio to demand radical revision? The answer may be found in the way the film structures the gaze of its characters to focus strongly on one woman's desire in regard to another woman, a desire that might easily be interpreted as homoerotic. According to Jackie Stacey, the film's gaze structure violates dominant Hollywood conventions that assign the look and accompanying mechanisms of desire exclusively to male characters; instead, *Desperately Seeking Susan* focuses on women as both actively desiring subjects and objects of the female gaze and of female desire. Stacey proposes that as a result of this unconventional gaze structure, the female spectator is implicated not only in Roberta's identificatory fascination with Susan as an ego ideal, but also in her intense, and for Stacey clearly homoerotic, desire for another woman.[18] The strong challenge to heterosexual norms found in the expression of this desire and the possibility of its being extended out to the female spectator through engagement with Roberta and her desiring fascination with Susan seem to have led the studio to insist on an ending that recuperates this threat by returning both women safely to their heterosexual lovers.[19]

Desperately Seeking Susan and the Female Spectator

Where, then, does all this position the female spectator in regard to the text of *Desperately Seeking Susan*? The studio's insistence on a more conventional ending indicates that studio executives felt the film had transgressive qualities that did not fit neatly with established Hollywood norms. One potentially transgressive aspect, for instance, is Roberta's idealizing transference relationship with Susan (a replication of the "wanna-be phenomenon"), which draws the female spectator into the possibly homoerotic pleasure that Roberta's fascination with the sexually provocative Susan involves. The end point of this transference relationship is a female victory that offers the viewer an empowering scene of female affirmation and autonomy.

The fact that the studio saw this empowerment as too subversive for mainstream audiences unless it was combined with a validation of heterosexual romance demonstrates how conservative Hollywood films really are. Actually, the political implications of Roberta's transformation are really quite limited. What the film presents is Roberta's personal development, confined entirely to the individual rather than the social level. She gets a job as an assistant to an incompetent male magician and replaces one man with another in a love relationship. The film seems to draw the spectator in through the promise of a radical change in Roberta's personality that never fully materializes. What *Desperately Seeking Susan* really offers its female viewer is a limited sense of empowerment that is used only to exchange and assist men. As Barish has said of her screenplay, it was easy to advocate self-development and liberation, but where this freedom would lead remained beyond her grasp, and apparently beyond Seidelman's as well. Although the film envisions a radical transformation of female identity, it cannot establish a suitable goal for that transformation. All it can do is show two women raising their hands aloft in celebration of their being "What a pair!" The liberating image is there, but the substance of that liberation remains illusive, and the studio seems to have found even this moderate stance too subversive unless combined with heterosexual romance.

Housekeeping

The Female Oedipal Drama

Whereas *Desperately Seeking Susan* connects female development to one woman's idealization of another woman as a role model, a second type of developmental female friendship film presents women's relationships within an intrafamilial context as a replication of the mother-daughter bond. Exemplary of this approach is Bill Forsyth's 1987 film adaptation of Marilynne Robinson's novel *Housekeeping*.[20] Forsyth served as both director and screenwriter, and his relationship to his literary source is a curious one. In interviews, he has expressed adamantly his determination to convert Robinson's novel to the screen as faithfully as possible. He has claimed to have conceived of his role as an adaptor in extremely limited terms: "I suppose there are any number of ways you can approach a novel in terms of adapting it but I simply wanted to make a promotional movie for the book so I was quite willfully slavish to the book. I didn't want to even have an attitude to the book or use it as raw material."[21] Yet Forsyth's determination to bring his, and only his, interpretation of Robinson's novel to the screen is apparent from his involvement in the project from its inception and his rejection of any interference with his designs for its execution.

Forsyth read the novel, obtained the rights from Robinson for the film adaptation, and wrote the screenplay himself. When Diane Keaton, slated for the film's starring role, sent him suggestions for the reconception of her character, Forsyth ignored her, and she dropped out of the production just six weeks before shooting was to begin. As Forsyth describes the incident:

> She [Keaton] liked the novel and said she liked the script but, in a normal kind of film starry way, she'd just presumed that she was going to have influence on it. She sent me pages of notes and, not knowing any better, I just read them and put them away. I didn't know that what I was supposed to do was re-write the script in order to put in all the kooky little scenes where Sylvie [Keaton's character] was really strange and wonderful. . . . I think, basically, I forgot to woo her.[22]

Forsyth goes on to say that he believes Keaton's leaving the project was to its benefit. Her departure represents for him her recognition that she was wrong for Sylvie's role, as Forsyth conceived it, and that he had no intention of changing that conception to appease her.[23] Thus, *Housekeeping* appears to be a film with a male writer/director who claimed to be simply transposing a highly regarded female-authored text to the screen yet was, in fact, strongly committed to filming his and only his interpretation of this work.

Both the novel and film versions of *Housekeeping* recount the story of two girls: Ruthie (Sara Walker), the narrator/protagonist, and her sister Lucille (Andrea Burchill). Ruthie and Lucille's experiences illustrate well the crisis of adolescent female development that psychologists have associated with female maturation. Both girls experience in their adolescent years a reactivation of their earlier Oedipal crises. Helen, the girls' mother, abandoned her preschool daughters before they had adequately weathered their childhood Oedipal dilemmas. She left them on their grandmother's porch and committed suicide by driving a borrowed car into a lake. As they approach adolescence, she represents a distant enigma to both girls, neither of whom understands her sudden inexplicable decision to kill herself.

Ruthie and Lucille are plagued by their sense of a lost maternal figure who cannot be replaced by a succession of inadequate mothers. Their grandmother, their first mother substitute, embodies traditional mothering nurturance. Although she provides a stable home environment, her mothering is suffocatingly constrictive. After her death, Ruthie and Lucille are placed under the supervision of their maiden aunts, who are at the same time too nurturing and too individuated. Although they worry constantly about their charges, they cannot accept the inhospitable environment of Fingerbone, the small, desolate town in the rural northwest where the family home is located. Eventually, they summon Sylvie (Christine Lahti), the girls' aunt and Helen's sister, to care for her nieces. Sylvie is an unconventional mother figure, yet she also embodies the qualities of relatedness and autonomy that psychologists describe as the object of the female adolescent's quest for a mature identity. Her individualism, which involves the mobile nonconformity of the transient, is rejected by the larger society, symbolized by the inhabitants of Fingerbone, who refuse to accept an autonomous woman who does not fit their conception of conventional womanhood.

Although Sylvie attempts to mother Ruthie and Lucille, she does so in ways that actually parody traditional maternal behavior. Forced to carry out "housekeeping" in order to raise her nieces, she subverts the system from within by living the life of a transient within a conventional domestic environment. She sees housekeeping merely as "accumulation" and decorates the house with empty cans and old newspapers.[24] When flooding occurs, she welcomes nature's invasion into her home. In both novel and film, she and Ruthie dance in the flooded kitchen, as if the water were not an intrusion, but a reason for celebration.

From Novel to Film

In her novel, Robinson converts her portrayal of these intrafamilial female relationships into a devastating critique of established conceptions of appropriate female development. Ruthie and Lucille embody alternative forms of female maturation, or Oedipal detachment from the mother. Glossing Freud's concept of the Oedipal crisis with his ideas concerning melancholia and mourning, Judith Butler defines two possible paths of female Oedipal development.[25] Ruthie assumes the melan-

In Housekeeping *(Forsyth, 1987), nonconformist Sylvie (Christine Lahti, center) walks through the streets of Fingerbone with her nieces, Lucille (Andrea Burchill, left) and Ruthie (Sara Walker).*

cholic, and Lucille undertakes the mourning pathway to female maturity. Having incorporated or encrypted her mother into her psyche, Ruthie is haunted by a desire to merge with another maternal figure. Lucille, on the other hand, having weathered maternal loss by introjection rather than incorporation, is able to regard her mother's death as accidental, rather than as a deliberate abandonment. This fabrication allows her to move out of her dyadic bond with her mother into conventional society, where she forms multiple relational bonds with others. As a result, she rejects Sylvie's unconventional motherhood as too smothering. For her, it signifies a regression to pre-Oedipal dyadism rather than a progression to nondyadic social integration.

In entering social life, however, Lucille also accepts the stifling conformity and conventionality of Fingerbone society, whose inhabitants live in fear of outsiders and of nature's constant threat to reclaim their "civilized" domain through flood and fire. In other words, Lucille enters a static, terrified, and intolerant society that sets itself up against nature, rejects difference, and insists upon complete conformity. Ruthie's and Sylvie's unconventionality, as well as their identification with and appreciation for the mysteries and beauties of the natural environment, identifies them as a particular threat to the citizens of Fingerbone, who see nature and natural instincts as frightening and destructive.

In the novel, Lucille's introjection of maternal loss thus allows her to achieve only a problematic maturity. Ruthie, on the other hand, remains trapped in her pre-Oedipal desire for merging with her lost mother, whom she finally replaces with Sylvie. On an overnight trip to a deserted homestead, Ruthie is able to forgive her mother for abandoning her and to accept Sylvie as a mother substitute, yet this bonding with Sylvie does not free Ruthie from her melancholic encrypted sense of maternal loss because Sylvie, too, possesses a melancholic psyche. Her melancholic dreaminess and unconventionality have propelled her outside of cultural relatedness into the individuation of transience.

Enmeshed in this melancholic bond with Sylvie, Ruthie achieves an Oedipal resolution that is just as unsatisfying as Lucille's. In addition to her isolation from society, she is plagued by an overwhelming sense of loss and a wish for death, which she sees as a means finally of merging with her dead mother. For both Ruthie and Sylvie, transience represents a way to connect with the family dead, and their decision to leave Fingerbone by crossing the bridge over the lake, where both Helen and her father perished, represents an attempt to do so. While they remain alive, they are plagued in their transient existence by an overwhelming sense of loss—the loss of Lucille. The novel ends with Ruthie's description of her subsequent life with Sylvie, their rejection of society's "ceremonies of sustenance, of nurturing," and their mourning for the loss of Lucille.[26] Ruthie and Sylvie, in fact, seem at this point to have almost completely retreated into their memories of past losses. Ruthie imagines that she and Sylvie are stalking the house in Fingerbone where Lucille has now established a conventional family, and Sylvie, equally obsessed, searches for Lucille's name in the Boston telephone directory. Finally, Ruthie envisions Lucille in a Boston restaurant: "No one watching this woman . . . could know how her thoughts are thronged by our absence, or know how she does not watch, does not listen, does not wait, does not hope, and always for me and Sylvie."[27] Clearly, the ones who do listen, do wait, and do hope for Lucille are Ruthie and Sylvie.

Through its enactment of Ruthie's and Lucille's troubled Oedipal development, the novel envisions female maturation as ending in one of two ways: acceptance of stifling conventionality or withdrawal into antisocial nonconformity. The first path, that taken by Lucille, involves an accompanying fear of nature's threat to an unnatural society that violates nature itself by excluding individuals like Sylvie and Lucille, who do not fit its norms. Ruthie's antisocial developmental path leads her, on the other hand, to feelings of autonomy and dyadic relatedness, but it involves an accompanying sense of loss that culminates finally in an intense wish for death. Hence, Robinson's critique of female development proposes no satisfying conclusion to female adolescence—women's entrance into adulthood under patriarchy. In the novel, the adolescent girl is unable to relate or to individuate successfully: either she loses something that haunts her forever or blocks out her sense of loss in order to conform to social requirements.

Although Forsyth's intentions may have been to re-create as closely as possible his novelistic source, the film version of *Housekeeping* alters the novel's portrait of female development significantly. Forsyth's film, unlike Robinson's novel, allows for the possibility of a fulfilling conclusion to the female quest for relatedness and autonomy. Remaining faithful to the novel until its very end, Forsyth radically recasts its conclusion. In the film, as in the novel, Ruthie and Sylvie form a strong twinship relationship as a result of their overnight trip to an abandoned homestead, and Ruthie overcomes her sense of maternal loss through bonding with her mirror image in Sylvie. In the film, however, this union leads the two women to move outside social constraints to a transience that is presented as mysterious and unknowable.

The film ends with Ruthie and Sylvie setting out on a liberating flight to a life that is, as Sylvie describes it when they leave Fingerbone, "not so bad" as the town's confining social environment. She tells Ruthie: "We'll go to Spokane, then to Portland. From Portland, you can take a train anywhere." They cross the bridge over the lake and disappear into the darkness. The film's final image of their tiny figures glowing in the distant night places the conclusion of their quest beyond the audience's comprehension. The viewer remains with Lucille, who in this version is the only one left behind with a sense of loss. She is given the film's final voice-over comment: "She always did that. She just wandered off."

Whereas Robinson's conclusion unequivocally rejects the notion that women can escape from conventional society without an enormous feeling of emptiness, Forsyth opens the text up to a reading that sees Ruthie and Sylvie's rejection of social constraints as an exhilarating flight from civilization. The film allows its audience to view these transient women as autonomous individuals who undertake an eccentric but triumphant escape from the confines of society. The novel, on other hand, questions the viability of just such a strategy of female liberation. For Robinson, no projected solution to the crisis of female development under existing social conditions seems completely satisfying. For Forsyth, merely "wander[ing] off," as Ruthie and Sylvie do, provides a perfect answer.

The Female Spectator and Forsyth's Representation of Female Oedipal Development

The differences between Forsyth's and Robinson's visions of female adolescent development have a significant effect on the subject positions each work offers its female audience. One might view Forsyth's changes as an expansion of Robinson's feminism. After all, the film's "happy ending" suggests, very much in contrast to the novel, that women can successfully escape the confines of a repressive social structure. Although Forsyth's conclusion is certainly more optimistic than Robinson's, this optimism actually seems to reduce her social critique. In the novel, women are presented as trapped, no matter which developmental path they pursue, by an unnatural social structure that forces them either to adopt Lucille's stifling conformity or to risk experiencing Ruthie and Sylvie's social ostracism. Forsyth, in contrast, envisions Sylvie and Ruthie as autonomous women who flee a repressive society for an exhilaratingly undefined transient future. This easy solution makes women's problems seem completely solved by a simple flight into nonconformity.

In addition, it is significant that Forsyth ends his film by breaking the spectator's connection with his triumphantly nonconformist heroines. In the film's final shot, the camera does not follow Ruthie and Sylvie as they cross over into a new life. Whereas the novel's focalization never deviates from Ruthie's first-person narrational perspective, Forsyth at the film's conclusion switches spatiotemporal attachment jarringly from Ruthie to Lucille. Ruthie's intermittent voice-over narration as well as the film's focus on her subjectivity up to this point have encouraged strong spectatorial engagement with her character. At the very end, however, the distant camera positioning that stops short of accompanying Ruthie and Sylvie over the bridge to their new transient existence, accompanied by the switch to Lucille's concluding voice-over comment, encourages viewers to abandon Ruthie as she goes off with

Sylvie and to remain behind with Lucille. Whereas the novel's conclusion focuses on Ruthie and Sylvie's lament for Lucille's loss, the film concentrates instead on Lucille's inability to sympathize with, or even to try to understand, her family's nonconformist behavior.

Ruthie and Sylvie depart for a distant, seemingly incomprehensible life of female liberation from which the film's spectator, like Lucille, is hopelessly barred. In this way, Forsyth positions his female viewers as onlookers, as uncomprehending as Lucille or perhaps somewhat more understanding of female nonconformity than she, but still merely looking on, as Forsyth may feel he is, as nonconformist women flee the existing patriarchal social structure. Although the film's female spectator may be encouraged to understand, she remains nevertheless excluded from participation in women's liberationist goals, which in the end are presented as distant and beyond her comprehension. With Forsyth, she is assigned to the role of observer—sympathetic observer perhaps, but never participant in women's strategies for liberation.

Mystic Pizza

An Adolescent Life Choices Film

Unlike *Housekeeping*, which examines the relationship between female bonding and female adolescent development in terms of a surrogate mother-daughter bond, *Mystic Pizza* revisits the traditional life choices formula of earlier woman's films, adapting it to the lives of three contemporary adolescent girls. A low-budget independent film with no major stars and a first-time director that became a surprise box-office hit, *Mystic Pizza* is based on an original story idea by Amy Jones filtered through the perspectives of three male screenwriters and a male director, Donald Petrie. Like *Desperately Seeking Susan*, *Mystic Pizza* achieved surprising success that was largely attributed to its youth appeal, especially to adolescent girls. The film focuses on the summer experiences of three young women who work as waitresses in a pizza restaurant in Mystic, Connecticut: the beautiful Daisy (Julia Roberts in one of her first roles), her college-bound sister Kat (Annabeth Gish), and their feisty friend Jojo (Lili Taylor). As the summer progresses, each girl experiences her own developmental crisis involving the twin components of autonomy and relatedness.

In adapting the life choices formula to contemporary adolescent female friendship, the film undertakes a revisionist stance. Unlike earlier

In Mystic Pizza *(Petrie, 1988), three friends—from left to right, Daisy (Julia Roberts), JoJo (Lili Taylor), and Kat (Annabeth Gish)—work at the Mystic Pizza Parlor.*

life choices films, *Mystic Pizza* does not use its presentation of different women's life alternatives merely to validate marriage as the only proper and ultimately fulfilling role for women. In *Mystic Pizza* the life choices formula operates, instead, to illustrate three very different young women's modes of development in their late adolescent years. As in *Housekeeping,* the goal for each of the film's protagonists is the creation of a female sense of self-in-relation. Unlike *Housekeeping,* however, *Mystic Pizza* investigates female adolescent development not only in terms of its young heroines' relationships with other women but also through an examination of their heterosexual romantic attachments. Each of the film's three protagonists in her own way undergoes an adolescent Oedipal transformation by differentiating herself from her mother: Daisy wants to leave the small-town environment of Mystic, Kat hopes to get a college education, and Jojo refuses to get married. At the same time they seek differentiation, they also desire relatedness. Not only do all three women experience romantic encounters in the course of the film, but they also find a surrogate mother. Leona (Conchata Ferrell), the owner of the pizza restaurant where the girls work, provides them with emotional support through their romantic crises and, at the film's conclusion, even offers Kat financial help with her college tuition.

Mystic Pizza is much more interested, however, in the girls' romantic crises than in their mother-daughter Oedipal relationships. In fact, the film's female friendship aspect is all but entirely obscured by its teenage romance component. The friendship among the three young women is largely reduced to providing the backdrop for their crucial relationships with the men in their lives. Each girl seeks to find both autonomy and relatedness in a relationship with a man. Jojo must resolve the conflict she experiences between her sexual attraction to Bill (Vincent D'Onofrio), her fisherman boyfriend, and her fear that she will lose her individuality by becoming his wife. Daisy cultivates a love affair with Charlie (Adam Storke), a rich young man who can provide her with both romance and a way out of what she sees as her dead-end life in Mystic, and Kat falls in love with Tim (William R. Moses), an older married man who employs her as a baby-sitter for his young daughter. In the same way that Daisy's wealthy boyfriend represents for her a life of independence away from Mystic, Tim, as a Yale alumnus and successful architect, signifies the autonomous life that Kat seeks as a college graduate.

Through the portrayal of these different romantic encounters, the film represents female adolescent development in ways that strikingly resemble theorists' accounts of women's real-life maturation. The experiences of all three of the film's young protagonists involve the creation of a core relational self-structure that can best be described as a self-in-relation. This distinctly female sense of self is discovered, experienced, and expressed through the formation of connections with others. By the film's conclusion, each of the female protagonists has grown up by enlarging her inner sense of relational being. Daisy learns to share her real feelings with Charlie. When she realizes he is just using her as a way to get back at his snobbish family, she confronts him and terminates their relationship. She not only learns to express her own feelings but becomes more sensitive to his as well. When he returns in the film's final moments to apologize for his behavior, she generously forgives him. While Daisy learns to express herself and to be more responsive to others, Kat comes to accept relational flexibility. When her married lover's wife returns, she is hurt by his decision to stay in his marriage but overcomes her disappointment, accepts the end of the relationship, and moves on to her college career. Jojo learns to work through relational conflict without abandoning a relationship that is important to her. She manages to overcome her fear of losing her identity in marriage and is able to commit to Bill.

An Adolescent Social Female Friendship Film

Mystic Pizza's portrait of female adolescent development ends by conveying a thematic message that places it in the category of the social female friendship film. By the film's end, each young woman is assimilated into what is presented as a reformed patriarchal social structure that offers women many different options in life. Unlike the traditional life choices film, which ends by proclaiming that marriage is the only real option for women, *Mystic Pizza* insists that women in today's society are offered not only romance but also the opportunity to express their individuality through education, social mobility, self-expression, and sexual desire.

The film's ending proclaims this message insistently. As Jojo's wedding reception takes place in the background, the three protagonists meet on the porch of the pizza restaurant to toast their uncertain futures. Daisy announces, ostensibly in reference to her relationship with Charlie, "Who knows? Anything can happen," but her words seem to apply to all of these young women's lives and even to extend out to the lives of the film's female viewers. Anything can happen for young women now that a reformed patriarchy offers them unlimited opportunities. The film ends by celebrating a female victory. It is a victory of uncertainty, in contrast to the old certainty of previous female life choices films. The female viewer is asked to rejoice with the film's protagonists because women are no longer limited by the certainty of only one option in life.

Although *Mystic Pizza*'s concluding celebration of women's right to personal fulfillment through the exercise of different life options may seem at first progressive, it should be noted that this thematic concept is placed in the context of the film's additional suggestion that these different life paths are fully available to women at the present time. Because the film proposes that a reformed social structure has granted women full access to the public sphere, it is left up to the individual woman herself to attain the level of personal development she needs to achieve whatever goal she sets for herself. In other words, the film neutralizes its affirmation of a woman's right to equal opportunity by connecting this message with the concept of a fully reformed status quo that allows women to do whatever they want. It suggests that women's struggle for equal rights and opportunities is over on a societal level and now exists only on a personal one. Each young woman must simply decide for herself which career or personal goal she wants to pursue, and the way is open for her to achieve success. This conception of women's position in contemporary society hardly accords with the reality of many women's experiences. Rather, it is a utopian picture of the advances women have made into the public sphere, a picture that in its optimistic celebration of women's glorious attainment of social equality can be very seductive to a young female audience.

Deconstructing the Traditional Life Choices Formula.

The recuperative elements in *Mystic Pizza* do not entirely obliterate the progressive changes the film makes in the earlier life choices formula. First of all, because the film presents women's development as involving the formation of a core self-structure based on a desire for autonomy as well as relatedness, it does not conclude by validating the domestic role as a woman's only proper and fulfilling life choice, nor does it suggest that marriage necessarily precludes a woman's undertaking other life options. Second, the film also repudiates the good girl/bad girl dichotomy. In fact, it takes pains to deconstruct this dualism. Daisy is initially set up as the bad sister in contrast to Kat's goodness. Daisy swears, smokes, drinks, and is sexually promiscuous, whereas Kat is a sexually inexperienced baby-sitter and an "A" student accepted for admission to a prestigious college, yet the film refuses to follow earlier woman's films in condemning Daisy and validating Kat; instead, it treats both women's crises of adolescent development sympathetically.

The portrayal of the female protagonists' relationships with men in *Mystic Pizza* also breaks decidedly with earlier stereotypes. The women do not compete for men, nor do they sacrifice themselves for men. Female sexual desire is expressed by each woman, and its expression is presented as natural and entirely appropriate. Daisy seduces Charlie, Jojo openly expresses her sexual attraction to Bill, and Kat becomes involved with a married man. The film never condemns their behavior; instead, it allows for female heterosexual desire's unfettered expression.

The film is also progressive in introducing class and ethnic issues into the female life choices formula. It not only foregrounds its protagonists' Portuguese American background, it also calls attention to problems arising from each girl's working-class status. Unfortunately, these class issues are resolved in ways that seem too easy and unrealistic. For instance, Jojo's opposition to marriage stems from her rejection of the empty lives led by the older working-class women she sees around her. When she finally decides to marry her fisherman lover Bill, however, she is suddenly convinced that her life as a working-class wife will be different, but the film never makes clear why she has come to believe that this will be the case.

Class issues are also raised in regard to Daisy's wealthy boyfriend, but again they seem to disappear miraculously when she stands up for herself and accuses him of using her as a way to rebel against his family. The fact that she is also using him as a means of escaping her working-class environment is never confronted. Similarly, Kat's difficulties in raising the money she needs to attend a prestigious school like Yale are also easily resolved when Leona suddenly offers to help pay her tuition. As a result of these facile resolutions, the problems related to class and ethnic differences that the film raises are so easily overcome that their social importance is actually minimized rather than accentuated.

Mystic Pizza and the Female Spectator

Mystic Pizza attempts to engage its female audience by extending the twinship transference relationship that exists among its three protagonists to the female viewer. The viewer is encouraged to relive her own developmental process as the film's three female friends undergo the trials of individuation/differentiation and the formation of their female core identity structures. The film uses its portrayal of late adolescent heterosexual romance to illustrate the formation of a female self-in-relation. Its three female protagonists achieve a sense of autonomy that is combined with relatedness and is formed within continuing love relationships with a maternal figure as well as with male love interests.

Although the film, like many earlier woman's films, promotes a spectatorial position that grants men a crucial influence on women's lives, it eschews the tendency of these films to place the female spectator in a masochistic subject position in regard to heterosexual romance. Although *Mystic Pizza*'s protagonists encounter problems in their romantic involvements, each is shown refusing the victim's role. Daisy has enough pride to reject Charlie when she realizes he is just using her, Kat does not let the disappointment of her first sexual experience interfere with her pursuit of a college career, and Jojo finally overcomes her fear of commitment and marries Bill.

Although it includes these progressive aspects, *Mystic Pizza* in the end does not construct a subject position that effectively critiques women's existing social situation. Its progressive aspects are wedded inextricably to its concluding message that gender and class barriers to women's success have been entirely eliminated or can be easily overcome. The film triumphantly proclaims that women's ability to attain their life goals rests entirely on their own personal development. In this way, it is able to offer its young female audience an affirmation of their bright future in a fairy-tale fashion, without seriously investigating how practically accessible this future really is to women of different racial, ethnic, and class backgrounds.

Concluding Comments

Female friendship films that investigate women's relationships within a developmental context can be divided into three categories: the "wanna-be phenomenon," the Oedipal drama, and the life choices formula. *Desperately Seeking Susan* stresses the importance of a female role model to healthy female maturation, *Housekeeping* emphasizes the female Oedipal drama and presents female relationships as surrogate mother-daughter bonds, and *Mystic Pizza* investigates adolescent friendships by looking at the life paths chosen by three different young women. All three approaches associate female friendship with the formation of the self-in-relation that psychologists identify as crucial to women's maturation. This connection of female friendship and women's development provides the films with an appeal to a younger audience than is characteristic of female friendship films in general.

The emphasis on women's needs for autonomy as well as a sense of relatedness renders the films discussed in this chapter somewhat more progressive than other types of female friendship portrayals. Like other films in the female friendship cycle, however, these films are still mixtures of progressive and regressive elements. Although they emphasize women's needs for both autonomy and relatedness, they have great difficulty envisioning the exact nature of the autonomy they advocate. As a result, they end up concluding with images that are emblematic of female liberation rather than providing substantive suggestions for how this liberation might come about or where it might lead. As scenarios of maturation, these films engage their female spectators by championing female development, but this development is presented as so individual, and its projected conclusion is so vaguely outlined, that the films really offer little challenge to the existing social order.

4 | The Political Female Friendship Film

Whereas sentimental female friendship films and those that focus on female maturation emphasize women's personal psychological development, other films of the 1980s move from the personal into the realm of the political. The initiating films in this category, *Nine to Five* (Higgins, 1980) and *Outrageous Fortune* (Hiller, 1987), embed their political themes within a comedy format that reduces their threatening nature. They still, however, manage to open up possible spectatorial positions that challenge existing social norms and encourage a rethinking of issues related to women's traditional societal roles.

In contrast to these 1980s comedic portrayals of political female friendship, suddenly in the early 1990s political female friendship films became deadly and deadly serious. Both *Thelma & Louise* (Scott, 1991) and *Mortal Thoughts* (Rudolph, 1991) make explicit political statements and do so within the context of women's violent reactions to their victimization. They take the political female friendship film away from the moderately progressive comedy format and place it in the realm of the "deadly dolls," creating potentially radical representations of women who kill.[1] The threat these films pose to the patriarchical status quo led to the female friendship film's subsequent retreat from the "deadly doll" format in the mid-1990s. This retreat was signaled by the release in 1992 of the highly recuperative *Leaving Normal* (Zwick), a film that seems almost a calculatedly conservative rewriting of *Thelma & Louise*.

Director Colin Higgins (right) confers with his stars, from left to right, Lily Tomlin, Dolly Parton, and Jane Fonda, on the set of Nine to Five *(1980).*

Nine to Five

The Working Woman's Comedy

Nine to Five, the first contemporary female friendship film with an overtly political message, examines the situation of women at work through the presentation of the work-related group friendship that is formed among three female office employees. As is the case with most female friendship films, *Nine to Five* is the product of combined male and female input. Produced by IPC, a production company formed by actress Jane Fonda and producer Bruce Gilbert, the film's screenplay was written by Patricia Resnick but reworked by director Colin Higgins. Produced outside of the major studios yet with strong Hollywood connections, *Nine to Five* focuses on an explicitly feminist issue, the exploitation and oppression of working-class women within the male-dominated workplace.

The film's three female characters represent different types of working-class women, and they experience different forms of oppressive working conditions. Violet Newstead (Lily Tomlin), a widow supporting four children, is a highly competent senior office manager. A faithful employee of the company for twelve years, she has been repeatedly subjected to sexual discrimination in regard to opportunities for promotion and assignment of office tasks. Violet's experiences of sexual discrimination are paralleled by Doralee Rhodes's (Dolly Parton's) encounters with sexual harassment on the job. Employed as personal secretary to the firm's vice president, Mr. Hart (Dabney Coleman), she is repeatedly subjected to his unwanted sexual advances. The final member of the film's trio of working-class heroines is Judy Bernly (Jane Fonda), a mild-mannered housewife with no office skills who is thrust into the working world when her husband divorces her for a younger woman.

The film's presentation of its characters' job experiences effectively exposes the disastrous effects on working women of male dominance and discrimination in the office environment and makes a strong argument for needed change by showing its protagonists' movement from passive acceptance of sexual discrimination to active initiation of reforms. It is their shared misery that finally brings the heroines together when they meet at a local bar and commiserate about their problems. The bond they form is based not on the personal intimacy and emotional intensity that characterizes sentimental female friendships, but rather on mutual recognition of shared oppression. As they get drunk and pass around a marijuana cigarette, the women exchange comic revenge fantasies against their oppressor, Mr. Hart. Their intimate exchange of unrealizable dream scenarios reflects not the formation of a sentimental bond between them but rather their feelings of powerlessness in a male-dominated work environment and their desire to take action against their oppression.

The portrayal of work-related female friendship in *Nine to Five* avoids many of the negative aspects found in sentimental and social female friendship portrayals. Unlike *The Turning Point* and *Rich and Famous,* for instance, which also deal with career women, the film is neither a throwback to earlier woman's film representations of female friendship nor a simple rehashing of established stereotypes. The female friendship portrayed in *Nine to Five* is not characterized by feelings of antagonism or betrayal, and the women are not presented as irrational, emotional creatures who eventually find fulfillment in dedication to men. When Violet accidentally puts rat poison in Mr. Hart's coffee and he threatens to report the incident to the police, the three women combine their efforts in a carefully constructed plan designed to expose his embezzlement of company funds. Until they can amass enough incriminating evidence to prove his guilt, they abduct him and lock him in his home. While he is held captive, they proceed to implement the reforms necessary to create a more efficient and hospitable workplace.

Unlike *The Turning Point* and *Rich and Famous*, which place women in glamorized careers only to show them finding nothing but disappointment there, *Nine to Five* affirms women's ability not only to succeed and find satisfaction in their work but also to create a better working environment. The changes that the film's protagonists implement, in fact, accord with cultural feminist visions of workplace reform. They establish child-care facilities, initiate a job sharing program, offer flexible hours, and implement a program for hiring persons with disabilities, reforms that are all based on such traditionally female values as connectedness and responsiveness to the needs of others.

As is often the case in female friendship films, these progressive qualities are recuperated and their radical potential reduced by their alignment with more conservative elements. First of all, the film's comedic form undercuts its political agenda. As a number of reviewers pointed out at the time of the film's release, *Nine to Five* deteriorates quickly from its initial attempts at social satire into slapstick farce, with Mr. Hart set up as an exaggerated male villain.[2] Hart is portrayed as an amalgam of negative masculine qualities; Judy sums up his composite character perfectly when she calls him a "sexist, lying, egotistical, hypocritical bigot." Mr. Hart's exaggeratedly stereotypical behavior is combined with a plot structure that relies so heavily on physical comedy that the film's underlying social message is all but completely obscured. When the women end up stealing and then returning a corpse, kidnapping Mr. Hart, and rigging up a preposterous contraption to keep him imprisoned in his home, the ideas behind the film are lost among its female characters' absurd antics.

The film does return to its social theme at its conclusion, when the women are congratulated by the company's president for turning their office environment into a model of progressive reform. Unfortunately, because it relies so heavily on slapstick comedy to bring about this transformation, the film's utopian happy ending seems unrealistic and contrived. By proposing kidnapping and tying up one's boss as a way to implement reforms in his absence, the film actually minimizes rather than accentuates the importance of the problem of sexual discrimination in the workplace.

Nine to Five and the Female Spectator

As James R. Baron suggests, *Nine to Five* engages its audience in ways that are reminiscent of ancient Aristophanic satire.[3] The protagonists in Aristophanes' plays gain the spectator's sympathy by concocting fantastic schemes in extemporaneous response to oppressive social situations. The audience derives pleasure from the hero's metamorphosis from a frustrated victim into a triumphant figure who brings about the fulfillment of his own fantasies. Unfortunately, the play's concluding fantasy victory mutes its satirical edge. Its theme gets lost under its happy ending.

Like Aristophanic satire, *Nine to Five* begins with an initial satirical presentation of its female characters' oppressive working conditions and concludes with a fantasy solution to their problems. The film's final celebration of a moderately reformist victory for feminist values in a male-dominated society works much more successfully as fantasy fulfillment than as sustained social criticism. In addition, the film's fantasy ending risks having a compensatory emotional effect on female viewers. The temporary liberation that it offers provides no practical solutions to the problems of working women, and may even encourage them to be satisfied with fantasies of revenge or with small reformist victories rather than significant change. In this way, the film actually works to stifle female discontent and to modify a desire for more extensive reform.

The limitations of *Nine to Five* as a work of social criticism should not, however, obscure its status as the only unequivocally political female friendship film to come out of Hollywood in the early 1980s. Although its political agenda is certainly limited, when it is compared with other Hollywood products of the period that deal with working women, such as *The Turning Point* and *Rich and Famous,* its accomplishments seem more pronounced. Its optimistic celebration of female solidarity and of moderately reformist feminist goals stands in welcome contrast to the use of female friendship in other films merely as a way to denigrate women's career achievements and affirm the primacy of men and domesticity in women's lives.

Outrageous Fortune
A Female "Male Buddy Movie"

The comedic format of *Nine to Five* is shared by another political female friendship film that found mainstream release in the late 1980s, *Outrageous Fortune*. This film was written by a female screenwriter, Leslie Dixon, but, like many other female friendship films, it was placed under the final control of a male director, Arthur Hiller. Dixon, in fact, took over the screenwriting project from a group of male writers who were unable to complete the script. The success of Dixon's screenplay can be attributed to her combination of female friendship with the male buddy plot formula. In fact, *Outrageous Fortune* is really a male buddy film that happens to star two women, Bette Midler and Shelley Long. Produced by Disney studios as part of a three-film contract with Midler, the film, according to Dixon, follows her original script very faithfully. Dixon claims to have benefited from a "studio regime [at Disney] that believes in getting the script right and then shooting the script combined with a director with the quaint, old-fashioned notion that you actually do shoot the script." Dixon says that her screenplay "was not only not rewritten," but director Hiller "shot the script almost verbatim" and even allowed her on the set during shooting.[4]

If Dixon's claims for the film's faithfulness to her screenplay are to be believed, *Outrageous Fortune* would seem to represent a female-conceived revision of the Hollywood male buddy formula. Its central dyadic relationship involves two women who are initially united only by their involvement with the same male lover, Michael (Peter Coyote). Upon learning of his supposed death, they discover that he was, in fact, involved in simultaneous affairs with both of them. At first, they despise each other, not only because they resent having shared the same man, but because they are very different types of women separated by class differences and career rivalry.

Both women are actresses, and they are enrolled in the same acting class. Lauren (Shelley Long) is an attractive, wealthy, well-educated snob, and Sandy (Bette Midler) is an earthy, working-class ex-waitress and porn star. When they discover that Michael was sleeping with both of them and that he is now mysteriously missing, they determine to find him so that he can choose between them. In the course of their search they grow to be friends, learn that Michael is a spy who was using both of them as part of his espionage schemes, and decide to foil

As part of their wildly comic escapades in Outrageous Fortune *(Hiller, 1987), Lauren (Shelley Long, left) and Sandy (Bette Midler) emerge from two industrial-size dryers, where they have hidden from their pursuers.*

his evil designs. Their quest involves endless complications and pro-longed episodes of physical comedy as they work together to defeat Michael and confiscate a deadly vegetation-destroying virus that he has stolen. In the course of their adventures, they learn that if they unite, they can triumph over male evil and save the world.

Absurd as the film's plot complications are at times, they provide the adventure format necessary in the buddy formula and allow the women to unite and prove their heroism by courageously overcoming the villainous opposition. Although the friendship that develops be-tween the women resembles sentimental female friendship in that it in-volves some intimacy and personal development, it can be classified as a political female friendship because it is primarily instrumental and ori-ented toward purposeful activity in the public sphere rather than re-maining solely a matter of individual personal development.

Outrageous Fortune, in fact, very much resembles such male buddy movies as *Butch Cassidy and the Sundance Kid* and *The Sting,* which Arthur Nolletti, Jr. describes as "films of male bonhomie."[5] In these films, as in *Outrageous Fortune,* the male buddy relationship is pre-dominantly characterized by a sense of adventure and fun. The buddies develop an unspoken loyalty, but very little intimacy or emotional com-mitment. What they exhibit most clearly, according to Nolletti, is a sense of "good ole American cool," which allows them to stay in control through endless adversity and countless chaotic adventures until their rugged individualism finally allows them to defeat their enemies.

In applying this male buddy formula to the female friendship film, Dixon creates an allegorical tale of developing feminist solidarity. Two women of different class backgrounds begin as enemies. They believe they have found their sense of identity in heterosexual romance, but their lover turns out only to be using them to further his own selfish ends and ultimately even to destroy the world. Once they discover that they are merely tools of his evil designs, they resolve their differences, unite, work together to defeat him, and in the process affirm themselves.

As a feminist allegory, *Outrageous Fortune* develops themes that pose significant challenges to the patriarchal status quo. The film's protagonists unite to further a positive political goal, the defeat of a villainous male scheme aimed at destroying the environment. They challenge male control of public space not only by entering the world of adventure, but by becoming heroes within it. They affirm female self-worth, take action against male dominance, disrespect, and destruction, and establish their personal sense of self in the process. The film's ending represents their final glorious triumph as female heroes. They track down the villain and defeat him, and in a coda are even allowed to achieve their career ambitions. In the film's closing moments, Lauren, who has always envisioned herself in the role of Hamlet, is seen taking her bows after just having played the role in a magnificently successful performance. Behind her is Sandy, who in acting class confessed that she did not even know any of Shakespeare's plays. Now she is in costume as Ophelia, sharing in her friend's acting triumph. The two women are not only heroes but career successes as well. Although the absurdity of the whole scenario is pronounced, so too is the female affirmation it provides.

Outrageous Fortune and the Female Spectator

The female viewer is clearly invited to join *Outrageous Fortune*'s two female protagonists in their adventures, participate vicariously in their escapades, and develop with them from insecure victims of male abuse into inspiring figures of female triumph and solidarity. This female-affirmative spectatorial positioning is tempered by the farcical nature of the film's formulaic caper plot. Its comedic treatment of women's issues lacks the bite that a serious presentation of these concerns might have, yet as a comic fantasy of female achievement, the film works very effectively, even perhaps too well. Like *Nine to Five, Outrageous Fortune* offers its female audience the pleasures inherent in a fantasy of female affirmation. Because the film undertakes no serious examination of the problems women face in contemporary society, however, the solutions it proposes are simplistic, and the affirmation it offers seems too easily won. For instance, Sandy and Lauren resolve the class differences that separate them simply by complimenting each other on their respective hairstyles and sharing an interest in fashion. Their common experiences seem to be all that is needed to resolve the differences between them, even though the issues that divide them are never even discussed.

Throughout most of the film, in fact, Sandy and Lauren's relationship is characterized only by negative stereotypes of female friendship. Antagonism between the two women prevails as they bicker at every turn; their behavior is also consistently irrational and emotional. They are united and propelled into action only by their shared victimization by a villainous male who is so bad that he drives them to each other. Even their goals are male centered. They initially want to find their lover because each of them wants to win him for herself. When they decide he is too evil to win, they determine to unite and defeat him. Lauren's final great career success is to play Hamlet, a highly coveted *male* role. The women act only in reaction to men and in order to be like them. Even the audience that cheers their career success is composed of their male acting teacher and the male CIA agents who previously chased them. What the film really offers its female spectator is the fleeting pleasure of watching women assume "male roles" in an impossible fantasy scenario that culminates in a spectacular female victory. Like *Nine to Five, Outrageous Fortune* demonstrates very clearly the limitations of comedic portrayals of female friendship. Such portrayals offer the female spectator the fantasy of women's success and solidarity, but situate it within a context that divorces these accomplishments from the everyday reality of women's lives.

Female Friendship and Violence

At the beginning of the 1990s, the political female friendship film suddenly underwent a significant change. Female revenge fantasies, presented comedically in *Nine to Five* and *Outrageous Fortune*, suddenly turned deadly, and female friendship became associated with violence in a way that it had not been previously. Two films, both released in

1991, epitomize this trend: Ridley Scott's *Thelma & Louise* and Alan Rudolph's *Mortal Thoughts*.

This sudden association of female friendship with violence represents a departure from earlier female friendship films, which focused much more on personal empowerment and psychological development than on women's revenge against men. Even films like *Nine to Five* and *Outrageous Fortune* that allow their heroines to take violent action against male oppression place this aspect of the film so completely within a comedy format that the women's behavior seems cartoonish rather than threatening. In the early 1990s, however, female friends became serious killers. This change partly reflects the development in this period of what Christine Holmlund has labeled "deadly doll films," which include a wide range of movies that focus on violent women. Some of the most popular films of this type include *Black Widow* (Rafelson, 1987), *Fatal Attraction* (Lyne, 1987), *Blue Steel* (Bigelow, 1990), and *The Silence of the Lambs* (Demme, 1991). As Holmlund points out, although female killers have always been a part of Hollywood cinema, they were previously confined to thrillers and presented either as unremittingly evil or as "innocent murderers" who were driven to their actions by extreme circumstances. This situation changed in the late 1980s and early 1990s, when the range of possible genres and the list of motivations for female violence expanded significantly.[6]

Both Holmlund and Helen Birch have speculated about the reasons for the sudden rise of the female film killer in the late 1980s and early 1990s. Both suggest, first of all, that there is no evidence that this increase corresponds to a sudden rise in the number of real female murderers; indeed, as Holmlund notes, the percentage of female killers throughout history has remained at the same low figure of 10–15 percent of all homicides.[7] Birch proposes that the films actually reflect not the frequency but the rarity of female homicides. Because women killers are so unusual, she asserts, they provide greater dramatic spectacle than the more common male murderer. Deadly doll films can also be seen as a response to a heightened awareness of the problem of domestic violence as a result of the work of women's groups in calling public attention to this issue.[8] Some filmic portrayals of female killers actually expose the prevalence of male violence against women by having their female killers act in response to male abuse. Others are merely sensationalist portrayals of female violence that contribute to the conservative backlash against women's achievements by converting female self-assertion into an unruly spectacle of female aggression. These sensationalized representations of female killers serve a conservative purpose simply by distracting viewer attention from the much more frequent violence perpetrated against women by men.

The release of *Thelma & Louise* and *Mortal Thoughts* in 1991 signaled the merger of the female friendship film's focus on women's personal development with the deadly doll film's violent scenarios of female revenge, making for an explosive combination. The explosive nature of these films is nowhere more apparent than in the debate that surrounded the most popular and controversial female friendship film to find mainstream distribution, *Thelma & Louise*.

Thelma & Louise

A Female-Authored Text

Thelma & Louise represents the combined efforts of a female screenwriter, Callie Khouri; a male director, Ridley Scott; and two very popular female stars, Geena Davis and Susan Sarandon. The film tells the story of two women friends, a housewife and a waitress, who set out together for a weekend trip to a mountain cabin. Along the way they stop at a bar, where Thelma (Geena Davis) dances with a man who later tries to rape her in the bar's parking lot. In coming to her friend's defense, Louise (Susan Sarandon) shoots and kills the attempted rapist, and the two women, afraid their story will not be believed, go on the run. After a number of experiences on the road, all presented to comic effect, the two women are finally confronted by the police on the edge of what they believe to be the Grand Canyon. Rather than turn themselves in, they decide to drive over a cliff into the canyon. The film ends with a freeze-frame of their car suspended in midair, followed by a montage sequence composed of earlier shots of the two women together.

Khouri, a novice screenwriter, wrote the screenplay for *Thelma & Louise*, her first, in the hope initially of directing the film herself. When she began to shop her script around Hollywood, however, she met with negative responses from producers until Ridley Scott offered not only to produce but also to direct the film. Khouri has suggested that it was his interest that saved the project. Although she has said that, failing to direct herself, she would have preferred a female director, she agreed to Scott because she knew that with his clout he would definitely get the film made. The key to the contract agreement, according to Khouri, was Scott's promise that the script's ending would not be altered.[9]

Khouri has stated that her initial inspiration for the story came from her negative experiences as a young actress and video producer. She became frustrated with the limited roles she saw offered to women:

> It is such a rare thing to go to a movie and think, God, that was a really interesting female character. I feel that the roles generally available to women in Hollywood films are incredibly stereotypical: the girlfriend, the wife, the moll, the prostitute, the rape victim, the woman dying of cancer. I wanted to do something outside these terms.[10]

Khouri decided that she "was fed up with the passive role of women. They were never driving the story because they were never driving the car," so she created heroines who did both.[11]

The *Thelma & Louise* Controversy

Thelma & Louise was without question one of the most controversial films of the 1990s. It stirred heated debate in the press, primarily in regard to three issues: its connection to feminism, its use of violence, and its presentation of male characters. In interviews, both Khouri and Geena Davis attempted to disassociate the film from feminism. According to Khouri, "*Thelma & Louise* is not about feminists, it's about outlaws," and Davis queried, "Why because [*Thelma & Louise*] stars women is this suddenly a feminist treatise, given the burden of representing all women?"[12] Yet Khouri seems definitely to have been motivated by feminist inclinations in writing the script. As noted above, her stated intentions were to provide new, more active roles for female characters—clearly a feminist position. How new her characters really are, however, and what exactly they stand for in terms of feminism are matters of some critical dispute.

Critics from both feminist and antifeminist camps have reached no consensus about the film. When it was first released, it immediately rated a cover story in *Time* magazine, which focused on the "white-hot debate [that] rages over whether *Thelma & Louise* celebrates liberated females, male bashers—or outlaws."[13] Reviewers both praised and condemned the film as a "butt-kicking feminist manifesto" that shows women fighting back against sexism, a brilliant depiction of the dire

In Thelma & Louise *(Scott, 1991), Susan Sarandon (left) and Geena Davis portray female outlaws. The film was criticized by some for advocating redemptive violence.*

straits contemporary women feel themselves to be in, an example of female escapism, a revenge fantasy, and a work that offers just enough "lite feminist fizz . . . to be pleasant without seeming pretentious."[14]

Some critics objected strongly to the film's presentation of women on feminist grounds. They felt the film actually violated the things that feminism really advocates, such as "responsibility, equality, sensitivity, understanding—not revenge, retribution, or sadistic behavior."[15] Others felt that it resorted to the same voyeuristic display of glamorous female bodies that has always been characteristic of Hollywood films, or that it attempted to empower women only by having them behave like men and act out a male fantasy of fast driving, hard drinking, loud music, and gunplay.[16] Finally, some saw the film as so pessimistic in its view of women's current social situation that it implied that few gains have really been won by feminism and conveyed a despairing message of patriarchy's invincibility.[17]

While feminist critics registered their objections, antifeminists criticized the film as feminist fascism that advocated transformative violence as the answer to women's problems, bashed men, and offered bad role models for female viewers. All of these criticisms were strenuously debated. Khouri responded quickly and cleverly to charges of antimale bias by arguing that the movie "isn't hostile to men, it's hostile to idiots."[18] She noted:

> You can't do a movie without villains. You have to have something for the heroines or anti-heroines to be up against, and I wasn't going to contrive some monstrous female, but even if this were the most men-bashing movie ever made—let all us women get guns and kill men—it wouldn't even begin to make up for the 99% of all movies where the women are there to be caricatured as bimbos or to be skinned and decapitated. If men feel uncomfortable in the audience it is because they are identifying with the wrong character.[19]

In spite of Khouri's disclaimers, *Thelma & Louise* does portray men largely in terms of negative stereotypes, including the obnoxious, domineering husband (Darryl); noncommittal, narcissistic boyfriend (Jimmy); irresponsible, sexually seductive bad boy (J.D.); woman-hating rapist (Harlan); infantile, harassing trucker; and paternalistic father figure (Detective Slocum). In fact, Marsha Kinder suggests that the film is more an attack on images of men in "media culture" than on men themselves. She points out that its "parade of treacherous male characters" corresponds perfectly to well-known figures from popular movies, ranging from the James Deanish outlaw figure and the foul-mouthed trucker to the sensitive, paternal cop.[20] The overwhelming negativity of the film's portrayal of men, like almost everything else about this film, has been open to dispute. Not only has Khouri denied that the film takes an antimale stance, but some critics have staunchly defended its characterizations of men. Tom Prasch, for instance, argues that both Detective Slocum and Jimmy are presented favorably and that J.D. is an ambivalent figure.[21]

The seemingly endless proliferation of debates in regard to this film marks it as a perfect example of the openness to multiple reading possibilities that characterizes so many of the most popularly successful female friendship films. As Harvey Greenberg suggests, *Thelma & Louise* contains an "exuberant polysemy." It not only addresses differing ideological agendas, from feminist to antifeminist and progressive to reactionary, it also "offers a wide range of possibility for contestation across the political spectrum over issues 'whose time has come' out of one contemporary circumstance or another."[22]

An Overtly Political Female Friendship Film

The controversy regarding *Thelma & Louise* is not entirely explained by the film's polysemy, as important as this characteristic may be in furthering the debates that have surrounded the film. The initiation of the controversy and its prolonged nature seem also to reflect the film's clearly political nature. As we have seen, an overwhelming number of female friendship films, while demonstrating some political qualities, fall in the end into either the sentimental or the social female friendship category. Few move out of the private realm of personal development to offer an overtly political critique of women's position in contemporary society. *Thelma & Louise* makes just such a move. The film refuses to fit into the usual categories of female friendship portrayals. It exalts the friendship between its heroines and places their intimate relationship squarely at the center of the narrative but at the same time violates the traditions of the sentimental female friendship film by never overly sentimentalizing their relationship or emphasizing the intimate self-disclosure characteristic of sentimental female friendship portrayals.[23]

In fact, *Thelma & Louise* seems to go out of its way to avoid sentimentalizing its female protagonists' friendship. Significant in this regard is Scott's decision to cut an important scene in Khouri's script, in which Louise confesses to Thelma that she had been raped in Texas.[24] Scott's refusal to have Louise reveal the nature of her past trauma provoked some critical disapproval. Lizzie Francke, for example, believes that the deletion blurs Khouri's original vision of the two women's intimate relationship.[25] Other critics have suggested further that Louise's reticence reduces the spectator's ability to empathize with her and to understand her murder of Thelma's rapist. According to Alice Cross, "Everything that happens in the movie is a consequence of that earlier experience, but because it is a hole, a blank, we are left detached where we ought to be most moved, angered, sympathetic."[26] Fitting the film squarely into the category of the sentimental female friendship film, Cross and Francke want Thelma and Louise to engage in an intimate discussion of their shared abuse: "Without such a sharing of the past, the kiss that Louise gives Thelma before they plunge into oblivion means little. It is like so much in this film, just the same old story artfully disguised to look like something new."[27]

Actually, in terms of the female friendship film, the intimate sharing of confidences that Cross and Francke want is not at all new; instead, it is what Scott has done in having Louise refuse to talk about her rape that takes *Thelma & Louise* in a new direction. By not discussing her experiences as a rape victim, Louise refuses to engage in the kind of intimate self-disclosure that would render her a powerless victim of male abuse; instead, as Lynda Hart points out, Louise remains throughout the film a powerfully subversive figure. Hart proposes that having Louise confess her rape would allow for the patriarchal recuperation of her criminality: "Filling the empty space of her trauma might facilitate her reintegration into the symbolic order, but Louise is not disposed to collaborate with 'justice.'"[28]

Using Sarah Kofman's distinction between the female criminal and the hysteric, Hart describes Louise as an unregenerate criminal, a figure Kofman sees as truly subversive of the patriarchal order. Like Kofman's conception of the unrepentant female criminal, Louise "knows her own secret" and refuses to share it because she is, or thinks she is, self-sufficient.[29] She will not submit to a psychoanalytic talking cure as the hysteric does, and it is this unwillingness to speak, as much as what she does, that criminalizes her. Her criminality stems from her refusal to allow Detective Slocum, the male police officer who wants desperately to save her, to do so. Not only does Louise refuse to be "saved," but she takes the younger, less experienced Thelma with her. As Hart points out, Louise thoroughly mistrusts the existing social structure and has to teach Thelma to do the same. Thelma is at first naive enough to believe that telling the truth will clear them, but Louise shows her that "the symbolic order is a masculine imaginary in which their truths have no credibility."[30] In this way, she takes Thelma, and the film as well, into a much more socially critical realm than the intimate self-disclosure of the sentimental female friendship film allows, and *Thelma & Louise* becomes as a result decidedly political.

Marsha Kinder argues, to the contrary, that *Thelma & Louise,* by refusing to "explore the repression of women in the context of larger issues of history and class conflict," fails to afford its viewers incisive political analysis.[31] Yet, as Elayne Rapping points out, although *Thelma & Louise* is not "an explicitly feminist movie, produced by politicos as an 'intervention,'" there still might be a reason for feminist critics to celebrate it. Rapping regards the film as an indication that feminist ideas have influenced the popular imagination to the extent that they are now part of "an oppositional way of thinking shared by a majority of women and lots of men." She adds:

The assault on this film must be read as part of a much larger political backlash against the real gains of feminism fueled by those for whom changes in gender power relations mean a serious loss of privilege and power. That they are so nervous proves to me that feminism has had a greater impact on this society than it sometimes seems in these politically dark days.[32]

In fact, *Thelma & Louise* does make a number of significant political points. First of all, in accordance with Khouri's stated intentions, the film grants its female protagonists central roles in driving not only the film's car but also its plot. They are granted agency in the narrative, challenging the traditional cinematic association of activity with masculinity. They remain in charge of their own fate throughout the film, frustrating all attempts at male control up to the very end, when they choose suicide over submission to male authority. While remaining resolutely heterosexual, they refuse to be defined entirely by their relationships with men; instead, they form at the film's conclusion a symbolic marriage of sisterhood.[33] Their sisterly bond, however, does not confine them to the private sphere of personal affection; instead, they move out into the public world as outlaws, attacking its laws and traditions, rejecting its traditional roles for women, and challenging men's control of public space. They bond for a cause beyond the level of personal attachment. Theirs is a union of two abused women who revolt against a society that has not adequately protected them from crimes of male violence.

Certainly, the most overtly political statement the film makes is its attack on the legal system's response to the crime of rape. Again, *Thelma & Louise* is not an incisive political analysis of the legal, psychological, and social questions related to the rape issue; instead, it is a popular culture expression of women's anger and frustration with the current situation in regard to this crime. As such, as both Carol Clover and Peter Lehman suggest, *Thelma & Louise* is a descendant of the low-budget rape-revenge movies of the 1970s and 1980s, films such as *Hannie Caulder* (Kennedy, 1972), *I Spit on Your Grave* (Zarchi, 1978), and *Ms. .45* (Ferrara, 1981).[34] As Lehman points out, these earlier rape-revenge films were aimed at a male audience and intended as popular entertainment rather than as serious considerations of the rape issue. They offer their male audience the spectacle of a beautiful woman "wrecking havoc on the male body." Lehman describes the films' formulaic plot structure: after an initial brutal rape scene, the film's rapists become victims themselves of the viciously vengeful woman whom they attacked. Their punishment is spectacularized in scenarios of excessive violence that Lehman believes offer the male spectator a "bizarrely pleasurable" viewing experience. According to Lehman, the films' address is not at all directed to female spectators, but to a male audience that takes pleasure in "a male masochistic fantasy so extreme that even brutal death can be part of the scenario."[35]

Thelma & Louise takes this generic configuration and transforms it to appeal not to a male but to a female audience. Rather than offering the protracted spectacle of a brutal rape, *Thelma & Louise* portrays in a decidedly nonvoyeuristic fashion a very brief near rape. The emphasis is placed on Thelma's response to the crime rather than on the rapist's pleasure. Lehman points out that low-budget rape-revenge films portray their rapists as physically repulsive in order to allow the male viewer to distance himself from their crime.[36] *Thelma & Louise* allows for no such convenient distancing; instead, it presents Harlan (Timothy Carhart) as a handsome, charming rapist from whom the male viewer cannot so easily disassociate himself.[37] Second, emphasis is not so overwhelmingly placed on the protractedly brutal punishment of the rapist. Harlan is shot efficiently and quickly, once in the chest.[38] The film's idea of female vengeance, as Carol Clover suggests, is related more to "the notion of corporate liability that makes every man pay" than to the concept of personal revenge.[39] This idea of "corporate liability" allows no male audience member to escape responsibility for the continuance of a rape culture that does not effectively prevent this heinous crime.

Clover argues that the transformation of the rape-revenge drama from the bracket of the B movie to the bigger-budget category creates a more "civilized version" of the story that loses sight of rape's effect on the raped woman herself and her need for retaliation.[40] Clover suggests that a big-budget rape-revenge film like *The Accused* (Kaplan, 1988) loses its political edge because it becomes a study of the workings of the legal system rather than of the crime of rape. *Thelma & Louise* avoids this pitfall and delivers a clear antirape message without losing sight of the individual victim.

The categorization of *Thelma & Louise* as a political female friendship film is very much tied to the nature of its conclusion. As we have seen, Khouri was adamant that Scott should not change her ending, and for good reason. The film's ending is crucial to its political critique. By choosing not to give up and, in Thelma's words, to "keep on goin'," the two women remain criminals, subversive figures to the end and beyond, never reintegrated into the existing social structure and forever unrepentant. Their friendship never becomes, as it does in the social female friendship film, merely a refuge that allows them to reintegrate into and better cope with the existing patriarchal order; instead, they remain throughout the film resistant to compromise with and recuperation by what they continue to view as an unreformed patriarchy.

Thelma & Louise and the Female Spectator

As a polysemous text stimulating wide controversy, *Thelma & Louise* draws in viewers of both sexes by opening itself up to readings that range over the ideological spectrum. It also creates a multiple address by integrating and reshaping film genres to create a work that is an incredibly multigeneric hybrid. Critics have pointed to the film as demonstrating qualities characteristic of an enormous number of genres: the male buddy film, outlaw film, road movie, deadly doll film, western, melodrama, gangster film, screwball comedy, and action/adventure film as well as the female friendship film. As a multigeneric hybrid, *Thelma & Louise* manages a remarkably broad address.

It also broadens its address by utilizing all three of the transference situations so often used in female friendship films to draw female viewers into its central female relationship. A mirroring transference is suggested by the emphasis on Thelma and Louise's development and rebirth in the course of their journey, an idealizing transference is evoked by the women's positioning as mythic figures at the film's conclusion, and finally a twinship transference is portrayed in the commonality that develops between them as they share experiences drawing on situations recognizably familiar to female viewers. Each of these transference relationships encourages the female spectator to react to Thelma and Louise with strong feelings of empathy.

What *Thelma & Louise* demonstrates most clearly is that the multiplicity of address and plurality of reading possibilities that so often characterize female friendship films do not inevitably mean that the films must sacrifice a political message. While *Thelma & Louise* allows for multiple readings, this multiplicity does not destroy the film's political significance. In fact, the controversy surrounding the film has added significantly to its social impact. *Thelma & Louise* has become not only the most controversial contemporary female friendship film made thus far, but also the most politically implicated. Its political message encourages its female audience not only to enter into the controversy surrounding its reception, but also, and most significantly, to take a critical stance in regard to contemporary U.S. society and its treatment of its female members.

Mortal Thoughts

Curiously Lacking in Controversy—and Popularity

In the same year *Thelma & Louise* appeared, Alan Rudolph's *Mortal Thoughts* also reached the screen, but not with the enormous explosion of controversy and popularity that accompanied the former film. In fact, *Mortal Thoughts* hardly made any impact at all. It was released with little fanfare and received mixed reviews of a very conventional nature, nothing like the highly charged polemics that accompanied the release of *Thelma & Louise*.[41] Although there was some critical disagreement about the film's quality, *Mortal Thoughts* sparked no ideological controversy and only moderate viewer interest.

Like most other female friendship films, *Mortal Thoughts* was developed with a certain amount of female involvement, if not in the writing process at least in the film's production. Demi Moore was initially involved as coproducer, although she is not listed as such in the final credits.[42] In fact, the film seems to have been conceived originally as a star vehicle for Moore, who is in almost every scene. As in so many other female friendship films, however, female involvement in the film's production was confined to a limited arena. Screenwriting and directorial tasks were placed entirely in male hands. The screenplay was written by William Reilly and Claude Kerven, with Kerven originally slated to direct. After only a week of shooting, Kerven was replaced by the more experienced Alan Rudolph, but the film's tight structure and murder mystery format do not seem to reflect Rudolph's visually stylized, narratively diffuse style, but rather its screenwriters' sensibilities. In any case, unlike *Thelma & Louise,* which benefited from significant female involvement, the major artistic influence on *Mortal Thoughts* was clearly male.

More Deadly Dolls

As another deadly doll film, *Mortal Thoughts* in many ways is remarkably similar to *Thelma & Louise,* yet it is also crucially different, and this difference perhaps largely accounts for its failure to provoke audience interest or critical response. The story is narrated by Cynthia Kellogg (Demi Moore), who as the film opens is about to be questioned in a police station interrogation room by two police officers, Detectives Woods (Harvey Keitel) and Nealon (Billie Neal). Her statement is also being videotaped, and the viewer occasionally sees her image captured in a video monitor as she speaks. Cynthia recounts the murder of James Urbanski (Bruce Willis), the abusive husband of her lifelong friend Joyce (Glenne Headly). According to Cynthia's story, which is rendered in flashbacks triggered by her voice-over narration, Joyce killed James, involved Cynthia in a cover-up of the crime, and later also killed Cynthia's husband, whom she feared would reveal her involvement in the murder to the police.

Having given her statement, Cynthia is escorted from the police station by Detective Woods, who makes it clear to her that he doubts the veracity of her story. As she sits in her car about to drive away from the police station, she experiences one more flashback to what really happened. Finally, the audience is allowed to see that it was Cynthia, not Joyce, who fatally stabbed James as he attempted to rape her. It was Joyce, however, who decided after Cynthia informed her of the incident that they should allow James to die rather than rush him to the hospital, and the two women together conspired to cover up his death. This memory leads Cynthia to return to the police station, apparently now determined to confess the truth. In the final shot of the film, we see her in the video monitor about to begin her testimony all over again.

Like *Thelma & Louise*, *Mortal Thoughts* eschews the emotionality of earlier sentimental female friendship films. Cynthia and Joyce have a long-standing, close relationship, which the home movie shots that open and close the film suggest extends all the way back to their childhood, yet the film refuses to emphasize the intimate, emotionally effusive, and nurturing aspects of their bond. Its portrayal of this working-class friendship between two New Jersey beauticians always maintains a hard-edged quality. Although the erotic overtones that often characterize sentimental female friendship films are present in the exchanges of looks between the two women and the accusations of lesbianism made by Cynthia's husband, these elements seem to reflect what Lynda Hart has described as the connection typically made in popular culture texts between female criminality and lesbianism, rather than the sentimentalization of the bond between the two women.[43]

Mortal Thoughts also resembles *Thelma & Louise* in its detailed

Unlike the intrepid Thelma and Louise, Joyce (Glenne Headly, left) and Cynthia (Demi Moore) in Mortal Thoughts *(Rudolph, 1991) react immediately with fear after the stabbing of Joyce's husband.*

presentation of women's violent reactions to male abuse. Both films are big budget rape-revenge dramas that deal with bloody murders in retaliation for attempted rape. Rather than flee as Thelma and Louise do, however, Cynthia and Joyce engineer a cover-up to escape punishment for James's murder. They are pursued by a male authority figure, Detective Woods, a paternalistic police officer who again, as in *Thelma & Louise,* is played by Harvey Keitel. Both films are also filled with stereotypically insensitive men. James is abusive and obnoxious, Cynthia's husband is probably best described, as he is by Joyce in the film, as a man who sold tools at his own wedding, and Detective Woods seems totally unsympathetic to the women's situation. The film even resembles *Thelma & Louise* in its attempt to add elements of comedy to its murder plot, although here the comedy is of a much darker hue.

The major difference between the two films lies in their endings. Unlike *Thelma & Louise, Mortal Thoughts* ends in a way that is strongly recuperative of the film's politically subversive potential. The concluding revelation that it was Cynthia and not Joyce who killed James has a significant effect on the film's thematic content. Cynthia's initial story is a paradigmatic rendering of negative stereotypes of female friendship as involving treachery, deceit, and betrayal. This type of female friendship portrayal warns women to distrust and fear members of their own sex and rely totally on men. Cynthia tells the police detective exactly what she believes he, as a figure of male authority, wants to hear. She proposes that Joyce not only murdered her own husband but also betrayed her best friend by killing her husband as well.

Unlike this initial story, which describes the dangers of manipulative female friendship, Cynthia's final version gives her friendship with Joyce a subversive dimension. The two women, ordinary working-class heroines, establish a primary bond to each other so strong that it outweighs their loyalty to their husbands, their families, and even the law. They unite and take strong, violent action against the existing social structure by fighting back against male domination and abuse. When Cynthia tries to betray her friend by blaming her alone for their actions, she is compelled by her sense of solidarity with Joyce to return to the police station and tell the truth.

This ending, suggestive of the political dimensions of the female friendship bond, is accompanied by extraordinarily strong recuperative elements. Although the film concludes with an affirmation of female solidarity, it also ends on a note of defeat. Typically, as a way to affirm their female viewers, female friendship portrayals end with an inspiring female victory. The only victory in *Mortal Thoughts* is a moral one: Cynthia returns to tell the truth and to share blame with her friend, yet her honesty and loyalty will not necessarily prevent the two women from going to prison for killing Joyce's brutal husband. Unlike *Thelma & Louise* and many other female friendship films, *Mortal Thoughts* at its conclusion does not offer its female spectators empowerment or female affirmation; instead, what it offers is an unjust female defeat at the hands of male power.

Whereas Thelma and Louise's final suicidal leap can be interpreted as a refusal to submit to male control, in *Mortal Thoughts* male authority triumphs completely. Cynthia and Joyce are reduced to typical female victims rather than elevated like Thelma and Louise to the level of mythic heroines. In the film's final scene, Cynthia is shown entrapped completely in Detective Woods's video monitor. He even usurps the power of her voice-over narration, and the film concludes with his voice-over command: "Ready. . . . Let's get started." Contrast this ending with the final shot of Detective Slocum running helplessly after the women's car as it speeds away from him in *Thelma & Louise,* and the recuperative nature of the conclusion of *Mortal Thoughts* becomes completely clear. Even the film's concluding validation of female solidarity is compromised. The film's ending takes the political charge out of the women's relationship and reduces it, instead, to a social female friendship. The bond Cynthia and Joyce finally share as they submit themselves entirely to the power of patriarchal law in the person of Detective Woods can offer them nothing more than temporary solace from their tragic fate. Their relationship is reduced to a way for the two women to commiserate with each other after their complete defeat by patriarchal law.[44]

The confessional narrative structure of *Mortal Thoughts* also renders it very different from *Thelma & Louise*. As noted above, a significant aspect of *Thelma & Louise*'s transgressive nature stems from the association of its female characters with the mythical figure of the female criminal, an autonomous woman on the margins of society who rebels against the established order. The figure of the criminal stands in contrast to the female hysteric, who represents through her bodily symptoms the history of female suffering. She has a "secret" of which she is ignorant and that she attempts to hide from herself and others, but that exhibits itself nevertheless through her symptoms.[45] It is the task of the male physician to cure her by making her aware of this concealed truth or "secret" and persuading her to accept it.

Both the criminal and the hysteric are antiestablishment figures in that they stand apart from the society from which they emerge and demonstrate to it through their actions or symptoms "the roots of a certain symbolic structure" that acts to condemn women to a position of silence and inequality.[46] They are also conservative figures, however, because most often they are silenced and returned to a position of social repression. Only the means by which they are controlled may vary. Whereas the criminal must be destroyed, the hysteric can collaborate with her oppressors and reacclimate to patriarchal norms. Significantly, not all criminals are destroyed, and not all hysterics are cured. Laughing at their pursuers, some criminals disappear or escape into an unknown future rather than submit to their execution.[47] Similarly, the hysteric can refuse treatment and reject reassimilation into patriarchal culture. Despite attempts to control their threatening nature, these resisting figures reject assimilation or destruction and remain threatening to the end because their ideology of resistance remains alive.

The heroines of *Thelma & Louise* and *Mortal Thoughts* resemble these mythical figures. As noted above, Thelma and Louise are criminals who rebel against society and create their own outlaw counterculture. Like the mythical figure of the female criminal, Louise has the hidden secret of her rape that she is determined not to share. Through their rebellious actions, the women expose the inequalities inherent in society's treatment of women. The film's ambiguous ending opens itself up to a conservative as well as a radical reading of their fate. Like the conservative figure of the criminal, they can be seen as completely destroyed at the film's conclusion when they plunge to their death, but a more radical reading allows them to escape, riding off to an unknown fate, laughing at their pursuers. After all, the film ends not with the fiery crash of their car as it hits the bottom of the canyon but with a freeze-frame in which they are suspended forever in time and space. According to this reading, Thelma and Louise resist destruction or reassimilation into the existing society and remain radical symbols of female resistance to the end and beyond.

Cynthia and Joyce, on the other hand, resemble not escaped criminals, but a hysteric and a punished criminal.[48] Cynthia, as a victim of attempted rape, represents, like the hysteric, the history of female suffering. By telling her story to the police, she relives the past and bears witness to her victimization, yet at the same time she tries to hide her "secret," the attempted rape and her retaliation against her male abuser. The male detective, acting as her physician, engineers her "cure," as well as her reassimilation into patriarchal society, by eliciting her confession and persuading her to accede to her punishment. Joyce, on the other hand, remains a criminal, but unlike Thelma and Louise, she is given no possibility of escape. She finally serves an entirely conservative function, acting as a figure of warning to those who would contemplate countering male abuse with female violence. Her fate suggests that this strategy can only end disastrously.

The Spectator-Text Relationship

The strongly recuperative ending of *Mortal Thoughts* ultimately offers the film's female spectator only one subject position, a conservative one that sees the women's actions and even their friendship as destructive. At the same time, however, its method of cultivating viewer engagement prior to its conclusion is very complex and opens the film up to a range of interpretive possibilities. First of all, the film draws in its female viewers through an engagement with Cynthia and Joyce's twin-ship relationship. The two women seem to be alter egos, even doubles, for one another. Taking to an extreme the idea that women possess more permeable ego boundaries and a greater capacity for empathy than men, Cynthia and Joyce demonstrate such a strong sense of attachment that they seem to merge, to become almost one person. As Lynda Hart notes, the two women are always "we" in Cynthia's narration. In fact, it is Cynthia's use of "we" to describe Joyce's actions that arouses Detective Woods's suspicions concerning the veracity of her story.

Cynthia's complete identification with Joyce makes interpretation of the two women's guilt or innocence difficult. As Hart points out, "Blurring of the boundaries between self and other, a typically 'feminine' problem for psychoanalytic femininity defined as a lack of the proper distance, abets both their violence and their deception. If we cannot tell the difference between them, how can we know which one of them did it?"[49] Additionally, if the female viewer, identifying with Cynthia and Joyce, cannot tell the difference between them, how can she differentiate between them and herself? The question of their guilt or innocence becomes also her own, and the female viewer is so strongly implicated in Cynthia and Joyce's twinship relationship that she seems intended to share even its homicidal character.

Spectatorial engagement with Cynthia and Joyce's friendship is further complicated by the film's narrational structure. The use of flashback visuals accompanied by Cynthia's voice-over narration is a complex structural device with a spectatorial effect that is both distancing and implicating. In *Mortal Thoughts,* the device seems to place the viewer in a mobile subject position, characterized by instability, fluctuation, and fragmentation. Although voice-over narration has a long cinematic history, much of which is associated with its use for granting power and authority to a single perspective and for implicating the spectator strongly in that perspective, in certain genres voice-over does not have such effects.[50] Notably in film noir and woman's films, two genres that utilize the voice-over device frequently and of which *Mortal Thoughts* is clearly an amalgam, its effect is hardly empowering.[51] In these genres, as in *Mortal Thoughts,* the voice-over and its accompanying flashbacks are associated with a confessional-investigative structure that is typically tied to a psychoanalytic therapeutic situation resembling the Freudian talking cure. The narrator is relieved of guilt and anxiety by attaining a sense of truth through a confession offered to a patriarchal authority figure, like Detective Woods in *Mortal Thoughts,* who grants the confessing narrator a sort of absolution. This authority figure typically interprets or even finishes the story of the narrator, who actually seems to become weaker as the narrative progresses.[52]

This narrational situation offers the spectator multiple, even conflicting, subject positions. The text really presents a narrational battle for control of the interpretation of events between the narrator and his or her listeners, and the viewer becomes involved in a very unstable viewing situation in which strong engagement with any one perspective is extremely difficult. What ensues in *Mortal Thoughts* is an oscillating subject position characterized by shifting spectatorial alignment with the perspective of Cynthia as narrator and the detectives as listeners. While Cynthia's voice-over allows the viewer to identify closely with her perspective, the presence of the two detectives as an internal audience for her account provides at the same time distancing figures of engagement who prevent complete involvement with Cynthia's point of view. The presence of the video monitor is yet another distancing device, foregrounding the viewer's voyeuristic positioning in regard to Cynthia's account of events.

This mobile subject position and its distancing effect on spectatorial engagement, accompanied by the film's strongly recuperative ending, prevent the female spectator from responding to the film intrapsychically in what Jackie Stacey has described as an introjective rather than a projective mode.[53] The great majority of female friendship films trigger introjective responses. Films ranging from the highly sentimental *Beaches* to the politically provocative *Thelma & Louise* encourage female spectators both to admire and to be inspired by their female characters. The films allow their female viewers to take into themselves aspects of these ideal characters' identities in ways that Stacey suggests can lead to permanent psychological and ideological transformation.

Mortal Thoughts follows not so much the female friendship film in this regard as it does another prominent female popular culture form, the soap opera. As Tania Modleski points out in her study of the relationship of female viewers to soap operas and romance novels, the soap opera villainess has a safety-valve effect on many of her female fans. Whereas identification with the soap opera villainess's subversion of patriarchal norms offers female viewers a temporary means of vicarious rebellion, her eventual punishment also allows them to condemn her behavior and to adopt in the end a patriarchally complicit stance that recuperates her subversive potential.[54]

Like the soap opera villainess, Cynthia and Joyce offer female spectators the temporary satisfaction of seeing two women rebel against male domination and abuse, but then the film's highly recuperative ending acts to prevent this rebellion from finally being seen as admirable or inspiring. Female viewers are, in effect, prevented by the film's ending and by the distancing effect of its strategies of subject positioning from introjecting into their own psyches the qualities of these rebellious characters; instead, the intrapsychic response the film finally encourages is what Stacey describes as transcendence.[55] The spectator experiences a very brief loss of self and a limited adoption of a character's persona in a temporary fantasy that exists only while the film is being viewed. According to Stacey, this type of spectatorial response, in distinct contrast to the introjective mode, is of temporary duration and provokes very little if any change in the spectator's permanent sense of identity.

The failure of *Mortal Thoughts* to produce the popular response that *Thelma & Louise* provoked can perhaps be at least partially explained by the different spectator-text relationships set up by the two films. The spectatorial positions offered by *Mortal Thoughts* render the film, in spite of its political implications, much less challenging to the patriarchal status quo and much less empowering to female viewers than *Thelma & Louise*. As a result, the film attracted fewer viewers and sparked much less interest or controversy.

Leaving Normal

Full Recuperation

The politically challenging nature of *Thelma & Louise* becomes even more apparent when it is compared with *Leaving Normal,* another women-on-the-road film that many reviewers perceived as a *Thelma & Louise* clone. Whereas *Thelma & Louise* was created with a significant amount of female input, *Leaving Normal* represents an unmitigated male fantasy of female friendship. It was written by Edward Solomon, co-screenwriter of the Bill and Ted adventure films, adolescent male buddy comedies. Edward Zwick, the film's director, found his greatest success as creator of the popular television serial *thirtysomething,* and some reviewers even labeled *Leaving Normal* the sitcom version of *Thelma & Louise.*[56] More important, however, *Leaving Normal* should be seen as the conservative version of *Thelma & Louise.* It is a film that seems to represent a calculated response to the earlier film and one that completely recuperates the female buddy road movie for patriarchy.[57]

"Thelma and Louise Would Have Blown These Bozos Off the Road"

Whereas *Thelma & Louise* clearly enters the realm of the political female friendship film, *Leaving Normal* remains safely behind in the patriarchally complicit social female friendship category. The film is remarkably similar to *Thelma & Louise* in its initial plot construction, but as it progresses it makes radical departures from the earlier film's evocation of female outlawry. The heroines of *Leaving Normal* are, in fact, never criminals at all. They are merely confused women who need to find some stability in their lives. Marianne (Meg Tilly), a very naive young woman, flees her physically abusive husband and meets up with Darly (Christine Lahti), a cynical, world-weary cocktail waitress. They set out on the road together, have some harrowing experiences, and meet a number of odd people along the way. They arrive finally at their goal, a plot of land in the Alaskan wilderness that Darly has inherited from her now deceased ex-husband. After some plot complications, they get jobs, settle down, build a house on Darly's land, and establish a pseudofamily that affords them the permanence and stability the film suggests they really want and desperately need.

The bond of female friendship formed between Darly and Marianne affords no challenge to the existing social structure whatsoever. It provides, instead, simply a way for the two women to be reintegrated into the existing society. In fact, very much in contrast to *Thelma & Louise, Leaving Normal* suggests that there is really nothing wrong with the social situation of contemporary women that cannot be cured by their taking a different attitude toward their problems. Whereas Louise makes it clear to Thelma when she begins to blame herself for their situation that if there is anything she should have learned from their experiences it is that what happened was not her fault, *Leaving Normal* preaches repeatedly its message that women's discontent with their lives is their fault. What is wrong is removed entirely from the societal level and reduced to the realm of personal decisions. Marianne and Darly have simply made bad choices in their lives, and, according to the film's logic, they need to realize not even that they should choose more wisely, which would at least give them some power to control their lives, but instead that they should not choose at all. They are instructed merely to let fate or natural forces take their course, and the

In Leaving Normal *(Zwick, 1992), Darly (Christine Lahti, left) and Marianne (Meg Tilly) are left stranded by the side of the road, a symbolic representation of their directionless lives.*

natural course the film envisions for women, if they keep themselves from ruining things by making needless and inevitably bad decisions, is one that leads inexorably to a domestic caring situation.

Leaving aside its wild improbability and gross sentimentality, the ending of *Leaving Normal,* again in stark contrast to *Thelma & Louise,* is highly supportive of the patriarchal status quo. By the film's end, the cynical Darly has become an unlikely mother figure to the still infantile Marianne, who seems to be slowly maturing under Darly's nurturing influence and in response to Darly's ability to provide the stability of a permanent home. Not only does Darly assume a motherly role to Marianne, but the two women also take in two Eskimo boys who have been squatting on Darly's land and who help them build their house. This strange group comes together to create a pseudofamily that provides both Marianne and Darly with the domestic bliss that the film suggests they have always craved but have prevented themselves from attaining through their "bad choices."

Like Louise in *Thelma & Louise,* Darly also has a hidden secret, but whereas Louise refuses to reveal hers, Darly is all too quick to inform Marianne that twenty years ago she abandoned her own daughter just two days after the child's birth and has made no attempt since that time to discover the girl's whereabouts. This decision the film clearly intends the viewer to see as yet another example of the bad choices these two women have made throughout their lives, choices that account for their current feelings of directionless desperation. The revelation of Darly's secret complements perfectly what has already been revealed about Marianne's childhood. In the film's opening sequences, Marianne and her sister are shown as children suffering the traumas of an unstable family life—quarreling parents and constant movement from one place to another. Marianne's failure to find stability as an adult is traced directly back to her childhood. What she needs, the film suggests, is to be nurtured by a stable domestic caretaker, and what Darly needs is to provide this domestic care. They are perfect for each other—Darly as the mother Marianne never had and Marianne as the daughter Darly lost. Both are healed and empowered by taking on their respective mother/daughter roles.

In stark contrast to *Thelma & Louise*, where the road becomes a symbol of the freedom the women have been denied by patriarchal society, the road in *Leaving Normal* represents only hellish instability and complete misery. What both women really want is the permanence that the film suggests can be found only in a home and family, even if it is a nontraditional one. The film's final creation of a female-centered family might be seen as a challenge to the conservative "family values" stance in that it eliminates the need for a father figure in the family construct, yet this interpretation is undercut by the film's presentation of its idyllic female-centered family as in no way representing a goal in itself.

Both Marianne and Darly are using their pseudofamily situation as a means of reintegrating into the existing social structure, rather than as a way to rebel against it. To this end, a conventional male love interest for Marianne is included in the film's plot. The family life she finds with Darly is presented as merely a stepping-stone for the younger woman toward the stability she needs before she can start a "proper" heterosexual relationship with Harry (Lenny Von Dohlen), a sensitive, shy trucker whom the two women met on the road and who is obviously the perfect match for Marianne. Darly, reduced by the film's end to a traditional asexual mother figure, is divested of her theretofore very evident sexuality. She is now preoccupied not only with "raising" Marianne and the Eskimo boys they have taken in, but also with making efforts to locate her abandoned child. In the meantime, the two women's friendship bond is reduced to an imitation of and ultimately a valida-tion of family life. It becomes merely a means of providing the familial foundation needed for the development of heterosexual relationships. Rather than presenting female friendship as an alternative for women to the absolute primacy of the domestic family situation, *Leaving Normal* uses female bonding to reaffirm strongly the highly conservative idea that the family is the core of women's healthy development and the source of their ultimate fulfillment.

Never Leaving "Normal" at All: *Leaving Normal* and the Female Spectator

Like so many other female friendship films, *Leaving Normal* draws in its female spectators by encouraging their identification with the nur-turing relationship that forms between its two protagonists. As a result, the spectator is led to follow the two women as they develop new iden-tities as a result of their friendship. Unlike *Mortal Thoughts,* which puts up barriers to the spectator's complete involvement in the women's re-lationship through its narrational frame, *Leaving Normal* implicates the female spectator strongly in its characters' nurturing friendship bond. Because the film's ending emphasizes the role the women's relationship plays in leading them to new healthier identities through the formation of a nontraditional family, the message of the appropriateness of women's domestic roles is forcefully propagated.

In fact, this propagation is so intensely made that the film does not at all possess the openness to various reading possibilities that is a major quality of many female friendship films, and that would seem at least partially to account for their popularity with a large and diverse female audience. *Leaving Normal* opens itself up really only to one very conservative reading. The film preaches its single message inces-santly and advocates it repeatedly throughout its narrative: women need to stop making bad choices in their lives and settle down to do-mestic caring situations. This is what they really want and need and where nature or fate in any event, if allowed to take its proper course, will inevitably lead them. The disastrous box-office performance of *Leaving Normal* suggests that its closing down of meaning in support of a heavy-handed conservative message was not at all a source of ap-peal to female viewers.[58]

Concluding Comments

Political female friendship films have played only a limited role in the development of the contemporary female friendship film. *Thelma & Louise,* in fact, stands alone as the one contemporary female friendship film that opens itself up to a political reading that cannot be easily recuperated. All the other films have their political implications strongly recuperated in the course of the narrative, by their comedic format, by a highly recuperative conclusion, or by an insistently ambiguous thematic stance. The essentially conservative nature of mainstream filmmaking is suggested by the fact that an extremely popular film like *Thelma & Louise* did not spawn a large number of imitators.[59] In fact, the association of female friendship with violence that the film initiated actually seems to have sounded the death knell for political female friendship representations in mainstream cinema. The year that *Thelma & Louise* was released, 1991, became both the high point and the end point of the political female friendship film, a branch of the cycle that proved even in its limited political implications too radical for mainstream representation.

5 | The Erotic Female Friendship Film: Lesbianism in the Mainstream

The 1980s represent a watershed period for the portrayal of lesbianism in mainstream American cinema. Prior to this time, lesbian relationships were largely absent from popular films, and when they were presented, they were branded as shameful, deviant, and unhealthy. It was only in idependent avant-garde cinema that more positive lesbian portrayals could be found, in the works of Jan Oxenberg, Barbara Hammer, Lizzie Borden, Sheila McLaughlin, and Su Friedrich, for instance.[1] The 1982 release of *Personal Best* (Towne) marks a significant transformation in mainstream lesbian representations. *Personal Best* took the popular lesbian film in new directions by offering at long last a positive mainstream portrayal of a lesbian relationship, even if this portrayal was in many ways extremely limited. This new direction was considerably expanded later in the decade. Lesbian films in the later 1980s and early 1990s offered innovative presentations of erotic female relationships that went well beyond earlier lesbian portrayals. The films of this period fall into two categories: openly lesbian films following in the path established by *Personal Best* and ambiguously lesbian portrayals influenced much more by the undefined sexuality earlier suggested, for instance, in *Julia*.[2]

The openly lesbian film is represented in the mid-1980s by the groundbreaking lesbian romance *Desert Hearts* (Deitch, 1985), the first mainstream lesbian film by a lesbian director and still by many accounts the most popular lesbian film ever produced. This film's notable success with both lesbian and heterosexual audiences might lead one to expect that it would have initiated a long line of openly lesbian romance films with crossover appeal to both gay and straight viewers. This, however, did not prove to be the case; instead, after *Desert Hearts,* mainstream lesbian portrayals nearly disappeared, and when a major lesbian feature film was finally released in 1992, it cultivated a crossover audience by retreating into the less potentially controversial arena of ambiguous lesbian representation. *Fried Green Tomatoes* (Avnet, 1991) gained vastly expanded distribution and was much more popular at the box office than *Desert Hearts,* but it accomplished this feat by closeting its lesbian content. It was not until the early 1990s that the openly lesbian film again reasserted itself, and *Go Fish* (Troche, 1994), an independently made lesbian romance directed by a lesbian director, entered mainstream distribution with some success.

Personal Best

A Lesbian Film or a Sports Film?

Personal Best, the first directorial effort of the prominent Hollywood screenwriter Robert Towne, was promoted not as a lesbian film but as a sports film dealing with the lives of female athletes.[3] Some critics even connected its lesbian content to then current sensationalized allegations of widespread homosexuality in women's sports.[4] Certainly, the use of lesbianism for purposes of shock and titillation is not new to mainstream filmmaking, but Towne added a dimension to his lesbian portrayal that lifts the film above the level of sensationalist exploitation. He presents his two central characters, female athletes who become involved in a lesbian relationship, as attractive, intelligent, and psychologically healthy young lovers who display toward each other genuine affection. Compared with earlier lesbian portrayals, this step represents a breakthrough in itself.

Towne combines his positive portrayal of a lesbian relationship with an attempt to attract a wide viewing audience. Not only did promotional material for the film minimize its lesbian content in favor of its portrayal of women's sports competition, but in interviews Towne insisted that the film was not about lesbianism. He described it, instead, as concerned with "two children . . . discovering who they are with their bodies."[5] Similarly, Patrice Donnelly, the actress and former athlete who plays Tory Skinner, one of the film's two lead roles, claimed that neither she nor her character is gay: "I had to believe that I could be attracted to Mariel's character in order to play those scenes, but that doesn't make either me or my character a lesbian. I think Tory may have affairs with men after she gets over Chris."[6]

The text of *Personal Best,* like its publicity material, seems carefully constructed to avoid alienating any potential audience members. Homosexual, heterosexual, female, and male spectators are all encouraged to engage positively with the film. As Chris Straayer's interviews with lesbian viewers indicate, many lesbians see the film as a rare sympathetic portrayal of a loving lesbian relationship.[7] Linda Williams suggests that heterosexual female viewers might also appreciate the film's "'positive' portrayal of (literally) strong female protagonists committed to excellence in their field."[8] As Straayer points out, however, the film's voyeuristic presentation of female athletic bodies in action seems aimed at attracting male viewers. Straayer believes the film's athletic sequences and lesbian scenes serve as "erotic spectacles" for heterosexual male consumption in much the same way the female body and lesbianism are presented for purposes of male titillation in art cinema and pornography.[9]

Recuperating the Transgressive Nature of a Positive Lesbian Portrayal

Personal Best's attempt to appeal to a diverse audience minimizes both the threat posed to the male spectator by the film's positive lesbian portrayal and its politically transgressive potential. A major reason for the paucity of lesbian representations in mainstream cinema is the challenge they present to heterosexist patriarchy. The very existence of a lesbian alternative to heterosexual relationships calls into question women's complete reliance on men for romantic and sexual fulfillment. Lesbian desire and its cinematic expression in the lesbian gaze also break the association of femininity with passivity and offer women access to an active desiring subjectivity that is independent of the male.

Because of the nature of this threat, *Personal Best* works to recuperate those elements that challenge male heterosexist dominance. It does so, first of all, by resolving the issue of lesbianism simply as a matter of sexual attraction rather than as a political or lifestyle choice. The relationship between Chris (Mariel Hemingway) and Tory seems to develop from their heightened physicality as athletes.[10] They meet after an athletic competition, talk, relax together, arm wrestle, kiss, and finally make love. Even more significant, their relationship is presented as a stage in their development toward adult heterosexuality, or at least it is

In Personal Best *(Towne, 1982), the sexual relationship between Tory (Patrice Donnelly, left) and Chris (Mariel Hemingway) seems to develop from their heightened physicality as athletes. Here, they are shown gazing into each other's eyes as they arm wrestle.*

for Chris. The film falls perfectly into what Richard Dyer has described as the central plot structure of the mainstream lesbian film.[11] The plot involves a struggle for the control of the central female character by competing female and male love interests. In *Personal Best*, Tory eventually has to compete with Chris's subsequent male lover, Denny (Kenny Moore), for Chris's affections. Chris is a character lacking in definition; she is "unformed . . . nothing, an absence," and because her sexuality is "malleable—she will be had by anyone." Tory, the lesbian competitor, is ultimately defeated in the struggle, suggesting, as Dyer indicates, that "the true sexual definition of a woman is heterosexual and that she gets that definition from a man."[12]

Personal Best adds to this plot construction an additional recuperating element by presenting Chris not only as sexually unformed but as childlike. As noted above, Towne commented that he considered both his female characters to be mere children learning about their sexuality. This attitude is clearly demonstrated in his construction of the film's one scene of lesbian lovemaking. Chris and Tory are shown in bed stroking each other's bodies, behavior that Chris describes as "tickling." She then comments that her brothers would consider both of them flat chested. After this "romantic" interlude, Chris encourages Tory to begin touching her by announcing, "It's my turn." As Christine Holmlund points out, many lesbian viewers reported in interviews that they found this portrayal of lesbian sex insultingly tame, the tickling inappropriate, and the lack of adult sexual passion ridiculous. Their overwhelming comment was, "So that's what they think we do?"[13]

The film actually portrays its lesbian relationship as alternating between childlike play and maternal nurturance. The presentation of Tory and Chris's relationship as a surrogate mother-daughter bond recalls psychoanalytic theories of lesbianism as a regression to the pre-Oedipal stage of childhood dependence.[14] Indeed, Chris's relationship with Tory seems to have an Oedipal dimension, with the older Tory providing maternal nurturance in response to Chris's childlike dependence. At the beginning of the film, Chris is shown to be dominated by her father, who serves as her coach. Tory precipitates Chris's break from paternal dominance, and her mothering seems to help Chris move closer to independence and maturity.

As their relationship progresses, however, Tory's nurturance becomes too smothering. She fails to grant Chris the autonomy she needs to reach full adulthood, and eventually Chris severs their relationship and moves on to a new male love interest, Denny. Unlike Tory's smothering maternal care, Denny's nonthreatening masculinity provides exactly the nurturance that Chris needs to learn to achieve her "personal best." The film's portrayal of Chris's progression from an unsuccessful lesbian involvement to a successful heterosexual relationship promotes a heterosexist message that views lesbianism as an inadequate adolescent stage in women's psychosexual development toward a more satisfying and fulfilling heterosexuality. As Linda Williams suggests, the representation of lesbianism as a return to "the non-viable, pre-oedipal dependence and narcissistic identification of mother and daughter" not only "renders the relationship safe in the eyes of the film's ultimately patriarchal system of values," but also dooms it to failure because of its regressive nature.[15]

Lesbianism and Female Friendship

Personal Best controls the challenge its lesbian portrayal poses for the heterosexist status quo by depicting lesbianism not only as a stage in the immature girl's progression to a more fulfilling adult heterosexuality, but also as appropriately replaced by a more acceptable female

friendship bond. In fact, *Personal Best* is much more politically challenging as a female friendship film than it is as a lesbian portrayal. After
Chris and Tory break up and Chris has become involved with Denny,
the two women meet again at the Olympic trials, where Chris easily
makes the Olympic team while Tory struggles. Disillusioned by her
poor performance, Tory contemplates quitting, but Chris motivates
her to continue and even jeopardizes her own position in the competition by taking out another runner so that Tory can win a place on the
Olympic team. This conclusion suggests that as friends the two women
can encourage and help one another in a way that they could not as
lovers, and the film's portrayal of lesbianism becomes merely a device
used to purify and exalt its final glorification of female friendship.

The representation of the lesbian gaze in *Personal Best* is also significant in this regard. The lesbian gaze's transgressive potential rests
on the challenge it offers to traditional cinematic ways of seeing and its
definition of an active, desiring female subjectivity. Chris Straayer describes it as setting up an exchange of female looks that create two-
dimensional, reciprocal sexual activity. It requires "a returning look, not
just a receiving look" that associates female subjectivity with equality,
reciprocity, and activity.[16] In *Personal Best*, the radical potential of the
lesbian gaze is entirely recuperated for patriarchy. The looks of the female characters are controlled by the masculinization of the film's gaze
structure. Although the sexual gaze is not restricted to the film's male
characters, it is granted to the female characters only on a very limited
basis. When Tory and Chris are involved as lesbian lovers, only Tory,
the more masculinized female character, gazes desiringly at her partner.
Her looks of desire are paralleled by those of the women's male coach,
Tingloff (Scott Glenn), and later by Denny's desiring gaze. The more
feminine Chris rarely gazes at Tory, and in the only scene in which she
actively pursues lovemaking, Tory accuses her of only doing it "because
you know it's what I want." The film not only seems to associate sexual
desire exclusively with its more masculinized lesbian character, it also
grants her possession of the lesbian gaze on an unequal, nonreciprocal
basis. As a result, the crucial differences between the lesbian gaze and
the male heterosexual gaze are effectively eliminated.

The film also draws a connection between the lesbian gaze and the
male gaze by associating both with "a downward slant in relation to
power."[17] The older Tory is constructed as empowering the younger,
less experienced Chris. Because the two women are never allowed to

look at each other reciprocally as a couple, the mutuality that Sue Ellen Case describes as essential to the creation of the coupled lesbian subject position is never achieved.[18] When the women's relationship is transformed at the film's conclusion into a female friendship, the dynamics of the gaze change dramatically. Suddenly, there is an exchange of looks between the two friends as Chris encourages Tory to continue in athletic competition. The film's gaze structure seems to suggest that it is only by reconceiving their relationship as a female friendship that the two women can achieve a bond based on reciprocity, equality, and mutual affection.

Personal Best actually ends by exalting female friendship at the expense of lesbianism. Female friendship is presented as a caring, supportive relationship that can encourage personal development, in contrast to lesbianism, which seems inadequate, nonviable, and inherently unequal. The film champions a female care ethic that it sees as successfully enacted in a heterosexual union, in a female friendship, and even in an athletic competition, but not in a lesbian relationship. As a female friendship film, *Personal Best* is, in fact, very female affirmative. It shows women achieving in the male-dominated sphere of athletic competition; represents the female athletic body as beautiful, graceful, and strong; and challenges the sexist association of masculinity with activity and femininity with passivity. It promotes gender equality not only by asserting the essential worth of the female, but also by advocating a reformed patriarchy tempered by nondominant masculinity, a female care ethic, and equality and reciprocity in heterosexual relationships. Unfortunately, all these points are made at the expense of lesbianism.

Personal Best is perhaps best characterized as a limit case demonstrating how far the female friendship film could go in the early 1980s. It illustrates the extent of the shift in female representations that occurred in this period. Female friendship could be shown to temper male dominance and even to reform it, but lesbianism was simply going too far. *Personal Best*'s highly compromised "positive" lesbian portrayal marks the extent of reformist sentiment that patriarchy would tolerate in 1982.

Personal Best and the Female Spectator

The limitations of mainstream lesbian representation as well as the attempt to attract a diverse viewing audience greatly influence the subject positions that *Personal Best* offers its female viewers. For both lesbian and heterosexual female spectators, *Personal Best* contains the "discursive consent" that typically characterizes mainstream lesbian portrayals. The film allows its female spectators to engage with the representation of a lesbian relationship rendered "safe" by the film's heterosexist narrative logic. The female viewer is encouraged by her spatiotemporal alignment with Chris throughout the film and by the attractions of Mariel Hemingway's Hollywood star persona to move with Chris through her lesbian experience to what the film posits as more fulfilling heterosexual and female friendship relationships. As a result, the heterosexual female viewer can vicariously participate in the sexual and emotional experience of Chris's lesbian involvement with Tory without having her heterosexuality challenged. Lesbian viewers can also experience these moments of "discursive consent," but at a significant cost to their self-esteem and sense of lesbian identity. The film, by representing lesbianism as an unsatisfactory stage on the road to more fulfilling heterosexuality, deauthorizes the lesbian perspective and attempts to invalidate spectatorial responses that would see lesbianism as a viable alternative to heterosexuality.

The determination of *Personal Best* to attract a diverse audience, however, also provides its spectator with myriad opportunities for subversive or oppositional readings. Audience studies of the film's reception by lesbian viewers demonstrate persuasively that these oppositional readings have, in fact, taken place among lesbian audiences. As Chris Straayer points out, lesbian viewers have become accustomed to performing subversive readings on films that present a heterosexist perspective. They simply ignore whole sections of such films and reenvision them to achieve the viewing pleasure they would otherwise be denied.[19]

Many lesbian viewers of *Personal Best* carried out just such an oppositional reading strategy. They "resisted the narrative's heterosexist closure and imagined what would happen to the characters in a lesbian future."[20] Responding to Tory's possession of the gaze, they identified her as the film's major character despite Mariel Hemingway's star status, narrative centrality, and greater amount of screen time. As Elizabeth Ellsworth points out, many lesbian viewers labeled as convincingly lesbian Patrice Donnelly's performance as Tory. They commented on the verisimilitude of her body language, facial expressions, use of voice, expression of desire, and strength in the face of male heterosexist dominance. With Tory the central character in the film, "the significance of key narrative events is altered in a way that makes it possible to interpret the film's ending as a validation of lesbianism" rather than of female friendship.[21]

For these lesbian "resisting readers," the film's ending allows for the possibility that Chris and Tory might reestablish their relationship sometime in the future, perhaps at the next athletic meet or at the upcoming Olympic games. They refuse to see the breakup of the lesbian relationship as complete or necessarily permanent. This reading is facilitated by the ambiguity of the film's conclusion. As noted above, when the women's relationship has been converted into a female friendship, Chris and Tory finally exchange reciprocal gazes, which seem emblematic of their close friendship, yet the gaze in the film up to this point has been so heavily invested with erotic overtones that it is difficult here at the end to divest it entirely of sexual significance. As a result, Chris and Tory's exchange of looks can be read as a suggestion of a continued romantic attraction between them, rather than of a newly established friendship bond.

The film's concluding scene also allows for an interpretation that sees Chris and Tory as possibly reestablishing their relationship sometime in the future. In fact, a minor dialogue change occurred as the film moved from its screenplay version to its final form, a change that is highly significant in facilitating a lesbian reading. Both the film and screenplay end with Chris and Tory on the winner's stand after having come in first and third, respectively, in the Olympic trials. In the screenplay, Tory tells Chris that Denny, whom we see looking on, is "awful cute." Chris responds "delightedly," as the script directions indicate, with a simple "I know."[22] This dialogue is changed in the film to Tory's suggestion that Denny is "awful cute . . . for a guy" and Chris's surprised questioning response, "You shittin' me?" Both screenplay and film suggest that Tory and Chris's relationship has moved from sexual involvement to friendship, but the screenplay closes down the possibility of a reactivated lesbian attraction, whereas the film does not. Tory's equivocal "for a guy" and Chris's surprised response in the film can be read as suggesting not only that Tory has maintained her lesbian orientation but also that Chris is surprised, perhaps somewhat dismayed, that Tory is so approving of her male lover. The screenplay's omission of Tory's equivocation and description of Chris's "delight" at Tory's remark make this reading much less likely. It seems clear from lesbian viewers' responses to the film that many of them utilize this small opening to resist the text's heterosexist closure.

Like lesbian viewers, heterosexual female spectators could also resist *Personal Best*'s attempts to place them in a particular subject position. For instance, they could reject the film's championing of a reformed nondominant patriarchy by interpreting its voyeuristic portrayals of female nudity and athleticism as symptomatic of a patriarchy that is not nearly as reformed as the film proposes. As Linda Williams suggests, *Personal Best* can be read, "for all its lyrically natural and guiltless sensuality, for all its celebration of women athletes as possessed of both excellence and integrity," as failing ultimately "to provide a genuinely feminist depiction of women in love or competition."[23] Thus, as a limit text that sets the boundaries beyond which mainstream female friendship portrayals could not go in the early 1980s, *Personal Best* unwittingly opens up avenues of interpretation that allow female viewers to read the film against the grain and contemplate possibilities significantly beyond the boundaries that the film attempts to establish.

Desert Hearts
A Groundbreaking Lesbian Romance Film

The positive lesbian portrayal in *Personal Best* did not stimulate a wave of popular lesbian films in the 1980s. In fact, it was not until 1985 that another lesbian film achieved wide mainstream release. In 1983, independent filmmaker John Sayles made *Lianna,* which deals with a young woman's discovery of her lesbian identity, but the film received only extremely limited mainstream distribution.[24] The next major step after *Personal Best* in the development of mainstream lesbian representation did not take place until the release of Donna Deitch's lesbian romance *Desert Hearts,* unquestionably the most popular mainstream lesbian film of the 1980s.[25] Although the popularity of *Desert Hearts* would seem to establish it as a significant advance in lesbian representation, it has received curiously little critical attention. Heterosexual critics ignore the film almost completely, and lesbian critics overwhelmingly condemn it.[26] Teresa de Lauretis, for instance, insists that *Desert Hearts* casts its lesbian love story squarely in the tradition of Hollywood heterosexual romance. For her, this repackaging of heterosexual conventions "as a commodity purportedly produced for lesbians, does not seem to me sufficient to disrupt, subvert, or resist the straight representational and social norms by which 'homosexuality is nothing but heterosexuality,' nor *a fortiori* sufficient to shed light on the specific difference that constitutes a lesbian subjectivity."[27]

Jackie Stacey is almost alone among lesbian critics in recognizing the importance of *Desert Hearts* not only as the most popular mainstream lesbian film in contemporary cinema but also as "the first lesbian romance which offers its spectators an unapologetic celebration of lesbian love" as well as "challenging the traditional definition of lesbianism as 'unnatural,' 'deviant,' 'predatory,' or 'depressing.'" Yet even Stacey sees the film as ultimately a failure. She believes that although it rejects older definitions of lesbianism, it "fails to introduce engaging new narrative formulae to replace these older unacceptable ones" and as a result lacks the emotional intensity viewers expect from screen romances.[28] I would argue, however, that the neglect and condemnation of *Desert Hearts* stem from a failure to investigate fully the film's obvious attraction to lesbian and heterosexual viewers alike and the pleasures its representation of lesbian love affords.

Desert Hearts was the first mainstream lesbian feature film in the contemporary period to be made by a lesbian director. Deitch, a photographer as well as an avant-garde and documentary filmmaker, spent six years developing the film from the time she initially conceived the project in 1979. Her struggle to get *Desert Hearts* off the ground began with the necessity of convincing Jane Rule, the well-known lesbian author of *Desert of the Heart,* the novel upon which the film is based, to grant Deitch the rights to film the story. Before Rule would agree, she required strong assurances that Deitch would not exploit the novel's lesbian content for pornographic purposes.[29] Deitch then spent two and a half years raising money for the production and is reputed to have raised, single-handedly, primarily from the gay and lesbian community, somewhere between $850,000 and $1.5 million.[30] In spite of Deitch's herculean efforts to obtain adequate financing for the film, its limited budget clearly affected its production values. It was shot in thirty-one days, with few retakes and little room for artistic flourish.[31] Once the film was completed, however, Deitch managed to obtain mainstream distribution through Samuel Goldwyn Productions.

A Lesbian Film Steeped in the Conventions of Heterosexual Romance

Based on Natalie Cooper's screenplay adaptation of Rule's story and set, like the novel, in 1950s Reno, Nevada, *Desert Hearts* recounts the story of a love affair between an eastern college professor, Vivian Bell (Helen

Shaver), and a western casino change girl, Cay Rivvers (Patricia Char-bonneau). Vivian comes to Reno in order to divorce her college profes-sor husband and meets Cay at the ranch where both are staying; they fall in love. Although the relationship between the two women is openly pre-sented as lesbian, a comparison of *Desert Hearts* to Jane Rule's novel clarifies sharply the film's extensive adoption of heterosexual conven-tions. The great majority of the changes made from novel to film render the story considerably less threatening to a heterosexual audience.

For instance, the film encloses Cay and Vivian's relationship within an environment dominated by idyllic heterosexual romance. Silver (Andra Akers), Cay's coworker and best friend, is involved in an intense heterosexual love relationship with her fiance, Joe (Antony Ponzini). Their romance parallels and comments upon Cay and Vivian's. It is after Silver and Joe's engagement party that Cay and Vivian first kiss, and their love affair is interrupted by their attendance at Silver and Joe's wedding. The paralleling of the two relationships renders the lesbian romance similar to, as intense as, and thus as natural and legitimate as the heterosexual love affair. It also, however, positions Silver and Joe's passionate heterosexuality as the norm by which the intensity of Cay and Vivian's homosexual relationship is appraised.

Although the novel, like the film, includes Silver and Joe's wedding, it depicts their relationship as much less idyllic than does the film. In fact, rather than serving as a heterosexual parallel to the novel's lesbian romance, Silver and Joe's relationship compares much less favorably with it. In the novel, Silver even serves as a rival to Evelyn (renamed Vi-vian in the film) for the affections of Ann (Cay in the film). Whereas the film's Silver is a failed singer who feels she has finally found her long-awaited true love in Joe, her novelistic counterpart is a former prostitute who is involved with a newspaperman who wants to become a porno-graphic author. During Joe's frequent absences, Silver invites Cay to spend the night with her, and the two engage in a clandestine lesbian af-fair. This affair continues throughout Silver's involvement with Joe, and she even invites Cay to stay with her on the very night before her wed-ding. Unlike in the film, which presents Silver and Joe's marriage as the consummation of their passionate love, in the novel their wedding is precipitated by Silver's unintended pregnancy.

In the film, Cay and Vivian's relationship is also implicitly com-pared to the heterosexual love affair that had existed between Cay's now deceased father, Glen, and her surrogate mother, Frances (Audra

Lindley). The character of Frances is greatly transformed from novel to film. In the novel, she is strongly supportive of Evelyn and Ann's relationship, whereas in the film she becomes a controlling, destructive surrogate mother figure who is determined to do everything she can to discourage Cay and Vivian's love affair. Frances's opposition to Cay and Vivian's relationship seems precipitated not only by her homophobia and possessiveness but also by her own unacknowledged sexual attraction to Cay, an attraction that seems to stem from Cay's resemblance to her dead father, Frances's ex-lover.[32] Frances tells Vivian that Cay strongly resembles Glen in both looks and personality. She describes her relationship with Glen in terms that Cay will later repeat to Frances to describe her relationship with Vivian. She says that Glen "just reached in and put a string of lights around my heart." Later, after Silver's wedding, when Frances tells Cay that she just cannot accept "two women together," Cay repeats Frances's earlier phrase, applying it to her feelings for Vivian and suggesting a parallel between Frances's heterosexual relationship and Cay's lesbian love.

Desert Hearts not only places Cay and Vivian's lesbian affair within an exclusively heterosexual context, it also presents the women's relationship as a matter of exclusionary sexual preference and never as a threat to the heterosexual relationships that surround it. Rule's novel, on the other hand, contains strong suggestions of both Ann's and Silver's bisexual rather than exclusively homosexual or heterosexual tendencies. In the novel, Ann is said to have ended a long affair with her male lover Bill (Darrell in the film) not because she realized that she was really attracted to women, as is the case in the film, but because she feared the exclusivity of the marital bond. Similarly, her clandestine lesbian relationship with Silver in the novel calls into question the exclusivity and passionate intensity of Silver's heterosexual union with Joe in a way that is completely eliminated from the film.

Deitch's recasting of the novel's presentation of a sexual relationship between Ann and Silver into a platonic friendship strongly indicates her determination to attract a heterosexual audience. The film contains only vague suggestions of Silver's possible attraction to Cay. For instance, in one scene the two women take a bubble bath together, and Silver gazes at Cay with obvious desire. Cay does not return the look, as she will later with Vivian; instead, the two women engage in a discussion about Cay's attraction, not to Silver, but to Vivian. Joe enters, and Silver turns her attention entirely to him, leaving Cay to look on with embarrassment as they proclaim their absolute devotion to one another.

The film replaces Silver as Ann's bisexual lover with Gwen (Gwen Welles), a lesbian one-night stand. Teresa de Lauretis suggests that Gwen serves as a "stock character whore" adapted from the conventions of the Hollywood western. She is coded by looks, pose, makeup, and speech as the "slut," in contrast to Vivian's role as the real love interest for Cay. As de Lauretis points out, "*Desert Hearts* does not distance this image and role or reframe them in a lesbian camp tradition or in the lesbian history of the forties and fifties, as it might have done, but only invokes a general fifties mood typical of many films of the eighties."[33] As a result, Gwen, a conventional Hollywood stereotype with whom a heterosexual audience could feel comfortable, replaces Silver, an unconventional bisexual character who might be potentially alienating to heterosexual viewers. The novel's presentation of Ann's relationship with Silver clearly posits lesbianism as existing within as well as next to heterosexual relationships, a much more subversive statement than the film's contention that the two sexual orientations coexist harmoniously in nonthreatening, mutually exclusive proximity.

The novel and film also differ in their presentations of the relationship between their lesbian lovers. In the novel, Evelyn and Ann's attraction is based primarily on their similarities rather than their differences from one another. Although there is a substantial age disparity between them, they still resemble each other enough that they are mistaken for mother and daughter. Not only are they remarked upon as mirror images of each other, they also share similar literary interests. Ann is a cartoonist (not a sculptor, as Cay is in the film), has an extensive library filled with literary classics, and writes poetry. Clearly, Evelyn, the college literature professor, represents a potential intellectual mentor to Ann, whom she initially describes as being "as young as a student."[34]

Whereas the novel places the women's relationship in what can be described as the "transgressive space" of lesbian sameness,[35] the film returns it to the more conventional heterosexual dimension of difference by accentuating the things that divide rather than unite the two lovers. Cay is from the West, and Vivian from the East. Cay is given to wild, spontaneous physicality, whereas Vivian represents sexually repressed intellectualism. Cay advocates risk, luck, and adventure; Vivian wants order, safety, and respectability. Cay is more aggressive sexually; Vivian represents a more traditionally passive femininity. These personality contrasts are not as evident in the novel as they are in the film. As Mandy Merck suggests, they represent "symbolic dichotomies" written into the film to make the lesbian relationship conform to heterosexual romantic norms by accentuating difference between the lovers rather than sameness.[36]

The Pleasures of *Desert Hearts*

Deitch's attempts to gain crossover audience appeal have led lesbian critics to emphasize the limitations of *Desert Hearts* and to ignore the real pleasures the film offers its female viewers, both lesbian and heterosexual. These pleasures can be elicited most fully if the film is placed in the context not only of lesbian representations but also of mainstream female friendship films. First of all, as a positive portrayal of lesbian romance, *Desert Hearts* succeeds in reversing the overt homophobia that previously characterized representations of lesbianism in popular cinema. Like *Personal Best,* it presents its lesbian romance as sincere and loving, but it goes beyond the earlier film by refusing to use lesbianism as a way to purify or show the superiority of heterosexual attachments. Nor does it follow earlier lesbian portrayals in depicting lesbianism as a regression to a childhood attachment to the mother or as a developmental stage leading to a more mature heterosexuality. The film allows its lesbian love affair to end happily, with both women transformed in positive ways by their attachment, rather than following older traditions in which lesbian lovers are ultimately punished or their love relationship is destroyed. These aspects alone would seem to render the film affirmative of lesbian viewers.

In addition, the gaze structure and representation of lesbian sexuality in *Desert Hearts* can also be seen as progressive. The exchange of erotic, desiring looks between Cay and Vivian permeates the film and presents a distinct challenge to mainstream cinema's dominant male gaze. Unlike *Personal Best,* where the looks exchanged between the two women are activated, complemented, and legitimated by the gaze of male characters, *Desert Hearts* creates and sustains an active, desiring female subjectivity independent of male control. Vivian and Cay engage in homoerotic visual interchanges that involve mutuality and reciprocity rather than dominance and submission. This lesbian gaze structure opens up to the female spectator the coupled lesbian subject position theorized by Teresa de Lauretis as characteristic of avant-garde lesbian representations.

Like more radical lesbian films, *Desert Hearts* creates a lesbian subject position that, in de Lauretis's words, offers "a place from where the equivalence of look and desire—which sustains spectatorial pleasure and the very power of cinema in constructing and orienting the viewer's identification—appears invested in two women, each of whom is both the subject and object of that look/desire."[37] Rejecting mainstream norms, the film refuses to recuperate this evocation of an active, desiring female subjectivity by punishing its female characters with death or the destruction of their relationship; instead, they are rewarded with a happy ending. Cay and Vivian not only end up together, but their relationship empowers them to take the necessary risks to find new directions in their lives. Vivian accepts her love for Cay and sets out to persuade her lover to accompany her back East. Similarly, at the film's conclusion Cay seems about to overcome her fears and embark on a new life with Vivian that will allow her to develop her creative talents fully.

The film's presentation of lesbian sexuality is more problematic than its evocation of the lesbian look. Much of its narrative tension is, in fact, sustained by the anticipation created by its long-delayed final love scene. Unlike Rule's novel, which contains several sexual encounters between Ann and Evelyn, the film creates emotional intensity by slowly building up to one climactic sex scene. Although this strategy works effectively to involve the audience strongly in the women's desiring subjectivity, the centrality of the love scene seems to define lesbianism primarily by its sexual dimension. The fact that Cay, coded as the more butch character, initiates the women's sexual relationship by actively pursuing the reluctant, more femininely passive Vivian also preserves norms of masculine dominance and feminine submission associated with heterosexual sexuality. As Jackie Stacey describes the film's presentation of lesbian seduction, it is "painfully reminiscent of pressure or coercion," a "battle of wills," with Cay representing confidence and spontaneity and Vivian repression and denial.[38]

The way the scene is shot also presents a complex mixture of progressive and regressive elements, and critics have diverged sharply in

In Desert Hearts *(Deitch, 1985), as she is about to board a train to go back East, Vivian (Helen Shaver, right) tries to persuade her lover, Cay (Patricia Charbonneau), to accompany her. When Cay finally agrees to get on the train at least until the next stop, the film provides a rare mainstream cinematic portrayal of a lesbian love affair with a happy ending.*

their reactions to it. The scene has been described, for instance, as portraying hygienic sex, as painfully naive, as sentimental, and even as reactionary. Christine Holmlund points out that it is

> restrained by the conventions of love scenes in the heterosexual woman's film. Lighting is never harsh. The use of close-ups and medium shots shows a distinct preference for the caress, the kiss and the gaze over anything else. Cunnilingus is, of course, out of the question. Sex, when shown at all, is never rough, and always takes place in relatively tame and traditional places.[39]

In spite of these qualities, other lesbian critics label the scene "one of the hottest bed romps in recent memory."[40] Although it begins with a pursuer/pursued situation reminiscent of representations of heterosexual sexuality, this encounter can also be read as decidedly lesbian, "a classic butch/femme, active/passive scenario which contemporary lesbians have come to associate with romance and sexuality between women in the 1950s."[41] As the scene progresses, it breaks down this active/passive dichotomy and conveys the mutuality of both women's attraction to each other. As Holmlund indicates, during its long, almost five-minute evocation of lesbian sexuality, "a space for homosexual desires for and identification with characters who openly acknowledge and live their homosexuality emerges in a way that it does not in most Hollywood films."[42]

It is not only as a reworking of traditional portrayals of lesbianism that *Desert Hearts* can be regarded as innovative. If seen in the context of female friendship film conventions, the film also contains progressive elements. It presents a dyadic female relationship that leads both women to change their existing unsatisfactory life situations. Although the empowerment resulting from the relationship remains primarily personal, with the women remaining isolated from the larger community, it does extend in significant ways out into the public sphere. Vivian not only overcomes her own internalized homophobic tendencies, but, in attempting to persuade Cay to accompany her back East, she seems also to have decided to fight openly against homophobic public opinion. Cay's decision to get on the train with Vivian, at least until the next stop, suggests that their relationship will lead her to take action to alter her life as well. In any event, she seems to be beginning to understand that, as Vivian tells her, she needs "to be with someone who realizes just how wonderful you are." It is on this note of female triumph and self-affirmation that the film ends. The conclusion is a victory for its female characters not only because it is implied that they choose to be with each other, but because their relationship seems to be leading them to greater personal development and self-fulfillment.

Desert Hearts and the Female Spectator

In accord with the film's attempt to attract a crossover audience, the address of *Desert Hearts* to its female spectators is intentionally diverse. Although this strategy of spectatorial engagement fails to cast light on the specific differences that constitute lesbianism, it contains the advantage of being able to offer the image of a desiring female subjectivity, not just to lesbian but to all female viewers. Homosexual and heterosexual female spectators alike are offered the "coupled lesbian subject position" that the film creates, and they are granted the "discursive consent" to adopt it. They can identify with the film's female characters as both desiring subjects and desirable objects of the female gaze that is so openly portrayed. Then they can retreat, if they wish, to seeing the film, as Deitch describes it, as "just a love story, like any love story between a man and a woman."[43]

In addition, *Desert Hearts* offers its lesbian spectators identification through the character of Cay with a primal scene of lesbian desire. As Teresa de Lauretis describes this scenario, it presents a restaging of the lesbian original fantasy, the "mise-en-scene of lesbian desire" as a drama of "the loss and recovery of a fantasmatic female body"—not the mother's body but the subject's own.[44] Lesbian psychosexual development, for de Lauretis, is distinctly different from heterosexual female development in that the loss of the pre-Oedipal mother is redoubled by the loss of the female body, a narcissistic wound that acts as a fantasy of castration threatening the subject with a loss of body ego, a lack of being itself. As a result of a maternal failure to validate the subject's body image, the lesbian subject through disavowal displaces the wish for the missing female body into a yearning toward other women.[45] Unlike traditional psychoanalytic accounts, which associate lesbianism with an enduring, active phallic attachment to the mother, de Lauretis's theory of the original lesbian fantasy has less to do with the recovery of the lost mother than with the loss and recovery of the female body, of the subject's own body image.

Through Cay's relationship with Frances, *Desert Hearts* enacts just such a scenario. Frances tells Vivian that Cay was rejected by her real mother and that Frances took her in, acting as a mother substitute. As we have seen, however, Frances's strong attachment to Cay stems not so much from her affection for Cay herself as from Cay's resemblance to her dead father. Thus, Frances's surrogate mothering redoubles Cay's loss of her real mother. Like the mother who rejected her, Frances rejects Cay's female body image and replaces it with Cay's father's. By loving Cay for herself, Vivian recovers for her not her lost mother, but her own body ego, her sense of self. Indeed, the nurturing aspects of their relationship, with Vivian both desiring Cay physically and offering her the intellectual stimulation she needs to develop her talents, complete this "mise-en-scene of lesbian desire." As a result, the film is able to offer its lesbian spectator a means of engaging with the text through its restaging of a lesbian primal scene as well as through the formation of a nurturing lesbian relationship.

The nurturing aspects of Cay and Vivian's love affair also engage both lesbian and heterosexual viewers in a mirroring transference relationship. As Vivian and Cay are shown to experience rebirth through their attachment to each other, the viewer is also empowered to aspire to the same therapeutic sense of self-discovery. The love relationship between the two women is not a refuge from the world, but a way into it. Vivian finds herself sexually, and Cay finds herself artistically. The viewer, nurtured by the film, as the women are by each other, is encouraged to do the same, to take the risk to find her real identity, to express her desiring subjectivity, to achieve a sense of positive self-esteem, and to reach her goals and ambitions.

The subject position offered by *Desert Hearts* is best summed up by the film's director, who inserts herself in the film in a brief, but important, cameo role as an anonymous woman identified in the film's credits as the "Hungarian gambler." Having won a jackpot at one of the casino slot machines, she is asked by Cay if she wants to play it off. She then pronounces what is clearly the film's central thematic statement: "If you don't play, you can't win." It is this risk-taking subject position that the film offers to its female spectators, irrespective of their sexual orientation. Like so many female friendship films, *Desert Hearts* is ultimately about female affirmation. In spite of its flaws, it offers its viewers, both lesbian and heterosexual, much to attract them to its evocation of female connection as a means of personal development; as such, its popularity is not at all difficult to understand.

Fried Green Tomatoes

The Retreat to the Ambiguously Lesbian Film

If the popularity of *Desert Hearts* might suggest that the mainstream lesbian film had finally come out of the closet and found wide acceptance, the years after its release were to see instead a retreat to ambiguously lesbian representation. It was not until 1991, in fact, that another lesbian film found substantial mainstream distribution, and then only by greatly minimizing its lesbian content. *Fried Green Tomatoes* (1991) was adapted by comedienne Fannie Flagg and Carol Sobieski with the uncredited assistance of producer/director Jon Avnet from Flagg's novel *Fried Green Tomatoes at the Whistle Stop Cafe*. It was a small Hollywood film financed by the fledgling all-woman production company Electric Shadows Productions. Initially marketed to appeal to older female viewers, it found a wide audience and became one of the most popularly successful female friendship films of the period.

To achieve this wide popularity, the film altered many of the more controversial aspects of Flagg's novel, including its lesbian, feminist, and racial themes.[46] Both novel and film contain a multilevel narrative

Novelist and screenwriter Fannie Flagg, surrounded by the stars of Fried Green Tomatoes *(Avnet, 1991). Standing, from left to right, Cicely Tyson, Mary Stuart Masterson, and Mary-Louise Parker; seated, from left to right, Kathy Bates, Fannie Flagg, and Jessica Tandy.*

structure that juxtaposes accounts of present-day and past events and focuses on two dyadic female friendships. In the present-day context, Evelyn Couch (Kathy Bates), a middle-aged women experiencing a midlife crisis, meets Ninny Threadgoode (Jessica Tandy), an older woman confined to a nursing home. In the past, Idgie Threadgoode (Mary Stuart Masterson), an unconventional young woman, forms a strong attachment to her more traditionally feminine friend Ruth Jamison (Mary-Louise Parker).

The accounts of both friendships fall into the sentimental female friendship category. The intimate and nurturing nature of the women's bonds, as well as their crucially important salvific quality is stressed. By telling Evelyn stories of Idgie and Ruth, Ninny helps her friend through a midlife crisis. At the film's conclusion, Evelyn decides in return to take Ninny in as part of her family, rescuing her from the sterile, uncaring environment of a nursing home. The two women's close friendship replicates in its salvific qualities the past relationship between Idgie and Ruth. In this friendship, Idgie rescues Ruth from marriage to an abusive husband and as a result is put on trial for his murder. Ruth then performs her own saving act by devising a strategy that prevents Idgie from being convicted.

The film's internal narrative, with its suggested, but unconfirmed, lesbian content, is encased in and granted thematic significance only in relation to the external narrative recounting Ninny and Evelyn's more conventional intergenerational friendship. This structure is very different from the one found in Flagg's novel, which is organized into three alternating narrative segments: Evelyn and Ninny's present-day activities; past events in the town of Whistle Stop, focusing not only on Idgie and Ruth but also on other members of the Whistle Stop community; and Dot Weems's Whistle Stop newspaper columns. In the novel, each segment has independent significance; no one part encompasses another, so that events in the past are given equal weight with those that occur in the present. In the film, however, the past relationship between Idgie and Ruth becomes merely an inspiring lesson for Evelyn in the present.

The subsumption of Idgie and Ruth's past relationship under Evelyn and Ninny's present-day friendship leads finally to an ending entirely altered from the one found in the book. The novel concludes with Ninny's death and Evelyn's subsequent visit to her grave to tell her deceased friend how much she misses her. Then, the last chapter switches the final focus to the aged Idgie, who is revealed to be still alive and working as the owner of a roadside fruit stand, where she continues to demonstrate her benevolent nature by giving a free jar of honey to a small child. Unlike the novel, the film keeps Idgie's story always confined within the Evelyn/Ninny narrative.

The film ends with a series of startling and manipulative revelations. First, Ninny recounts in maudlin detail the tearful story of Ruth's tragic death from cancer. The narrative then moves to what appears to be Evelyn's discovery of Ninny's sudden demise in the nursing home. After the viewer's heartstrings have been pulled by this paralleling of Ninny's death with Ruth's, we learn that Ninny is not dead at all. It was her roommate who died, and Ninny has merely left to return to her former home. Evelyn follows her there, knowing that Ninny will find that her house has been condemned and demolished. In response to this new catastrophe, Evelyn offers to take Ninny into her own home, where she will care for Ninny herself. Apparently, the filmmakers did not see even this strong resolution as tying things up enough. Ninny and Evelyn proceed to visit Ruth's grave, where they find next to her tombstone a jar of honey and a loving note from Idgie, who it is suggested is not only alive but is really Ninny.

From a Political Female Friendship Novel to a Social Female Friendship Film

The concluding series of sensational revelations in *Fried Green Tomatoes* serves two important functions: it disavows the lesbian content of the internal story of Idgie and Ruth while at the same time reducing the feminist dimensions of Evelyn's struggle. By finally repositioning Evelyn back in the domestic sphere as Ninny's caretaker, the film undercuts significantly the novel's theme of women's need for a sense of independence outside the home. In the film, Evelyn's personal struggle ends not with her finding success in the work world, as it does in the novel, but with her return to the domestic sphere as she replaces her husband and son with Ninny as a surrogate family.

In this way, the film transforms the novel's presentation of political into social female friendship. The novel suggests that its female friends carve out for themselves their own niche within a larger patriarchal society. The sense of security and self-confidence they gain from their relationships with each other inspires them to challenge an inhospitable, and even at times openly hostile, outside world. Evelyn, inspired by Ninny's tales of Idgie and Ruth's courage, changes her life by losing weight, working to improve her relationship with her husband, and seeking employment as a cosmetics representative. Her career success is prominent at the novel's conclusion as she drives up to the cemetery to visit Ninny's grave in the pink Cadillac that she had always wanted. Similarly, Idgie and Ruth's challenge to male power involves not only their defiance of Ruth's abusive husband but also their establishment of the Whistle Stop Cafe as a successful business venture.

Whereas the novel's female relationships culminate in the women's discovering how to enter into and transform the public sphere in ways that help them meet their needs, the film presents a less politically challenging picture. It suggests, instead, in the tradition of the social female friendship film, that the niches the women carve out for themselves do not so much lead them into the larger society as provide them refuge from the outside world of male abuse, hostility, and neglect. Although the film follows the novel in suggesting that the social structure both in the past and in the present does not meet women's needs, it fails to argue, as the book does, that women can establish more fulfilling lives in the public sphere if they are inspired by the courageous lives of women in the past. It proposes instead that women both in the past and in the present can find solace from the outside world in their relationships with each other.

From Openly Lesbian Novel to Ambiguously Lesbian Film

The reduction of the feminist message in *Fried Green Tomatoes* from that found in Flagg's novel is complemented by the film's minimization of the novel's lesbian content. The creators of *Fried Green Tomatoes* transformed an openly lesbian novel into an ambiguously lesbian film. The book portrays clearly, if not in sexually explicit terms, a butch/femme lesbian marriage. The novel's Idgie, openly dressing in masculine attire and engaging in male pastimes, falls in love with the more conventionally feminine Ruth. They live together, run their own business, and raise Ruth's child as if he were their own.

The novel can even be read as a celebration of lesbian butch courage in its idealization of Idgie's character. As a number of lesbian theorists have recently suggested, the significance of the butch role in pre-women's liberation lesbian working-class communities is currently being rethought. It is no longer seen, as it so often was in the past, as an embarrassing imitation of masculinity, "evidence of the backwardness, conservatism, and confusion of working-class lesbians, who were generally depicted as victims of patriarchal brainwashing" by lesbian feminists of the 1960s and 1970s.[47] Judy Grahn, for instance, argues for the "persistent construction of the butch as 'magical sign,'" as a "shaman figure," and as part of the "core or heart group" against which others in lesbian culture measure themselves.[48] For lesbian theorists such as Grahn and Joan Nestle, the butch figures as a heroic statement of lesbian independence, a woman who "refuses femininity and takes on the dress of the male . . . to announce her sexual identity to the world."[49] In Flagg's novel, Idgie is just such a heroic figure.

Within this context, *Fried Green Tomatoes at the Whistle Stop Cafe* can be read as a celebration of the working-class butch lesbian's courage in presenting herself in ways that she feels are authentic and standing up against male domination. Idgie is without doubt the most heroic figure in the novel. Not only does she save Ruth from her husband's abuse, she also masquerades as Railroad Bill and secretly distributes food to the poor from moving railroad trains. The novel presents her as the embodiment of the subversive figure of the butch lesbian, who confirms the fact that, as Joan Nestle suggests, "in some sense, lesbians have always opposed the patriarchy: in the past, perhaps most when we looked like men."[50]

The subversive potential of this portrayal is largely recuperated by the film's refusal to represent Idgie and Ruth's union unequivocally as a lesbian bond; instead, it converts their relationship into what the film's press materials suggest is "the deepest bond of friendship" between a "young maverick unrefined by etiquette and untamed by men" and a "God-fearing woman."[51] As David Ehrenstein points out in his review of the film, "So much for 'butch' and 'femme.'"[52] The film's lesbian content is, indeed, restricted to what Christine Holmlund has called "cliched counter-conventions of continuity editing" marked as possibly indicating lesbian desire: "shot/reverse shots of two women looking longingly at each other, point of view shots where one woman spies on another, and two shots where two women hug, romp, or dance together."[53] All of these visual markers of suggested homoerotic desire can just as easily be interpreted, and certainly are by many viewers, merely as indicators of admiration and affection between friends.

Additionally, the film's gaze structure works to contain the lesbian look within the internal narrative and to prevent its extension out to the female viewer. The erotically charged looks exchanged between Idgie and Ruth are mitigated by those between Evelyn and Ninny, which lack erotic overtones. Finally, the erotic implications of Idgie and Ruth's exchange of looks are strongly disavowed by the film's ending, which identifies Idgie with the heretofore decidedly heterosexual Ninny, who previously regaled Evelyn with stories of her long-term happy marriage to her now deceased husband and her motherly devotion to her mentally handicapped son.

In the film, the suggested lesbian relationship between Idgie and Ruth also becomes heterosexually mediated in that it is centered on both women's dedication to the memory of Idgie's beloved older brother, Buddy (Chris O'Donnell). In both novel and film, Idgie's "masculine" behavior is traced to her extremely close childhood relationship with Buddy, who as an adolescent is killed in a train accident. The film takes this scenario one step further and suggests not only that Idgie adored her brother but that Ruth was also in love with him. In a radical departure from the book, both Idgie and Ruth, whom Ninny describes as Buddy's "true love," are present at Buddy's death. In fact, he is trying to retrieve Ruth's lost hat when he is struck by a railroad train and killed while the two girls watch in horror. Clearly, it is implied that the attachment the two women share in later life stems from their over-whelming need to maintain a connection to Buddy, an idealized, lost male figure.

Fried Green Tomatoes and Race

Like the novel's feminist and lesbian content, the importance of its African American characters is also minimized in the film. Although the novel's presentation of racial issues is far from entirely progressive, it does pursue as a major plotline the victories and defeats of several members of a black family as they move from rural Alabama to city life in Birmingham. The wide range of black characters presented and the active agency they display in furthering the narrative are progressive aspects of the novel that are completely eliminated from the film. In the film, the African American characters are reduced to three, and their roles as active narrative agents are minimized significantly.

However, the film does maintain all of the novel's problematic elements in terms of race. Its major African American characters are Ruth and Idgie's housekeeper, Sipsey (Cicely Tyson); Sipsey's son and Ruth and Idgie's cook, Big George (Stan Shaw); and Sipsey's younger sister, Naughty Bird (Enjolik Oree). As Christine Holmlund points out, the film visually codes each of these characters as less important than the white characters and presents them in accord with negative racial stereotypes.[54] For instance, Sipsey is a mammy figure whose only concern is to serve her white mistresses. Her devotion eventually leads her to murder Frank Bennett, Ruth's abusive husband, in order to prevent him from taking Ruth's baby. Similarly, Big George represents the buck stereotype, the large, muscular black man, and Naughty Bird is the pickaninny. Although the novel also contains these stereotypes, its wider range of black characters tends to reduce their prominence.

Even more significant than the reduction of the black characters to stereotypical representations is the minimization of their active roles in the narrative. The novel grants its African American characters major influence on the lives of their white superiors. Not only does Sipsey kill Frank Bennett, but it is Big George who concocts the scheme to cook Frank's body and serve it as barbecue at the cafe. Later in the novel, when Ruth is dying of cancer, Onzell, George's wife, performs an act of euthanasia to release her from her suffering. The film preserves only Sipsey's killing of Frank and keeps her performance of this act offscreen.

As a result, her heroic actions are reduced to the level of the whodunit, and then this mystery is submerged under what is set up as the more prominent final enigma of Ninny's identity.[55] The novel's other two instances of black agency are completely eliminated from the film. In the film, it is Idgie, not Big George, who thinks of the plan to cook Frank's body, and Ruth dies a natural death.

As a result of these changes, the film's racial presentation is transformed into "a relatively rosy picture of black servitude."[56] The black characters demonstrate total devotion to the whites, who repay them with paternalistic protection. Even though the film contains scenes of racial prejudice culminating in a Ku Klux Klan raid, racial problems are never really confronted on a societal level. The racism that is portrayed is simply countered by Idgie and Ruth's compassion and decency in their treatment of their devoted black servants. Private concern and paternalism seem to be the only model offered for rethinking racial inequality. In fact, the film does not really even portray racism as a continuing social problem; instead, it is presented merely as a rather curious past "tradition."[57] The novel, on the other hand, makes a point of extending its portrayal of racial discord to the present time by tracing the history of Big George's descendants as they struggle to combat contemporary racism. This is not to say that the novel is entirely progressive in its treatment of racial issues. Like the film, it presents black characters in stereotypical ways, emphasizes their roles as devoted servants, and confines their importance largely to their effect on the white characters. What is significant is that the film's departures from the book never render its treatment of African Americans more progressive; instead, the changes consistently make this treatment less so.

Fried Green Tomatoes and Women's Issues

The limited and largely unsuccessful efforts of *Fried Green Tomatoes* to deal with issues of social import extend beyond its treatment of race and sexual orientation. The film also strongly focuses attention on such women's issues as spousal abuse and aging. Ruth is physically and mentally abused by her husband. When he attempts to prevent her from leaving with Idgie, graphic evidence is provided of the brutality of his attacks. At the same time, however, this scene provides a vivid example of how limited the film's approach to the issue of spousal abuse actually is. First of all, Ruth's determination to remain with Frank in spite of his abuse in order to provide a home for her ailing mother is presented as noble and courageous, rather than foolhardy and dangerous. Second, her final resolution to leave him involves not her own actions so much as the help of others. Presented largely as a helpless victim, she relies on Idgie to come and take her away. Third, the private nature of this rescue suggests that the solution to the widespread social problem of spousal abuse is individual action rather than societal change.

In dealing with the problems of the elderly, the film again presents its solution on a personal rather than a societal level. Certainly, *Fried Green Tomatoes* takes an unusual step for a mainstream film in focusing so much attention on characters who are not young or glamorous. The narrative deals not only with Evelyn's fear of menopause, but also with Ninny's need in her old age for decent living conditions, companionship, and a sense of self-worth. Again, however, the solutions presented to these problems are rendered totally on a private level. The personal relationship that develops between Evelyn and Ninny solves everything. Ninny inspires Evelyn to go on with her life, and Evelyn in return provides Ninny with the loving home she needs.

The solutions the film offers to the issues it raises in regard to women are not only restricted to the private sphere of individual action but are also backward-looking. *Fried Green Tomatoes* idealizes a past society presented as filled with loving, caring, generous people who promote harmony and tolerance among persons of different races, classes, and sexual orientations. This mythical idyllic past is contrasted to a present in which disrespect, intolerance, and selfishness dominate. Evelyn's failed attempts to solve her problems by attending what the film describes as a "women's group" illustrate well the contrast set up between past and present. This organization's meetings are presented as pointless and even somewhat ridiculous. The women sit around inspecting their vaginas, discussing masturbation, and learning new ways to please their husbands. This simplistic reduction of feminist consciousness-raising to the level of laughable self-help tips is contrasted to Ninny's more effective form of feminist inspiration. Her successful recipe for helping Evelyn involves finding inspiration in the lives of strong women of the past, like Idgie and Ruth, who it is suggested can provide contemporary women with useful models of female courage and caring. This strategy of looking backward for inspiration advocates a retreat into a mythical past of female achievement that serves as a means of escape from rather than a way to confront current social problems.

Fried Green Tomatoes and the Female Spectator

The attempts to deal with contemporary social issues in *Fried Green Tomatoes,* as superficial as they may be, represent nevertheless one way the film achieves an address to a wide audience. It raises issues important to women and then resolves them on a personal level that is unlikely to alienate any particular audience group. Different types of audience members are also drawn in by the provision of multiple entry points into the text. The film contains four female figures with whom very different female spectators might identify: Evelyn, who finds the strength and sense of self to triumph over the problems of middle age; Ninny, who remains vital and vibrant into old age; Idgie, an independent young nonconformist; and Ruth, a traditional young woman emboldened by her love for her "friend." Each woman in her own way triumphs over adversity and provides the viewer with an idealized portrait of female success. Just as Ninny inspires Evelyn with the story of Idgie and Ruth's courage, so too is the viewer intended to be inspired by identifying with one or more of these idealized characters.

Although the address of the film is multiple, the subject positions offered are actually quite uniform. The spectator might enter the text from a number of entry points, but all of these positions are eventually united as the voice-over narration and the concluding series of shocking revelations draw the spectator out from the internal story of Idgie and Ruth and into the external one of Evelyn and Ninny. Whether the spectator identifies with Ninny as narrator or Evelyn as narratee, the effect is similar. The spectator is empowered by the story of Idgie and Ruth as inspirational figures from the past, but to what end? Although a number of potential responses are possible, by ending with Evelyn taking Ninny home with her, the film attempts to limit its inspirational effect to the domestic realm of interpersonal relationships.

Within this structure, the lesbian content of *Fried Green Tomatoes* is largely subsumed under the umbrella of female friendship, just as Idgie and Ruth's story is contained within Evelyn and Ninny's. This subsumption has led some critics to condemn the film for its "delesbianization" of Flagg's novel in order to court a homophobic viewing audience.[58] Others, however, have championed it as providing a positive lesbian portrayal; the film even received an award from the Gay and Lesbian Alliance against Defamation as the best gay filmic portrayal of 1991. It could also be argued in the film's defense that *Fried Green*

Tomatoes serves as a dramatization of Adrienne Rich's "lesbian continuum."[59] By presenting Ruth and Idgie's relationship as ambiguously lesbian and connecting it with Evelyn and Ninny's friendship, the film portrays lesbianism and female friendship as woman-centered relationships that are not so easily separated. The two forms of female attachment exemplify different levels of women's resistance to patriarchal control that have existed continuously throughout history. *Fried Green Tomatoes* illustrates both the advantages and the disadvantages of Rich's formulation. On the positive side, lesbianism is not marginalized as a matter only of sexual preference or lifestyle choice but is portrayed instead as behavior that strongly resists male dominance and abuse. At the same time, however, the differences that constitute lesbianism as a unique form of psychosocial subjectivity are denied and swept under the rug of female friendship.

In many ways, *Fried Green Tomatoes* is a paradigmatic sentimental female friendship film. It takes no unequivocal stand on any issue, tries to remain on a personal rather than a societal level, and attempts to appeal to viewers of as many different dispositions as possible. Its success indicates that it largely achieves its goals. It is a lesbian text to those who choose to read it as such and a female friendship film to those who do not. Perhaps this is, in fact, the essential point about mainstream lesbian representation in this period. Each of the films we have examined thus far pulls back from unambiguously saying anything in order to say different things to different people. One thing they seem to say unequivocally, however, with the notable exception of *Desert Hearts,* is that in spite of the similarities between them, the boundary that "purifies" female friendship and renders it "acceptable" within mainstream representation is located at the point where it begins to move into the realm of lesbian eroticism and active female sexual desire.

Go Fish

The Struggle to Represent Lesbian Lives Realistically

Three years after the release of *Fried Green Tomatoes,* a film that seems to represent a retreat from openly lesbian mainstream representations, the development of the popular lesbian film took yet another radical departure. If *Fried Green Tomatoes* is the epitome of the Hollywood ambiguously lesbian film that tries to be different things to straight and lesbian audiences, *Go Fish* (1994), the debut independent feature of

Creating a lesbian film about lesbians for lesbians
by lesbians. Director Rose Troche (left) and screen-
writer/star Guinevere Turner in a publicity still for
Go Fish *(1994).*

lesbian director Rose Troche, goes in an entirely different direction by
aiming specifically at a lesbian audience. Due to the rise of independent
films in the 1990s and a greater willingness among distributors to accept films targeted at specific audiences, it became easier for an independent film like *Go Fish* to be discovered on the festival circuit and
picked up for at least limited mainstream distribution.

In fact, *Go Fish* was preceded by the disastrously inept lesbian-
directed *Claire of the Moon* (Conn, 1992), a low-budget independent
lesbian film that found limited mainstream distribution even though it

received scathingly negative reviews in both the mainstream and alternative presses. *Claire of the Moon*'s unenthusiastic reception among lesbian audiences, however, quickly led to its demise.[60] It seems significant only as a failed precursor to the transformation in lesbian cinema initiated by Troche's much more accomplished effort. *Go Fish* was written by two young first-time filmmakers, Rose Troche and Guinevere Turner. Troche directed and Turner starred in the grainy black-and-white film, which they shot on location in Chicago on a minuscule budget. Neither Troche nor Turner envisioned the film as a mainstream success. They expected it to play only at lesbian and gay film festivals, but it became the first lesbian feature film to be screened and a sleeper success at Robert Redford's prominent showcase of independent filmmaking, the Sundance Film Festival. There, it was picked up for mainstream distribution by the Samuel Goldwyn Company.[61]

Go Fish's popularity with gay and straight audiences alike led critics to see it as a breakthrough lesbian film;[62] indeed, it seems to be a significant event in the development of popular lesbian cinema, accomplishing a major transformation in mainstream lesbian representation. In interviews, Turner and Troche have indicated that in writing the script, they wanted to do something different. According to Troche, they were determined not to write "another agonized tract about coming out" or a movie in which women "only have sex under excruciating circumstances."[63] What they created instead was a refreshingly new look at lesbian life.

A Lesbian Film by Lesbians for Lesbians

Go Fish represents an innovation in mainstream lesbian cinema both narratively and stylistically. It is, first of all, a romantic comedy that presents lesbian love from a witty, lighthearted perspective. It details the progress of a budding romance between a hip, young aspiring writer, Max (Guinevere Turner), and a slightly older, shy veterinary assistant, Ely (V. S. Brodie). The romance takes place entirely within the lesbian community. In fact, the two women's relationship is engineered by their lesbian friends, who introduce them and then proceed to observe with avid interest the development of their love affair, even at times working to facilitate its progress.

As Turner suggests, she and Troche set out to write "a happy script. . . . to just for once have a movie [about lesbians] that's plain old tra-la-la."[64] The film's light comic tone contrasts decidedly with the seriousness that characterizes previous mainstream lesbian portrayals. *Go Fish* is innovative not only in its use of the comedic mode but also in its stylistic qualities. In fact, the film seems to achieve almost effortlessly an artistically satisfying mix of naturalism and experimentation. The majority of the film's narrative segments are presented in a down-to-earth, naturalistic, pseudodocumentary style that is complemented by the use of grainy black-and-white film stock and a nonprofessional cast and crew. These raw qualities provide a stylish yet unpretentious feel.

Juxtaposed with naturalistic sequences are more experimental segments. As Troche moves episodically from scene to scene, she intercuts images that seem to represent directorial flights of fancy or abstractions vaguely related to the previous or forthcoming scenes. For instance, interspersed among narrative segments are images of the turning pages of a book, a child jumping up in the street, two hands clasping, and a glass of iced coffee as milk is being added. The film also contains two dream or fantasy sequences. The first is a Kafkaesque trial scene. In a dark, nightmare setting, Ely's sexually promiscuous roommate Daria (Anastasia Sharp) is interrogated by an assembly of lesbians who condemn her for calling herself a lesbian and still having sex with men. The second is a fantasy wedding sequence in which Max, dressed in a wedding gown, is kissed by a succession of women. The scene is accompanied by Max's voice-over commentary, expressing her fear that social pressure might lead her to abandon her lesbianism for heterosexual marriage. The film also contains another stylistic flourish in its repeated use of talking heads sequences in which four women are arranged as if they are lying on the floor in a star formation, with their heads touching at the top. In these scenes, Max and Ely's matchmaking friends assemble as a pseudo-Greek chorus to comment on the progress of their nascent love affair.

Go Fish departs from previous mainstream lesbian representations not only stylistically but narratively as well. Unlike earlier lesbian portrayals, the film is not a coming-out narrative. The main characters are all quite happily and well-adjustedly "out." As Michelle Kort indicates, they are shown contentedly living emotionally satisfying lives "completely inside of a lesbian space."[65] In fact, *Go Fish* is not only a chronicle of a lesbian romance but also a representation of lesbian community. Its opening sequence places it immediately within the context of lesbian history. Max's roommate Kia (T. Wendy McMillan), a college instructor, is shown discussing with her class the paucity of accurate in-

*In stylistically innovative talking heads sequences, director Rose Troche
shows her characters in* Go Fish *engaging in extended discussions of love, life,
and sexuality while lying in a star formation.*

formation available about lesbian lives, past and present. She has her
students list women who might be lesbian. As they compile a very
speculative list, one student proposes that the attempt seems pointless
because it is so entirely speculative. Kia responds by suggesting the lesson behind the exercise:

> Throughout lesbian history there has been a serious lack of evidence
> that'll tell us what these women's lives were truly about. I mean les-
> bian lives and lesbian relationships—they barely exist on paper, and
> it is with that in mind and understanding the power of history . . .
> that we begin to want to change history.

Because this scene, periodically interrupted by the credit sequence,
serves as a preface to the film's narrative action, *Go Fish* is situated
within the context of this history of inaccurate or simply absent information on lesbian lives, and the film seems to offer itself as an attempt
to change this history.

The main way in which *Go Fish* acts to alter the history of lesbianism, at least in regard to its cinematic representation, is through its celebration of lesbian community. The film breaks decidedly with a popular cinematic tradition of isolated lesbian lovers who struggle alone

against a hostile heterosexist world; instead, *Go Fish* surrounds its lesbian couple with a group of loving friends who unite to bring them together. Ely's friend Daria is joined in her matchmaking efforts by Max's roommate Kia and her lover Evy (Migdalia Melendez). This group of lesbian friends hang out together, share ideas and gossip, and form what one critic has called "an almost Utopian picture of a republic of gay women . . . set in a free floating, multiracial woman-world."[66]

Go Fish and the Lesbian Spectator

The portrayal of lesbian love and friendship in *Go Fish* is a clear attempt to construct a lesbian spectatorial position that is engaged not only with the film's lesbian lovers but also with its portrayal of the lesbian community. The film encourages, first of all, a "coupled lesbian subject position" by crosscutting between the daily lives of Max and Ely. Although Max's voice-over readings of passages from her diary make her subjectivity most accessible to the viewer, several scenes are also included that reveal Ely's feelings as their romance progresses. In addition, spatiotemporal attachment and subjective access to the lives and thoughts of the couple's friends Daria, Kia, and Evy are also provided. The audience is led to respond empathically not only to Max and Ely as they gradually become romantically involved, but also to their matchmaking friends as they anxiously monitor this involvement. By leading its spectator to engage not just with one of its lesbian characters but with all of them, the film's advocacy of lesbian community is extended out to its viewer.

Go Fish also draws in its lesbian spectator by introducing issues of interest to a lesbian audience. As Jonathan Romney points out, it seems almost to represent "a communal bulletin board, avid to cram in every topic. . . . very much angled not at a viewer but at an audience, with one eye on the arguments in the bar afterwards."[67] While the film raises issues that it considers of interest to the lesbian community, its "assertively undoctrinaire" stance keeps it from becoming tendentious.[68] There is no attempt to resolve every problem or to confront every issue. Even in regard to the matter of defining lesbianism itself, *Go Fish* simply takes the sexual orientation of its characters for granted and presents them as comfortable with that orientation. There is no tortured self-doubt or internalized homophobia represented. As Max casually tells Ely during a discussion they have about gay cinema, she prefers to see positive gay images on the screen because, as she puts it, "I'm queer, and I'm finding it relatively easy not to hate myself." Although the film may not try to define lesbianism, it provides, nevertheless, a picture of lesbian life that extends well beyond previous mainstream representations. Earlier films, as we have seen, simplified their portrayal of lesbianism by reducing it to a stage on the road to mature heterosexuality, to a personal matter of sexual preference, or to a form of genital sexuality. *Go Fish,* in contrast, offers a portrait of lesbianism that defines it both sexually and politically.

In terms of its representation of lesbian sexuality, the film manages at the same time to be both graphic and nonvoyeuristic. Like *Desert Hearts, Go Fish* builds to a climactic sex scene, the consummation of Max and Ely's romance. Sexual encounters between Kia and Evy, as well as between Daria and both male and female lovers, are also portrayed, and the characters discuss sex frequently. The film's graphic sexual portrayals are constructed, however, in ways that reduce the possibility of their being incorporated by a male viewer into a heterosexual pornographic fantasy. The scenes are edited at such a fast pace and are so fragmented in form that they resist voyeuristic expropriation. The light comic tone also reduces the sexual representations' pornographic potential. One of the film's boldest strokes is the casting of the androgynous and conventionally unattractive V. S. Brodie as Ely. Her appearance seems intended, as David Ansen has pointed out, as "a rebuke to Hollywood romantic conditioning," as well as to the cinematic tradition of presenting lesbians as highly charged sexual symbols.[69] Although cute and definitely hip, even Max in her baggy shorts and backward baseball cap is no conventional female sex symbol.

The film's final sex scene involves yet another interesting technique that reduces the voyeuristic potential inherent in portrayals of lesbian sexuality. The viewer is not initially shown Max and Ely as they make love. They are seen kissing, and then Troche cuts to a pan up their naked bodies just before Ely gets up, covers Max with a sheet, and leaves. The actual sex scene is shown only later in flashback as the two women tell their inquisitive friends what happened. In this way, the film demarcates its portrayal of lesbian sexuality as belonging to the lesbian community. It is intended to be shared by the lesbian characters and their projected lesbian audience, and not to be incorporated into the pornographic fantasy life of the male heterosexual viewer.

Although the film spends a significant amount of time on the sex lives of its characters, it includes other elements of the lesbian lifestyle as well. Most important, all the characters share a strong sense of woman-identification. Not only are they woman-loving, but they live woman-directed and woman-centered lives. The film, especially through Max's diary entries, also explores lesbianism as a lifestyle choice and as a rejection of the expectations of heterosexual femininity. Because *Go Fish* represents lesbianism as composed of various elements, it is able to shed light on lesbian difference in a way that is not found in earlier mainstream lesbian films. By placing its lovers within a lesbian community and immersing the spectator in the life of that community, the film is able to do much more than just cast its female characters in the standard heterosexual romance plot and label them lesbians.

Go Fish ends with an extended montage sequence that reaches out specifically to the lesbian viewer and draws her into its narrative. This upbeat conclusion, described by one critic as a "lesbian music-video ending," begins with scenes of Max and Ely spending an idyllic day together.[70] It then moves to rapidly intercut shots of various of the film's characters kissing, and finally ends with a grainy close-up of Max and Ely as they embrace. This last shot is accompanied by Max's voice-over:

> Don't fear too many things—it's dangerous. Don't say so much—
> you'll ruin everything. Don't worry yourself into a corner and just
> don't think about it so much. The girl you're gonna meet doesn't
> look like anyone you know, and when you meet her, your toes might
> tingle, or you might suppress a yawn. It's hard to say. Don't box
> yourself in. Don't leave yourself wide open. Don't think about it
> every second, but just don't let yourself forget. The girl is out there.

This voice-over direct address to the lesbian spectator strongly draws her into the film's lesbian romance. It announces the possibility of actually realizing the ideal that the film repeatedly champions. It tells the lesbian viewer that, like Max and Ely, she too can "find someone." The concluding voice-over seeks to inspire in its spectator the desire to reach this goal, to find both lesbian love and lesbian community.

Go Fish and the Heterosexual Female Spectator

Go Fish not only envisions a lesbian spectator but also refuses to court a heterosexual audience, or even really to acknowledge its existence. This is without question a story demarcated as by lesbians, about lesbians, and for lesbians that still found substantial mainstream distribution. In interviews, Guinevere Turner expressed both surprise and mild dismay at the film's appeal to heterosexual viewers: "To have it supposedly appealing to a heterosexual audience is fascinating to us. It makes us a little nervous because neither of us would want any lesbian to think we made it as some public-service announcement to the heterosexual world or to cash in on lesbian chic."[71]

In spite of its filmmakers' seeming disregard for what straight viewers might think, *Go Fish* still managed to find a crossover audience. The film's appeal to both gay and heterosexual viewers can be attributed to its portrayal of the lesbian community as characterized by a significant amount of diversity. The characters portrayed in the film include women who are different in terms of age, profession, race, and ethnicity, yet they all also belong to a hip twentysomething lesbian youth culture with a strong attraction to a young audience. The film's romantic and friendship themes also have crossover appeal, and even its very disregard for the heterosexual viewer may be an attraction. *Go Fish*, after all, affords its straight audience, as Martha Baer suggests, a privileged view of "what a bunch of dykes do when no straight people are looking, where they live, what they like, how they fuck (or don't), and what they wear when dating."[72] One of the film's major attractions for heterosexual viewers could be that it offers an insider's view of a lesbian subcultural experience from which they are otherwise excluded.

The implications of *Go Fish*'s seemingly unintentional crossover appeal are highly significant for the future of lesbian representations. The film achieved popular success without altering its lesbian portrayal to court a heterosexual audience. It was able to represent the difference of lesbian lives and still draw both heterosexual and lesbian viewers alike into its female-centered community. *Go Fish* is, indeed, a breakthrough film for mainstream lesbian representations, and one that should assume a prominent role in the development of contemporary lesbian cinema.

Concluding Comments

In contrast to other categories of female friendship films, lesbian representations seem to show significant progress throughout the contemporary period. If one compares *Personal Best* with *Go Fish*, the movement from a heterosexually conceived male representation aimed at heterosexual viewers to a lesbian-affirmative portrayal made by lesbian filmmakers for lesbian audiences becomes very clear. It should be noted, however, that these changes reflect primarily the influx of films from the independent sector into mainstream distribution. Progressive changes in lesbian portrayals are largely restricted to low-budget independent films. The situation in regard to Hollywood films, where we see only a progression from *Personal Best* to *Fried Green Tomatoes,* is far less impressive. Optimism about the development of the lesbian film must also be tempered by the fact that although many more independently made films are beginning to reach mainstream audiences, their distribution in comparison with Hollywood products is extremely limited.

The progressive influence of lesbian directors on the development of lesbian films also seems highly significant, but again their impact is confined to the independent sector. Lesbian directors Donna Deitch and Rose Troche have taken lesbian portrayals in new directions, just as female independent filmmakers such as Claudia Weill and Allison Anders have made major contributions to transforming female friendship portrayals. Female input into Hollywood films, on the other hand, has been much less transformative. Fannie Flagg and Carol Sobieski's involvement with *Fried Green Tomatoes,* for instance, did not prevent the film's delesbianization of Flagg's novel. The force of Hollywood conventions, as well as the power of male producers and directors, obviously overshadows the impact of female influence.

A final issue that emerges from an examination of mainstream lesbian portrayals relates to Teresa de Lauretis's proposal that a radical break exists between lesbian and female friendship films. As I noted in the introduction to this volume, de Lauretis takes exception to Jackie Stacey's claims that the two types of films are intimately related, with many female friendship films also expressing homoerotic desire between women. My inclusion of a chapter on lesbian films here obviously suggests that I believe a connection exists between the two types of films. Clearly, however, the emphasis in lesbian films, especially those directed by lesbian directors and aimed at a lesbian audience, is on desire between women, whereas in female friendship portrayals the focus is much more on identification. Yet the very existence of ambiguous lesbian films like *Fried Green Tomatoes* and female friendship films with homoerotic overtones like *Julia* suggests that the break between the two categories of films is not as decisive as de Lauretis claims. Although we should not ignore de Lauretis's fear that the establishment of a strong connection between female friendship films and lesbian films can prevent a recognition of the differences that constitute lesbianism, it remains true nevertheless that the two types of relationships, as well as their cinematic representations, possess a component of woman-centeredness that inevitably unites them. It seems most productive, therefore, to recognize a connection between lesbian films and female friendship films while at the same time acknowledging the differences that exist between them.

6 | The Female Friendship Film and Women of Color

The portrayal of people of color in American cinema has been as conflicted as the relationship between dominant white and other ethnic and racial minorities in the society at large. Critics have argued persuasively that minority representation in mainstream films has been and continues to be disproportionately rare and distorted. With the advent of more minority directors within both independent and mainstream cinema, the hope is that the representational picture of minority racial and ethnic groups is moving in a progressive direction and will continue to do so, yet critics argue on the negative side that control of the film industry is so completely in the hands of a white male majority that the single step of putting people of color in the director's chair, although important, will hardly work a miraculous transformation.

The female friendship film as a product of American culture reflects in many ways this larger cinematic failure in regard to representations of minority groups. The portrayal of women of color on the screen remains particularly susceptible to neglect or distortion because those minority directors who have emerged in both mainstream and independent cinema are overwhelmingly male. In fact, only very recently, with the release of *Waiting to Exhale* (Whitaker, 1995), has a female friendship film finally been directed by a minority director, and he was a man.

The films that I have discussed thus far in examining the contours of the female friendship film cycle for the most part ignore the issue of

179

race entirely. Typically, female friendship films deal with white characters and are aimed at a white audience. When they are portrayed, which happens infrequently, minority characters are relegated to the background of the narrative, as they are, for instance, in *Fried Green Tomatoes*. Additionally, minority characters are represented almost exclusively by African Americans; other minority groups are almost completely absent. Consider, for example, the representation of race in *Thelma & Louise*. The only African American character in the film is a black Rastafarian bicyclist who is on the screen for just a few minutes. He comes across a police officer whom Thelma and Louise have locked in the trunk of his squad car. This character's brief appearance seems intended to provide comic relief as the tension created by Thelma and Louise's flight from the police grows, yet the comic moment he provides is based on his association with a negative racial stereotype. As he rides up to the police car, he is seen smoking a marijuana cigarette, and when he hears the police officer's pleas for help, he responds by blowing smoke through a hole in the lid of the trunk.[1]

According to Yvonne Tasker, the association of black characters with drugs has become one of the most frequent Hollywood stereotypes used to keep African Americans connected in the minds of white audiences with marginality and criminality.[2] This association seems particularly incongruous in a film like *Thelma & Louise*, which argues for a fairer, more equitable society. It is, however, not at all uncommon in white-dominated mainstream cinema for filmmakers, regardless of the thematic content of their films, to remain unaware of, or unconcerned with, the racism inherent in their portrayals of people of color.

A small number of female friendship films do take as their central focus relationships that involve minority women. Once minority characters actually become part of the primary plot structure of a film, racial consciousness seems to be heightened and attempts are made to avoid obvious negative stereotypes and racially insensitive portrayals, yet these attempts are still often problematic. Female friendship films that deal with women of color fall into two categories. Intraracial or intraethnic female friendship films deal with friendships among women of color themselves. These films have been very rare in both mainstream and independent feature filmmaking. The idea of minority women uniting in bonds of friendship seems to be so potentially challenging to the existing social structure, where women of color are positioned as the most disempowered group, that its cinematic expression has been suppressed.

This type of film is represented in the Hollywood context only by Steven Spielberg's *The Color Purple* (1985) and in the arena of independent feature filmmaking by Allison Anders's *Mi Vida Loca* (1994).

The second type of female friendship portrayal that deals with women of color is the interracial female friendship film, which is also quite uncommon in both independent and Hollywood cinema. It is represented in this period only by John Sayles's independent feature *Passion Fish* (1992). Very recently, however, several films have been released that deal with interracial lesbian couples: *The Incredibly True Adventures of Two Girls in Love* (Maggenti, 1995), *Boys on the Side* (Ross, 1995), and *Watermelon Woman* (Dunye, 1997). Only in *Watermelon Woman,* however, is the issue of race given any extensive consideration as a thematic element. Both *Incredibly True Adventures* and *Boys on the Side* introduce minority characters and then proceed to ignore the issue of race entirely. In addition, to my knowledge there is no prominent contemporary example of an interethnic female friendship film.

The Color Purple

The Quintessential Hollywood Director Renders a Prominent Black Feminist Novel into Film

The unique position of *The Color Purple* as the first contemporary Hollywood female friendship film to focus on friendships among women of color has largely been ignored. Its ranking with *Thelma & Louise* as one of the most controversial films of the 1980s has obscured the strong focus the film places on African American sisterhood. Like *Thelma & Louise, The Color Purple* provoked bitter attacks in the press, not primarily because of its treatment of women's issues but because of what were labeled its unfair portrayals of men. Unlike *Thelma & Louise,* however, which initially appeared to be a harmless female buddy comedy that went on to provoke heated debates in the press, *The Color Purple* seemed destined from its inception for a controversial reception.

Based on African American author Alice Walker's popular feminist novel, with a score written by the noted black composer Quincy Jones, and with an entirely black cast in its major roles, *The Color Purple* contained a remarkable amount of African American input for a Hollywood film of the 1980s. Directorial control, however, was placed squarely in the hands of a white male director with a quintessential Hollywood style and reputation, Steven Spielberg. With such blockbuster successes as *Jaws* (1975), *Raiders of the Lost Ark* (1981), and *E.T.—The Extra-Terrestrial* (1982) as prior film credits, Spielberg was perceived at the time as the creator of lucrative but very superficial popular entertainments, rather than as a director with serious artistic aspirations. Clearly interested in changing this image, Spielberg not only sought to direct *The Color Purple* but was also instrumental in initiating the project. He has even proposed in interviews that if it had not been for his clout, no studio at the time would ever have risked making a film with such an overwhelmingly black cast and subject matter.[3]

Controversy was bound to be stirred by a white male director known for his entertaining but lightweight adventure films supervising the film adaptation of an issues-oriented, women-centered, and highly controversial black feminist novel. Spielberg, however, never expressed the slightest concern about his involvement in the project. He seems to have approached his directorial role with a color blindness that can only be described as willfully myopic given the novel's strong racial content. In interviews, he has indicated that he undertook the project without the slightest qualms because he was convinced that the novel is not even concerned with the issue of race but is rather a story about generalized humanity: "This is a human story, and the movie is about human beings. It's about men and women. This is a movie about the triumph of the spirit—and spirit and soul never had any racial boundaries."[4]

African American critics almost without exception have virulently attacked Spielberg's direction of the film.[5] Jacqueline Bobo, for instance, proposes that Spielberg was simply too divorced from black experience to be able to portray it accurately. As a result, he both distorted the story's portrayal of African American life and divested it of much of its original thematic significance. According to Bobo, Spielberg did not even try to understand Walker's literary portrayal of a courageous African American woman's struggle against oppression; instead, he transformed it into a "conventionalized melodrama of heightened emotionalism induced by music and heart-tugging moments."[6] What he carelessly abandoned was the indictment of sexism, racism, and social oppression that Alice Walker authored.

The Controversy Surrounding the Film's Portrayal of Black Men

The controversial reception of *The Color Purple* was precipitated only in part by Steven Spielberg's involvement in the project. More important in generating opposition to the film was the provocative content of

Walker's original text itself, as well as Hollywood's long-standing tradition of presenting distorted cinematic portraits of African American culture. Many black critics attacked the film for reinforcing already strongly established negative white preconceptions of black life. Walker's focus on problems within the African American community, such as incest, spousal abuse, and rape, filtered through the vision of a white director and submitted to the scrutiny of a white audience struck many African American critics as objectionable. Although Walker's novel itself had been criticized for presenting African American men and the black family in an unfairly and unrealistically negative light, critics could point to the pervasive presence in her work of white racism as one of the major underlying causes for the problems she examines.

Spielberg, however, divests the film of much of Walker's condemnation of white racist sentiments and as a result alters significantly her already highly critical portrait of black men, and it is in regard to this portrait that the film's major controversy emerged.[7] Whereas Walker makes it clear that the development within the black community of a code of masculinity involving the systematic abuse of women and children is the African American male's response to his disempowerment within a white racist society, Spielberg leaves his male characters' brutally abusive natures unexplained.[8] Consequently, the film's portrait of African American men increases Walker's negative portrayal by rendering its black male characters either inexplicably evil or quintessentially so. In addition, the film's portrayal of black men seems to be authenticated as true to life "by the signature of a black and female writer."[9]

Spielberg's Distortion of the Female Characters in *The Color Purple*

The controversy surrounding the representation of black men in *The Color Purple* obscured the fact that both the novel and the film are centrally concerned not with men at all, but with the strong and enduring bonds formed among a group of African American women. At the center of the narrative is Celie (Whoopi Goldberg), the abused wife of a black landowner who finds empowerment through her relationships with three women: Shug (Margaret Avery), a free-spirited blues singer; Nettie (Akosua Busia), Celie's beloved sister; and Sofia (Oprah Winfrey), Celie's strong-willed stepdaughter-in-law. Not only did the film's controversial reception ignore the importance of women in the film, it also obscured the alterations Spielberg made to the novel's female characters. As Jacqueline Bobo illustrates in her careful comparison of novel and film, Spielberg greatly transforms each of Walker's major female characters. These changes weaken the women's natures and allow them to be presented in accord with racist Hollywood stereotypes.[10]

Through her struggle against racist tyranny and male abuse, Celie, the novel's protagonist, represents the symbolic victimization of all black women by sexism, racism, and patriarchal privilege. By the novel's end, when she finds the strength to triumph over her oppression, Celie becomes a very empowering image of African American womanhood. Spielberg, however, strips Walker's text of its political and social context by rendering Celie an individualized rather than a representative figure. She becomes not a model of empowered womanhood in the face of overpowering social forces, but merely the fortunate survivor of unfortunate personal circumstances.[11]

Shug also undergoes a radical revision in moving from novel to film. Spielberg's Hollywood sensibility led him to cast Margaret Avery, a very beautiful, light-skinned African American actress, in the role, even though the novel's Shug is clearly described as a dark-skinned black woman who is not conventionally attractive. As a result, whereas in the novel Shug gets her power from her usurpation of male privilege and from her sense of accomplishment as a blues singer, in the film she exerts influence in typical Hollywood fashion, through her physical beauty.[12] Whereas Spielberg's characterization of Shug allows her to fall into the established stereotype of the lascivious black temptress, her character in the novel represents an innovation in the literary portrayal of the sexual African American women. Jacqueline Bobo even goes so far as to call the novel's Shug the "most acceptably received sexual Black heroine created in literature," and SDiane A. Bogus places her within a long tradition of African American literary representations of the "Queen B figure."[13] Based on real-life female blues singers of the 1920s and 1930s such as Gladys Bentley and Bessie Smith, the figure of the "Queen B" expresses a distinctive African American sensibility through her music. She lives her life based on a strong sense of freedom, autonomy, and unself-conscious sensuality that includes open bisexuality. The novel's Shug clearly draws on this tradition, and the strong impact her friendship has on Celie demonstrates the empowering nature this figure has in black women's cultural history.

Spielberg works systematically to reduce Shug's image as a figure of black female strength and autonomy. Not only does she seem in the film to get her power primarily from her light-skinned, glamorous

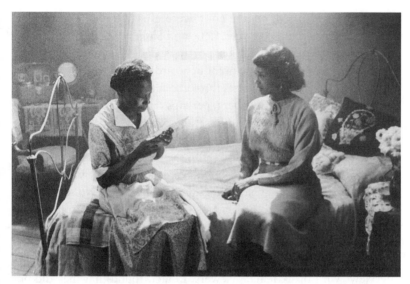

In The Color Purple *(Spielberg, 1985), Celie (Whoopi Goldberg, left) and Shug (Margaret Avery) share an emotional moment when Celie first reads her letters from her beloved sister, Nettie. As this scene indicates, the film minimizes the importance of the lesbian attachment between the two women and reduces Shug's role to acting merely as an instrument of Celie's reconciliation with her biological sister.*

looks, but her sense of independence is also reduced. Spielberg adds to the film a subplot not found in the novel that involves Shug's relationship with her father, a local minister who has disowned her. Throughout the film, Shug is preoccupied with obtaining her father's forgiveness and regaining his love. Finally, near the film's conclusion father and daughter are reconciled in a climactic musical production number that provides such a spectacular context for this event that it is given particular importance in the narrative.[14] Not only is this reconciliation scene a strong affirmation of patriarchal values and their continuing influence on women's lives, it also weakens Shug's character significantly. In the novel, she is an independent, self-possessed, autonomous woman who is determined to exercise the same rights and privileges that men have, but in the film she becomes an insecure, lascivious sinner who desperately seeks the approval of her righteous father and of the religious establishment he represents.[15] These changes reduce the effectiveness of her portrayal as a model of female self-assertion for both Celie and the female spectator.

Spielberg also reduces the empowering nature of the lesbian attachment that develops between Celie and Shug in the novel. As many critics have pointed out, Walker portrays Celie's sexual relationship with Shug as a crucial turning point in regard to her developing sense of self-love, and Celie demonstrates throughout the book a continuing sexual attraction to Shug.[16] Spielberg, perhaps due to his own or his fear of his audience's homophobia, trims the women's sexual relationship down to a very brief and ambiguously presented incident. Marcia Pally describes the encounter as follows: "In the one scene where they [Celie and Shug] tentatively kiss, they bobble at each other like woodpeckers and the camera pans to wind chimes and poppy fields. No show of affection is repeated; the scene remains so isolated and embarrassed that one wonders to what it alludes."[17] The reduction of Celie and Shug's sexual relationship to a single ambiguous incident leaves the question of the nature of their attachment very unclear. Jacqueline Bobo, in her interviews with black female viewers, in fact, found that they did not even perceive the relationship between Celie and Shug in the film as necessarily a lesbian one, and one viewer even expressed resentment at this implication.[18]

The final major female figure whose character Spielberg alters significantly is Sofia, Celie's spirited stepdaughter-in-law. In the novel, she is presented as another model of female strength and resistance. Interested only in a marriage of equals, she refuses to be beaten by her husband, Harpo, Celie's stepson. Insulted by the mayor's wife's unsolicited and condescending attention to her children and by her request that Sofia become her maid, Sofia lashes out at the woman and is punished severely with imprisonment, forced labor as the mayor's housekeeper, and estrangement from her family. In the novel, she becomes a martyr to racist and sexist injustice who is saved from prison when the black community, led by its female members, comes together to work for her freedom.

In the film, Sofia is no longer a model or a martyr; instead, she is reduced to the stereotype of the Sapphire figure, the overbearing, emasculating matriarch.[19] She becomes a warning of the danger of too much female self-assertion, a grim reminder of the fate that awaits women of unbridled independence. Significant in this regard is Spielberg's portrayal of Sofia's altercation with the mayor's wife. In reacting to the woman's insults, Sofia becomes so upset that she seems totally out of control, indiscriminately lashing out at anyone who comes near her. Finally, when she is beaten down with a club, she falls to the ground and is pictured with the skirt of her dress blown up over her head. These images of female hysteria and humiliation represent Spielberg's distorted version of what Walker presents in the novel as an act of courageous defiance in the face of blatant white racism.[20]

How Could This Film Be Popular?

In light of Spielberg's devastating alterations to Walker's original material, it is difficult to believe that anything is left in the film to appeal to either black or white female viewers, yet statistics attest to the film's remarkable popularity with a crossover audience.[21] Jacqueline Bobo even interviewed black women to find out just what attracted them to a film that seems so clearly to violate its African American literary source. Bobo concludes from these interviews that black female spectators' positive responses to the film stem from their ability to be highly selective in responding to what they see on the screen. According to Bobo, they in effect create their own text by accepting aspects of the film that appeal to them and rejecting those that do not.[22] In essence, they utilize what black feminist critic bell hooks has in another context called the black "oppositional gaze."[23]

According to hooks, African American women spectators learn from a lifetime of Hollywood filmgoing experiences either to turn completely away from the negative and distorted images they see of themselves on the screen or to recast these images in a more favorable light. Bobo claims that, starved for positive images of black women, her interviewees took the latter course in watching *The Color Purple*. Inspired by the empowering images of black women that African American female writers such as Alice Walker had already provided for them, these women read the film very selectively. In essence, they created their own African American woman-affirmative film from fragments of Spielberg's text.

Although Bobo's argument for oppositional readings of the film is to a certain extent persuasive, at least in regard to the film's African American female audience, it does not account for the enormous crossover appeal of *The Color Purple* for white female viewers. Bobo's harshly critical view of the film also leads her to minimize the importance for audience appeal of what Spielberg actually maintained in moving from novel to film. Critically important in accounting for the positive viewer response the film received is Spielberg's preservation of one crucial aspect of Walker's novel, its representation of female friendship and sisterhood. Although he altered substantially the thematic significance of this representation, Spielberg at the same time increased its emotional impact. In order to investigate how the maintenance of this important aspect of the novel may have affected the film's reception, it is necessary to look at *The Color Purple* as other critics have not—as an African American female friendship film.

African American Women Bonding

In both its novel and film versions, *The Color Purple* has many of the characteristics of high sentimentality that became increasingly associated with the female friendship film as it developed in the contemporary period. Both novel and film celebrate idealized, emotionally effusive, and psychologically empowering female friendships contained within a highly melodramatic narrative structure. In addition, Spielberg's Hollywood sensibility led him to accentuate the sentimentality found in Walker's already melodramatic story. He emphasizes, for instance, highly emotional moments of loss and reconciliation, morally polarizes his characters by fashioning the film's narrative as a struggle between good women and evil men, and employs Quincy Jones's music on the film's sound track to support the mood of heartrending pathos.

Although the film relies heavily on its emotional impact, it does not remain entirely on the level of sentimental melodrama. As we have seen, many female friendship films begin as purely sentimental portrayals, but as their narratives develop they move out of the realm of the personal and into the category of political or social female friendship. *The Color Purple,* in both its novelistic and filmic incarnations, undertakes this movement, but the directions taken are different in the two works. Walker's novel is unhesitatingly political in its themes. It openly attacks an American society plagued by the twin evils of sexism and racism. Walker emphasizes the importance of female bonding in order to fight women's oppression and abuse by tyrannical patriarchs, affirms the essential worth of all black women, critiques the injustices done to them, and advocates female solidarity and economic independence as a way for black women to develop a sense of identity and self-respect.

Especially important for the formulation of Walker's political themes are the novel's portrayals of the dyadic female bonds that Celie forms with Nettie, Shug, and Sofia. They lead not only to Celie's personal growth but also to the formation of a female solidarity network.

It is this network of female friends that wages a strong challenge to racist patriarchal domination. It offers the sexually and racially oppressed woman an alternative to basing her identity solely on her familial relationships and provides the support she needs to take action against abuse and discrimination. In the novel this female friendship network acts effectively to transform the larger society. It unites the black community to save Sofia from racial oppression and supports Celie as she struggles against the tyranny of her husband, Albert (Danny Glover). The novel ends with a chastened and disempowered Albert, its most cruelly sexist patriarch, sitting on Celie's porch, helping her with her sewing.

Although Spielberg maintains some of the political implications of Walker's novel, he alters them just enough to render his film a social rather than a political female friendship portrayal. Significant in this regard are his addition of the subplot dealing with Shug's father and his recasting of the novel's ending. As noted above, Shug's profound longing for a reconciliation with her father suggests, in contrast to the novel, that women have a desperate need to be accepted by patriarchal power figures. The film further develops this theme by granting Albert a central role in the story's conclusion that he does not have in the novel.[24] The film ends with a scene that occurs much earlier in the book: Celie's dramatic reunion with her beloved sister and children. In contrast to the novel, the film shows Albert watching this episode from a vantage point in a distant field. With this change, an earlier scene not found in the novel but added to the film finally becomes clear. In that scene, Albert is shown entering an immigration office, apparently to arrange for Celie's family to be allowed back into the country from their missionary work in Africa. Now, he gazes with paternal affection over their joyous reunion.

In one fell swoop, Spielberg transforms Albert in the film's final moments from the novel's chastened abuser into the film's benevolent savior. Coupled with Shug's father's "generous" forgiveness of his wayward daughter in spite of her "sins," Albert's final transformation promotes the idea of a reformed patriarchy that perhaps at times in the past has been somewhat harsh in its treatment of women, but has now seen the error of its ways. All that was needed to make the male power structure aware of its overly harsh behavior was for women to ask forgiveness for their rebelliousness and return submissively to the patriarchal fold. With these changes, the film eliminates the novel's insistence that the whole value system of a racist and sexist society needs to be altered fundamentally in accord with feminist values for any really significant change to take place. Men must sit down with women, as Albert finally does in the novel, and help them with "female" jobs. They must relinquish their attempts to dominate and to "save"; instead, they must just help. The impetus for this change in Walker's novel is the power of sisterhood. In Spielberg's film, however, sisterhood does not triumph; instead, Celie is saved by the salvific force of male benevolence.

Although Spielberg converts Walker's narrative from a political into a social female friendship portrayal, this transformation does not reduce the emphasis placed on female bonding. In fact, the idealization of Celie's relationship with her sister Nettie is stronger and the moments of their separation and reunion even more emotionally wrenching in the film than they are in the novel. What are reduced are the politically empowering aspects of the female relationships that are presented. The film displaces Celie's bond of female friendship with Shug from the position it holds in the novel as the crucial relationship in her life and replaces it with her idealized biological sisterhood with Nettie. Whereas Celie and Shug in the novel set out to destroy patriarchal power, Celie and Nettie in the film are concerned instead with restoring rather than challenging the patriarchal family structure. In this way, Spielberg repositions the politically subversive female bonding found in Walker's novel within the traditional confines of domesticity. He returns Walker's revolutionary female characters to their traditional familial roles without sacrificing the novel's emphasis on sisterhood and the strong appeal this theme has for female viewers.

Attracting a Female Audience

Cheryl Butler provides convincing evidence that the evocation of African American sisterhood in *The Color Purple* was indeed important in eliciting black women's support for the film. Butler has described a class discussion in which she participated as a student at the University of Pennsylvania. After viewing the film, several white female students in the class criticized both the film itself and Walker for having endorsed it.[25] In reaction to this criticism, black female students refused to contribute to the class discussion, standing, as Butler suggests, in a bond of "sistern" with Walker that was inspired by the film's portrayal of black female solidarity.[26] What Butler describes is the film's strong appeal to its black, if not its white, female audience in terms of its portrayal of female bonding. This appeal affected these African American women viewers so strongly that it initiated a show of black female unity against what the women perceived as white-initiated attacks on one of their black sisters.

The appeal of *The Color Purple* to white female spectators, on the other hand, might seem difficult to explain given Butler's classroom experiences, which suggest that white female viewers are much more openly critical of the film than their black counterparts. It should be noted, however, that white graduate students in a university setting represent a very elite segment of the filmgoing population. The group that Butler describes utilized highly cultivated feminist sensibilities to analyze carefully the relationship between the novel and the film. It seems likely that these women represent exactly the type of spectator to whom *The Color Purple* would not appeal and who would have made up a very small part of its audience. Spielberg's film aims to attract not those who would carefully analyze and compare its political message to the novel's, but rather those who would respond to the strong emotionality it evokes, without much concern for a message that extends beyond the personal level of individual empowerment.

As Jane Shattuc suggests, the film effectively utilizes three methods that have been typically employed to cultivate white identification with black characters without in any way challenging preconceived racial attitudes.[27] Shattuc labels these three approaches the solidarity, pity, and imitation stances, and she finds all of them operative in *The Color Purple*. The solidarity stance allows a white female viewer to identify with black women's experiences as indicative of shared female oppression while ignoring the particular problems faced by black women due to racism. The pity stance initiates feelings of compassion and guilt in the white spectator for the plight of black women while at the same time reinforcing her sense of pleasure and good fortune in being white. Finally, the imitation stance involves an idealization of the naturalness and simplicity of black as opposed to white culture with no investigation of the real differences between them.

It would seem that the box-office success and crossover popularity of *The Color Purple* largely resulted from its white male director's determination to alienate no potential female audience members. This determination, however, led Spielberg to eliminate the unrelenting attacks on racist and sexist oppression found in Walker's novel and to replace them with a feel-good affirmation of a reformed patriarchy and a female-affirmative message that remains entirely on the level of personal empowerment. The highly compromised version of black women's life experiences found in Spielberg's film may have led to its box-office success, but the movie failed to initiate a new cycle of Hollywood intraracial female friendship films. In fact, *The Color Purple* stands alone as the only Hollywood intraracial female friendship film of the 1980s.[28]

Mi Vida Loca

An Intraethnic Female Friendship Film

It was not until 1994 that an intraethnic female friendship film reached mainstream audiences. *Mi Vida Loca (My Crazy Life)* also has the distinction of being the first film about Chicanas and about girl gangs to achieve wide distribution. Although *Mi Vida Loca* and *The Color Purple* are alike in that they both have white directors, the two films are in every other way quite different. The modestly budgeted *Mi Vida Loca* was written and directed by independent filmmaker Allison Anders, whose credentials contrast startlingly with Steven Spielberg's. Whereas Spielberg is the essence of the successful mainstream Hollywood director, Anders is an iconoclastic, antiestablishment female filmmaker, described by one reviewer as a "lavishly tattooed and pierced high-school-dropout single mother of two who went from white trash welfare to UCLA film school."[29] The film was financed by HBO Showcase as a "gangxploitation movie," but Anders provided, instead, a realistic look at Chicana gang subculture.

Anders has called her approach to her material "romantic realism," a style that tries to capture the external nuances of the characters' experiences while at the same time penetrating into their inner emotional lives.[30] Although she insists that *Mi Vida Loca* is a melodrama and not a social problem film, Anders still went to great lengths to portray Chicana gang culture in a way that feels authentic.[31] For this reason, her style has been likened to the social realist tradition of Latin American cinema, yet Anders distances herself from the gritty look of social realism.[32] She aestheticizes an inner-city Chicano/a lifestyle that for too long has been demonized in mainstream films. As Rosa Linda Fregoso notes, *Mi Vida Loca* is filled with "opalescent and luminous shots" woven into a "tapestry of music, death, and melancholy, attending meticulously to the stylistic nuances of Chicano gang culture."[33]

This tapestry is composed of a three-part episodic structure that also seems to imitate unformed reality. The film begins with the story of a dyadic friendship between two female gang members, Sad Girl (Angel Aviles) and Mousie (Seidy Lopez). The strength of their relationship, which extends back to their childhoods, is put to the test when both become pregnant by the same man, a local gang member and drug dealer named Ernesto (Jacob Vargas). The film's second segment widens the cast of characters to include the gang of homegirls to which Sad Girl and Mousie belong and switches its focus to concentrate on their struggle to achieve some direction under the leadership of an older gang member, Giggles (Marlo Marron). This emphasis on group friendship extends into the film's final segment, which has a twofold plot structure: interconnected to a narrative of intergang rivalry over the ownership of a flashy custom truck is the story of the tragic romance between one of the homegirls and an ex-convict. The three episodes are united by setting and common characters, yet no one figure emerges as the film's protagonist. The stories are told by multiple voice-over narrators, both male and female, whose commentaries segue into each other, forming a mosaic of different voices pieced together to tell the tale of the Echo Park neighborhood and the lives of its young inhabitants.

Anders's realism includes her use of actual gang members as actors and story consultants on the film; the lead roles of Mousie and Whisper (Nelida Lopez) are played by women who actually are from Echo Park.[34] Anders has stated that her gang consultants advised her on everything from the style, gestures, and speech of her characters to the music she used on the sound track. She based at least one of the stories in the film on real-life events that she and her daughter observed in the Echo Park neighborhood:

> I used to see these two girls at each other, with these babies on their hips. They were like 14-year-olds. One day I said [to her daughter], "Devon, what's up with those girls?" She says, "Well, you see, Marty and Christine were best friends. Then Marty had a baby by Ernesto, and then Christine had a baby by Ernesto, and now they don't get along." This was literally the Sad Girl and Mousie story.[35]

In spite of Anders's attempts to create a realistic, nonexploitative portrayal of Chicana gang life, her film has been criticized by mainstream and Chicano/a critics alike as a paternalistic and voyeuristic investigation of what is presented as an "alien" subculture. Many mainstream critics have condemned the film for offering a stereotypical portrait of urban minority teenagers living aimless lives that involve irresponsible sex, teenage motherhood, crime, and drugs.[36] Rosa Linda Fregoso's lengthy analysis of the film in *Cineaste* is representative of the unfavorable response it has received from Chicano/a critics. Fregoso emphasizes not so much Anders's use of stereotypes as her inability to capture the substance of Chicana gang culture. Fregoso proposes that the film is flawed by Anders's reliance on her own autobiographical experiences to form her stories. In publicity material for the film, Anders indicates that she based the doomed love affair between La Blue Eyes (Magali Alvarado) and a prison inmate on her own failed relationship with a white rock star, and that the custom truck plotline came from a short script by another of her white male former lovers.[37] According to Fregoso, this reliance on non-Chicano/a material led Anders to distort the lifestyle of the Chicana homegirls she was trying to portray by reducing them merely to "pretexts for [her] own fantasies."[38]

Fregoso presents two particularly strong examples of Anders's distortions of Chicano/a gang life. First, she proposes that by centering her film on gang rivalry over an expensive custom truck, Anders entirely misses the point of gang warfare, which results not from frivolous obsessions with luxury consumer items, but from the scarcity of basic economic resources in the barrio. Second, Fregoso points out that Anders also completely overlooks the importance of intergenerational female relationships in Chicana culture. Fregoso asserts that the homegirls' survival in the difficult environment of the barrio depends heavily on elaborate female intergenerational kinship networks through which older women pass on to the younger homegirls practical help and crucial survival skills gained from their own experiences in the neighborhood.[39] Again in this regard, Anders's reliance on autobiographical material rather than her knowledge of the culture she is trying to portray interferes with her presentation of Chicana experience. Anders seems to have projected onto the homegirls' lives the lack of parental guidance she found in her own life. In interviews, for instance, she has stated that she identified with her young female characters because she felt she shared with them a lack of a parental presence.[40] This identification led Anders to portray her female characters as entirely self-sufficient, with little or no adult guidance, and to ignore the importance of intergenerational female relationships to women's survival in the barrio.

Mi Vida Loca (Anders, 1994) begins with what appears to be a typically senti-mental account of an intimate dyadic relationship between two best friends, Sad Girl (Angel Aviles, left) and Mousie (Seidy Lopez). Here we see them struggling to maintain their childhood friendship after each has had a child with the same man.

Mi Vida Loca as a Political Female Friendship Film

Mi Vida Loca begins as a sentimental female friendship portrayal. It ini-tially engages its female viewers by presenting what appears to be a typ-ically sentimental account of an intimate dyadic relationship between two best friends, Sad Girl and Mousie. Their idyllic childhood bond is disrupted by the conventional device of their becoming rivals for the same man. After this initial episode, however, the film moves into the realm of political group friendship as it comes to center on the home-girls' attempts to unite under the leadership of Giggles, an older girl re-cently released from prison. Having served a four-year prison term be-cause of her involvement in a crime committed by her now deceased male lover, Giggles is determined to make it on her own and not rely on a man. She becomes the guiding force behind the homegirls' attempts to take care of themselves by organizing a female gang.

The coming together of the homegirls to take charge of their own lives seems to represent the heart of Anders's film. She effectively relates this theme to the dyadic friendship between Sad Girl and Mousie by portraying the solidarity network that the women organize as a natural outgrowth of women's tendency to reconcile their differences rather than resort to violence. This tendency is represented on a dyadic level by

Sad Girl and Mousie's reconciliation and on a group level by the formation of the gang under Giggles's leadership. This emphasis on female solidarity does not lead to a fantasy happy ending, however, as it does in so many female friendship films, because Anders refuses to indulge in a simplistic glorification of female bonding.

Consequently, some reviewers have criticized the film as fatalistic or nihilistic,[41] but rather than conveying a hopelessly negative view of barrio life, the film's ambivalent ending seems to represent instead a realistic, thought-provoking attempt to show that the problems with which it deals are in reality far from solved. As Anders has shaped *Mi Vida Loca*'s conclusion, the homegirls form a gang that they feel will work for their benefit and for the benefit of their children. Sad Girl announces in her concluding voice-over:

> By the time our boys are 21, most of them will be disabled, imprisoned, or dead. We need to learn new skills for the future because we can't count on the boys to take care of us and our kids. We have our own meetings now—our own operation and we defend our own neighborhood. By the time my daughter grows up, Echo Park will belong to her, and she can be whatever she wants to be. The homegirls have learned to pack weapons 'cause our operations have become more complicated. It makes me nervous to have so many guns around the kids, but we are safe and practical. Women don't use weapons to prove a point. Women use weapons for love.

Sad Girl's sentiments express a real energy and determination among the homegirls to take charge and change their lives. They have assumed a position of agency and refuse to remain passive victims of their environment, yet the direction they have adopted is presented as fraught with mortal danger. As Sad Girl's optimistic voice-over concludes on the audio track, the screen shows something very different. A car pulls up before a local grocery market, and a young woman in the car pulls out a gun and shoots at a homeboy in revenge for the gang-related murder of her lover. Missing her targeted victim, she accidentally kills a small child who is playing nearby. Sad Girl's assertion that women can control weapons better than men because they kill for love and not to make a point is seriously called into question by this incident.

Anders's attitudes toward her material are complex, and never more so than here at her conclusion. While demonstrating considerable sympathy for her female characters, Anders's perspective always maintains a certain distance, a reflection perhaps of her status as an outsider to the subculture she portrays. Her sympathetic, though not entirely empathic, stance seems to reflect a calculated decision to maintain a nonjudgmental perspective in regard to her material.[42] As a result, Anders stands back from her film's tragic conclusion and allows for considerable ambiguity in interpretation. Certainly, Sad Girl's voice-over narration indicates that the homegirls feel empowered by their commitment to female solidarity, and Anders seems to admire their attempts to take charge of their own lives. The method they have chosen, however, replaces reliance on men with doing what the men do—only better. The flaws in this strategy become apparent when a woman is shown slaughtering a small child on the street.

The film's ending actually raises a number of troubling questions about female involvement in gang culture. It suggests, first of all, that women's assumption of agency may not be enough to end a cycle of male gang violence that seems to be self-perpetuating. Women in the film repeatedly take on traditionally male roles, but their imitation of male behavior is not presented as necessarily positive in its consequences. Whisper gets involved in Ernesto's drug business and ends up with a disabling leg injury; Giggles serves her prison time "like a man" and then after her release cannot find a job to support herself and her daughter; finally, the homegirls "pack weapons" like their male counterparts, only to find that violence enacted by a woman is just as destructive as that perpetrated by a man.

Anders's final questioning of women's adoption of violent male behavior is part of a larger interrogation running through the film. Much of *Mi Vida Loca* investigates the romantic notions that dominate the lives of the film's young female characters. Like Sad Girl, whose sentimental idea that killing for love can make a difference is challenged by the film's tragic ending, many of the other homegirls, in spite of their tough attitudes, also seem tied to a romantic view of life, which is shown to be particularly destructive when wedded to the violence endemic in gang culture. For instance, just before she is to meet Sad Girl in a shootout to resolve their conflict, Mousie gives an impassioned, highly romanticized speech to Ernesto:

> . . . and now I have to kill my friend. She was my friend even before I knew you and now we're not friends no more. Now, she's a bitch. I'm scared. What if she kills me tonight? What about our son? You have to tell him, Ernesto. You've got to tell him about his mother.

Maybe, he'll remember all the cute toys I got for him. I used to comb his hair. I'd sing to him before he'd go to sleep. You've got to tell him about his mother if anything happens to me, Ernesto. Tell him how his mother died for love.

Although these words could easily have been presented as an ironic critique of Mousie's destructive romanticism, Anders pulls back from such a judgmental attitude. In interviews, she has said that it was actually the "intense sense of tragedy" her female characters had about themselves that drew her to them. She felt that the only way she could "get away with [the] melodrama and high romantic tones" that dominated their lives was to have the story told through their eyes, so she developed the idea of using multiple voice-overs from the perspectives of various characters as a narrational device.[43]

Anders's nonjudgmental stance is also evident in her refusal to end the film on a note of empty moralizing by fashioning an entirely uplifting or wholly tragic denouement; instead, she creates a realistic portrait of women who have the energy and determination to change their lives, yet are tragically caught in a cycle of violence that their romanticized worldview only works to support. Anders refuses to offer the type of cinematic fantasy resolution found in mainstream Hollywood films like *The Color Purple* that rely for their happy endings on a retreat from social and political issues into the realm of personal relationships; instead, *Mi Vida Loca* at its conclusion confronts head-on the problems of minority inner-city gangs—problems that the film suggests are not easily solved. Anders opts for a complex and ambiguous ending that seems intended to open up a discourse on women's position in gang culture rather than merely offering a blindly affirmative statement of female solidarity that would in effect shut this type of discourse down.

Mi Vida Loca and the Female Spectator

In spite of its attempts to grapple with serious issues in an intelligent and thought-provoking manner, *Mi Vida Loca* did not find a wide audience. It was received indifferently by critics and found little success at the box office. There seem to be several reasons for the film's lack of popularity with female viewers. Its failure, first of all, reflects mainstream audiences' conditioning by Hollywood norms. By 1994, when *Mi Vida Loca* was released, female friendship films had already established a set of conventional audience expectations for the cycle. These expectations include, as we have seen, a fantasy resolution that is strongly affirmative of women, even if this affirmation is patently contrived and artificial. *Mi Vida Loca*'s refusal to provide this blindly affirmative ending may in itself have doomed the film's chances for mainstream success.

The film's refusal to resort to blind affirmation extends to its depiction of its female relationships, all of which represent imperfectly realized and inadequately resolved transference situations. Sad Girl and Mousie's friendship, the film's most sentimental relationship, initially represents a mirroring transference that nurtures both girls through their childhood and adolescent developmental crises. The relationship fails, however, as they reach early adulthood and fall prey to stereotypical female behavior as they become rivals for male affection. Although their friendship is eventually renewed, they never recover the intimacy of their lost bond and for the remainder of the film engage in constant and pointless bickering.

As the film moves in its last two sections from a focus on dyadic to group friendship, its portrayal of gang life involves not so much mirroring as idealizing and twinship transference situations. The female gang members, for instance, idealize their leader, Giggles. She is seen after her release from prison as a savior who they believe will provide new answers to their problems. Although Giggles does offer them some leadership, she does so only with reluctance and, as the film's conclusion indicates, with mixed success. Finally, even the female solidarity that the girls find in their gang experiences does not bring about an ultimate solution to their problems. As the film's concluding song, "Girls, It Ain't Easy," suggests, there are no simple solutions to the problems of inner-city youth culture. Thus, *Mi Vida Loca* seeks at its conclusion to convey the message of a continuing struggle rather than to provide an ending marked by empty affirmation.

The imperfectly resolved transference situations that characterize the relationships among the film's characters are extended out to the female spectator's connection to the text of the film itself. First of all, *Mi Vida Loca*'s episodic narrative structure, with its fragmented, loosely constructed plotline, has a substantial distancing effect. In addition, the multiple voice-over narrational device prevents the spectator from primary engagement with any one character; instead, it offers many different points of view for potential audience identification. This distanced spectatorial positioning allows viewers to stand back and adopt a more thoughtful perspective in regard to the issues raised by the film than they would if they were strongly implicated in the emotional experiences of a single character. Hollywood conventions, however, have led audiences to expect strong implication into the emotional life of a central character who is engaged in a compelling linear narrative. These mainstream audience expectations make the type of intellectually stimulating distanciation effect that Anders tries to achieve in *Mi Vida Loca* anathema to mainstream viewers.

Anders's realism may have also prevented the film from finding a Chicano/a audience. Fregoso's response suggests that Anders's attempt as a white woman to present a realistic portrait of Chicana culture may have distanced more Chicano/a viewers than it attracted. *Mi Vida Loca* represents an odd mixture of narrational distance, faithfulness to the nuances of the subculture presented, and story lines drawn from Anders's observations of Echo Park gang life as well as from her own experiences. The intermingling of these different elements may have created for many Chicano/a viewers the sense of betrayal that Fregoso expresses in her critique of the film. To see a film that is so faithful to the external particularities of one's culture fail to capture the essence of that culture cannot but be a very alienating experience.

The film's relation to its white audience appears to have been equally alienating. Unlike *The Color Purple*, *Mi Vida Loca* refuses to offer white viewers the opportunity to relate to its minority characters without having their racist views of minority groups challenged. Although a white woman may adopt a relationship of solidarity with the female characters presented in *Mi Vida Loca*, she is never allowed to forget the particularity of their situation within the Chicana gang subculture. The film also makes no attempt to provoke pity in its white female viewers by encouraging them to feel sorry for its characters or to feel guilty or responsible for their plight. Anders also refuses to idealize Chicana culture as more natural, simple, or straightforward than white culture; instead, the viewer is encouraged to recognize and deal with the real differences between the two cultures.

The failure of *Mi Vida Loca* to attract an audience is particularly unfortunate given the film's many accomplishments. Anders constructs a serious, complex, and sympathetic treatment of Chicana gang culture. As the first mainstream treatment of a minority experience that has otherwise been either vilified or ignored, the film deserves a larger audience than it has gained. Anders has said that her goal in making the film was "to humanize people who don't get represented on the screen," and in spite of its flaws, *Mi Vida Loca* still succeeds admirably in achieving this end.[44] It is an indication of the deleterious effects of American film exhibition's saturation with Hollywood films and the pervasive influence on audience expectations of Hollywood filmmaking norms that more people have not seen or appreciated Anders's film. A film like *Mi Vida Loca* that stimulates thought about important social issues should not be ignored simply because its director refuses to pander to mainstream tastes by offering a fantasy ending and providing easy identification with characters. It should also not be rejected by the Chicano/a community simply because Anders let her own experiences interfere too much with her presentation of another culture. There are too few filmic treatments of intraethnic female friendship for one that achieves so much to be so readily dismissed.

Passion Fish

A Rare Look at Interracial Female Friendship

The interracial female friendship film is an even rarer commodity than its intraracial counterpart. There are, in fact, no mainstream films released in the 1980s that focus on the portrayal of an interracial female friendship.[45] It was not until 1992 that writer/director John Sayles's independent feature *Passion Fish*, which deals with the relationship between a white woman and her black nurse, found mainstream distribution. By the time he made *Passion Fish*, Sayles was a very well established independent filmmaker with a reputation for being sensitive to political and social issues and for approaching them from a leftist liberal perspective.

Passion Fish focuses on a dyadic friendship between two women: May-Alice (Mary McDonnell), a former soap opera star who has been crippled in an auto accident, and Chantelle (Alfre Woodard), her African American nurse. Chantelle is a rehabilitated drug addict who sees her job with May-Alice as a way to pull her life back together and regain custody of her child. May-Alice, embittered by her sudden paraplegic state, has rejected physical therapy, retreated to her dead parents' country estate on the Louisiana bayou, and become an alcoholic. The film recounts the slow development of a friendship between the two women as they gradually become more intimate, begin to depend upon one another, and offer each other the practical help and emotional

In Passion Fish *(Sayles, 1992), the friendship between the paraplegic May-Alice (Mary McDonnell, right) and her nurse, Chantelle (Alfre Woodard), progresses without any discussion of the racial barriers between them. In this scene, the two women enjoy a picnic lunch together in the film's picturesque bayou setting. Photo by Bob Marshak.*

support they need to heal their wounds. It is an indication of the failure of American cinema to confront racial issues seriously that the only mainstream female friendship film to approach the theme of interracial relationships advocates as one of its primary thematic messages an escape from the problems of public life into the personal. In fact, *Passion Fish* goes to great lengths to avoid social issues and to limit itself entirely to the level of personal uplift. Viewer attention is distracted from the film's racial elements by the focus on May-Alice's struggle to deal with her disability as well as by the local color aspects of the film's Louisiana bayou setting.

In spite of these distracting elements, however, *Passion Fish*'s portrayal of a racially mixed female friendship cannot help but make a statement about racial relations. Although Sayles seems at times to be trying to reformulate stereotypical portrayals of his black and white characters and of their relationships with each other, the film's narrative content nevertheless often falls into established patterns for presenting interracial friendship, patterns that fail to confront racial difference with any degree of thoughtfulness.[46] Although the friendship between May-Alice and Chantelle develops slowly and tentatively, the barriers between them are never examined and their eventual connection is portrayed as entirely divorced from matters of race. In fact, the film goes out of its way to pull back from moments when racial issues seem on the verge of being confronted. In one instance, during a visit from May-Alice's former soap opera costars, a black female actress initiates a private conversation with Chantelle. Each woman interrogates the other concerning the nature of her relationship with May-Alice, and both seem reluctant to admit to being her friend. The scene ends with each women confessing only that she has spent "a lot of time with her," rather than admitting to feelings of friendship. Although this incident raises important questions about the barriers that prevent interracial friendships, the topic is never again introduced.

Even more problematic than Sayles's refusal to have his characters discuss racial issues openly is his attempt to deconstruct the power relationship between May-Alice and Chantelle. Sayles's intentions in his portrayal of interracial female friendship seem to involve a reconception of the mistress-slave relationship as a mutually beneficial friendship bond. May-Alice's soap opera character is even named Scarlett, a reference to Gone with the Wind's Scarlett O'Hara that can hardly be unintentional, yet the new type of interracial female relationship that Sayles creates between May-Alice and Chantelle still has unfortunate racist implications. For instance, one device that seems to be employed to equalize the two women's situations is May-Alice's disability. This seems to suggest that in order for a white woman and a black woman to be on an equal footing, the white one must be severely handicapped. In addition, the women's sequestration from the outside world implies that a reconciliation of racial differences can be accomplished only on a personal level and in a situation of isolation from societal influences.

The most problematic aspect of the film's approach to racial issues is its ending. May-Alice refuses an offer to return to her career in New York, decides to remain in her ancestral home on the Louisiana bayou, and offers Chantelle the opportunity to stay with her. The implication is that Chantelle will now be able to regain custody of her daughter because she can provide a suitable home for her, or at least May-Alice can. This ending represents the kind of fantasy resolution that African American critics have identified as characteristic of works that present interracial relationships from a white perspective.[47] The emphasis is placed on May-Alice's decision rather than Chantelle's, which reduces Chantelle's significance in the narrative to the role of providing a learning experience for her white friend. In addition, the film seems to suggest further that the best way for its black central character to gain respectability is to place herself in the custody of her benevolent white protector, who can provide her with a proper living environment.

In many ways, *Passion Fish* simply applies the formula that is characteristic of Hollywood biracial male buddy films to a female friendship portrayal. As Ed Guerrero notes, biracial male buddy films typically place one black and one white character in an unpleasant situation that both would rather have avoided. In order to solve the problems they face, these characters are forced to work together, and the growing understanding and cooperation that develop between them lead to a racial reconciliation that allows the black character to gain acceptance on white terms.[48] This formula is perfectly dramatized in *Passion Fish*. Neither Chantelle nor May-Alice wants to be in the situation in which she finds herself, but the two women learn to work together and to understand each other. In the end, May-Alice provides Chantelle with a suitable "white" home life that will allow her to find acceptance on white terms and to regain the respectability she needs to be reinstated as a suitable mother for her child.

But Is Race or Gender Even the Issue Here?

Although *Passion Fish* certainly can be read for its unfortunate implications concerning race and gender, it does not seem interested in creating a female spectator who is concerned about either of these issues; instead, race and gender are used to draw the spectator into an acceptance of a thematic stance that does not really deal with either of these issues directly. What Sayles seems most ardent about presenting is a scathing critique of contemporary American society as so dangerous, potentially crippling, and false that the only alternative available is to retreat into personal relationships and the solace of a natural rural environment. Ideas of sisterhood and racial harmony, with obvious social implications, are appropriated ironically only to advocate flight from social problems. Perhaps this retreat from public life is the only reaction Sayles felt was open to a leftist liberal like himself when faced with the growing conservatism of Reagan-era America.

It seems significant, however, that Sayles couches his idea of a necessary retreat from involvement in public life in the form of the female friendship film, applying it to female rather than male characters. As a result, the film supports, perhaps inadvertently, a very conservative agenda in regard to both racial and women's issues. If read in terms of its message about gender, *Passion Fish* offers a strong warning to women to flee the dangers of public involvement and return to the less threatening sphere of intimate personal relationships. In terms of race, it positions its spectator in an equally problematic position. While failing to confront seriously the social issues involved in interracial relations, the film proceeds nevertheless at its conclusion to resolve these issues simplistically through an unrealistic and essentially racist ending. What *Passion Fish* demonstrates most clearly is how far the female friendship film has to go before it even begins to provide the important subject of interracial relations with the thoughtful consideration it deserves. In advocating a flight from social issues into idyllic antisocial isolation and proposing white benevolence as a way to bridge the gap between the races, *Passion Fish*'s investigation of interracial female friendship unfortunately represents only an embarrassing failure.

Concluding Comments

The history of the female friendship film's presentation of racial and minority issues within the contemporary period is not encouraging. The most popular female friendship film to deal with racial issues has been without question *The Color Purple,* an extremely flawed bowdlerization of Alice Walker's important novel. *Mi Vida Loca,* in contrast, which represents a serious, if flawed, attempt to portray Chicana gang culture, failed to attract an audience because, unlike *The Color Purple,* it refused to pander to Hollywood-created viewer expectations. The intraracial female friendship film, however, has recently experienced a landmark development with the release of *Waiting to Exhale,* the first Hollywood intraracial female friendship film directed by an African American director, Forest Whitaker, and cowritten by an African American screenwriter, female author Terry McMillan.

Based on McMillan's best-selling novel, the film found a wide, primarily black, female audience and seems to have attained almost immediate cult status with African American women viewers. Although its substantial box office success may have the important political effect of precipitating the production of more mainstream intraracial female friendship portrayals, in terms of the political implications of its narrative content *Waiting to Exhale* is in fact extremely limited. The film is preoccupied with its female characters' troubled heterosexual romances and seems primarily concerned with expressing black women's frustrations with their relationships with black men. The film's female friendship component is all but lost in the process, and in any case is presented in the social rather than the political female friendship film tradition. Female friendship in *Waiting to Exhale,* following the conventions established by other social female friendship films, serves as a place of refuge for African American women from their problematic romantic entanglements with what are presented as insensitive and irresponsible black men.

Interracial and interethnic female friendship portrayals are even rarer and more problematic than their intraracial and intraethnic counterparts. *Passion Fish*'s position as the only representative of the interracial female friendship film in this period suggests a strong reluctance by the film community even to approach this issue. The regressive nature of *Passion Fish*'s tentative attempts to confront interracial relations indicates further that the foundation has not even been laid for future attempts to grapple with this important subject.

7 | Backlash: The Anti-Female Friendship Film

The manipulative female friendship film portrays a destructive female relationship that mocks the possibility of women's forming the bonds of loyalty and affection that characterize other female friendship portrayals. These films often rejuvenate antiquated stereotypical representations of female relationships from woman's films of the 1930s and 1940s. They represent women's friendships as plagued by jealousy, envy, and competition for men, and they teach women to beware of and fear one another. By focusing so strongly on conflicts between women, they obscure other issues related to women's position in society, relieve men of any responsibility for women's problems, and suggest, instead, that women should grant men primary importance in their lives because they are the only ones upon whom women can rely.

In response to the growing political conservatism of the 1980s and 1990s, one might expect a major backlash against the female friendship film, and the most obvious form of backlash would be the rise of a significant number of manipulative female friendship portrayals. Curiously, however, this category of the female friendship film is represented only by a small group of films, all confined to the single year of 1992. There is a marked absence of mainstream anti-female friendship films extending throughout the period from the late 1970s to the early 1990s, when the female friendship film gained its enormous popularity with female audiences. No major anti-female friendship film appears until the release of Curtis Hanson's *The Hand That Rocks the Cradle* in 1992, and even this film's popular success did not initiate a trend.[1] It was followed in the same year by two films, *Single White Female* (Schroeder, 1992) and *Poison Ivy* (Ruben, 1992), but in succeeding years the category of the anti-female friendship film has not gained wide cinematic expression.[2]

This paucity of manipulative female friendship portrayals suggests that the backlash against the female friendship film did not take the directly confrontational form represented by blatantly anti-female friendship portrayals; instead, what we see throughout the period of the female friendship film's rise in popularity is an erosion of its political dimensions in favor of much less politically challenging social female friendship portrayals. Because of the growing dominance of social female friendship films that support rather than challenge the status quo, no compelling reason existed for the development of anti-female friendship films attacking the idea of female friendship directly.

By the mid-1990s, the female friendship film had already developed almost exclusively into a socially conformist cinematic form that presents female bonding as a useful means of social integration, guiding women into acceptance of the existing social structure. As such, the female friendship film came to represent no apparent threat to the way things are and therefore warranted no direct attacks. In 1992, however, in the wake of *Thelma & Louise*, the most politically transgressive film that the cycle has offered thus far, direct challenges in the form of manipulative female friendship portrayals did materialize. Interestingly, however, the female friendship film's polysemous quality, its tendency to seek a wide appeal to diverse audiences, as well as the influence of female input on its production, most often renders the anti-female friendship film a strange, amorphous creature that in more instances than not disintegrates in its own polysemous ambiguity.

The Hand That Rocks the Cradle

The Nanny from Hell

None of the three films that make up this 1992 wave of anti-female friendship films received critical acclaim, and only the first, *The Hand That Rocks the Cradle*, attained substantial box office success. *The Hand That Rocks the Cradle* also provoked the most controversy of the three films, with reviewers attacking it as a blatantly reactionary attempt to play upon working women's fears of inadequate child care.

Susan Faludi, for instance, has condemned the film as part of an anti-feminist movement that she describes in the subtitle of her book *Backlash* as "the undeclared war against American women." She believes the film sets out to convince female viewers that they were better off isolated back in their homes before feminism released them to the ugly outside world of work and career achievement.[3]

Amanda Silver, screenwriter of *The Hand That Rocks the Cradle*, however, claims that she intended to, and believes she actually did, write a progressive film. In discussing her inspiration for the screenplay, Silver has suggested that, like Callie Khouri's revision of the male road movie in *Thelma & Louise*, her script was crafted to transform the male-dominated thriller formula by placing female actors in its major roles. In an interview, Silver described her intentions as follows: "Men get to be everything in the movies, they get to be good, they get to be bad, they get to be friends and they get to be enemies. I feel that women should get to play all those parts. They should be allowed to be strong, they should be allowed to be vicious." Silver, who calls herself a feminist, insists that she never intended to fashion the film as a message to working women about the dangers of leaving their children with child-care workers; instead, she says she wanted to prompt discussion about issues important to women. She also has stated that she did not feel that it was her responsibility to worry about what is "politically correct or not."[4]

What Silver does seem to have felt was her responsibility was the creation of a script that would sell, so she determined to write a thriller with women at its center. As she has described her technique, she developed the idea of two women in conflict and then "milked it for all it was worth," looking for "juicy opportunities to exploit."[5] Her greatest triumph of exploitation is her creation of a truly monstrous female friend in the person of Peyton (Rebecca De Mornay), the film's dementedly evil nanny. Peyton is introduced to the audience in a deceptively sympathetic light as the victimized pregnant wife of a debauched gynecologist who kills himself after he is publicly accused of molesting his patients during office visits. Traumatized by her husband's suicide and his failure to provide for her and their unborn child after his death, Peyton suffers a miscarriage.

Having lost her husband, her home, and her child, Peyton determines to take revenge on Claire (Annabella Sciorra), the patient who first reported Peyton's husband's misconduct to the police. Claire is in

Manipulative female friendship appears in The Hand That Rocks the Cradle *(Hanson, 1992). Peyton (Rebecca De Mornay, left) masquerades as Claire's (Annabella Sciorra) loyal friend while secretly plotting to destroy her happy family life.*

possession of what the film presents as an ideal upper-middle-class family life. She and her husband, Michael (Matt McCoy), a genetic engineer, have a happy marriage, two thriving children, and a beautiful old home. When Claire's interest in horticulture leads her to advertise for a nanny so that she can have time to build a greenhouse in her backyard, Peyton seizes the opportunity to destroy Claire's familial bliss. Assuming a position not only as Claire's employee but also as her devoted friend, Peyton does everything possible to destroy Claire's happy home.

Although the character of Peyton is not really a new addition to cinematic constructions of women, it does represent a variation on an established theme. In fact, Silver admits to having based the character on male-conceived images of evil childless women, "monstrously perverted versions of the stereotypical nurturing and caring female."[6] The twist that Silver adds is to reincarnate this figure, traditionally portrayed as an unattractive older woman, the "old maid," as a beautiful and sexy female friend. This alteration, crucial to the film's anti-female friendship component, obviously worked, because Silver found it, as she says, "embarrassingly" easy to sell her script to Hollywood Pictures.[7]

Silver claims that the film, directed by Curtis Hanson, is true to her original vision. One wonders, however, after reading her description of this vision, how accurate her interpretation of the film really is and how much Silver is deceiving herself into thinking that her original idea was maintained. In addition to feeling that *The Hand That Rocks the Cradle* provided "juicy" parts for female actresses and that it has served to stimulate discussion of women's issues rather than merely played on their fears, Silver also has asserted that she intended the film as a mild satire directed at her "too saintly to be true" upper-middle-class heroine and hero, "smugly ensconced behind the white picket fences and lovingly tended gardens" that isolate them from the world around them.[8]

Although the film allows for this possible reading, its satiric edge is not at all as sharp or clear as Silver apparently imagines it to be. Silver has described story conferences with male production executives concerning the film that suggest not only how much the script may have been changed by male input but also the lengths to which Silver would go to deny to herself that her initial intentions were being transformed:

> A lot of it was compromise—but I felt good because I didn't feel that the original vision had been compromised at all, it was only little things. Though during the rewriting process there would only be myself and one other female production executive in a roomful of men . . . I felt very lucky with the group of men I was working with. One of them was my husband [who was executive producer on the film] and the Hollywood Pictures people were very "hands off" for them. I felt that everyone was making a big effort not to impose sexist or male fantasies on Peyton.[9]

Although Silver seems sure that her initial vision was not altered by male studio executives, one has to wonder in looking at the film whether this male input might have had more deleterious effects on the satiric dimensions of Silver's plot than she is willing to admit. For instance, Silver points out that one of the "little things" that was changed was her original conception of Peyton as "an almost campy, over the top figure." Peyton's character was toned down in the course of various rewrites and rendered more realistic.[10] The effect of this change alone on the possibilities of a satiric reading of the film is devastating. Another possibility, of course, is that Silver's original story conception, intended to "milk" her topic for every "juicy" possibility available, was already so clearly based on "sexist or male fantasies" that tampering with "only little things" was all that was necessary to allow her script to be transformed into a full-blown masterpiece of misogyny.

Attacking Female Friendship

The plot of *The Hand That Rocks the Cradle* functions in many ways as an attack on narrative elements associated with the sentimental female friendship film. Rather than benefiting psychologically and practically from her intimacy with Peyton, Claire finds her self-confidence and family life slowly undermined by Peyton's machinations. Rather than offering her friend affection and loyalty, Peyton instead disguises hatred and malice under the veneer of love and admiration. Whereas the female friendship film advocates a sense of women's solidarity based on their common interests, *The Hand That Rocks the Cradle* promotes, instead, distrust and hatred between women based on the envy, antagonism, and betrayal that it suggests inevitably result from their similarities. The film actually encourages women to fear the most those whose desires are most like their own, and these desires are presumed to be a secure home, children, and a faithful husband.

Whereas the female friendship film presents relationships between women as a source of strength that helps them to cope with the problems they face in the larger society, manipulative female friendship portrayals blame all of women's problems on other women. As a result, issues related to women's social roles under patriarchy escape consideration. *The Hand That Rocks the Cradle*, for instance, begins by pointing to the abuse of women by the male power structure. It opens with a harrowing scene in which Claire is molested by her gynecologist during an office visit. After the film's opening sequences, however, this issue is completely dismissed as the focus shifts entirely to Peyton's malice and her plot for revenge. The psychotic woman driven mad by her thwarted desire for a husband and family, rather than the male abuser, becomes the villain.

In fact, the manipulative female friendship film returns with a vengeance to the tradition of 1930s and 1940s woman's films, which reaffirm strongly the primary importance of husband and family in women's lives. Whereas other forms of the contemporary female friendship film offer friendship between women as an alternative to heterosexual romance and family life, *The Hand That Rocks the Cradle* seems obsessed with repositioning women in their traditional role as domestic caretakers. The film is, in fact, so insistent that a women's place is in the home that it even goes so far as to cut off its major female character's access to the outside world. It suggests that just by going into her backyard to build a greenhouse for her own enjoyment and creative satisfaction, Claire has neglected her family to the extent that they have been placed in the hands of a homicidal maniac. Claire does not have to go to work outside the home or even venture very far from her family to endanger them. Any type of outside endeavor appears to interfere with the total dedication required of the truly devoted wife and mother.

The Hand That Rocks the Cradle on the Other Hand

In spite of what appears indisputably to be a portrayal of a manipulative female friendship, as noted above, screenwriter Amanda Silver claims that she never intended the film to be an attack on female friendship at all, but regarded it instead as a study of the differences between true and false female relationships. Significant in this regard is the figure of Marlene (Julianne Moore), Claire's other female friend and a character Silver claims to have fashioned as a counterpoint to Peyton.[11] In many ways, Marlene is indeed a glowing example of true female friendship. She warns Claire from the beginning to beware of Peyton's possibly evil designs and is the first to discover Peyton's true identity. Even though Claire, influenced by Peyton's insinuations, falsely accuses Marlene of having an affair with Michael, Marlene still heroically tries to save Claire from Peyton's machinations and is killed for her efforts.

At the same time, however, Marlene is given some of the most regressive dialogue about women contained in the film. She tells Claire never to let another woman assume a position of power in her home and mouths the sentiment, also suggested in the film's title, that women gain their greatest power by confining themselves to the domestic sphere: "The hand that rocks the cradle rules the world." She is a hard-boiled career woman who sees the modern working woman's role as so demanding that in order to be considered a success she must "bring in $50,000 a year and still make time for blow jobs and homemade lasagna." Marlene, in fact, fits perfectly into the stereotype of the overachieving, stressed-out career woman set up to contrast with Claire's always smiling and relaxed (at least until Peyton turns up to torment her) homebody. The undesirable nature of Marlene's lifestyle is indicated perhaps most clearly by her incessant smoking and her unnecessarily rude beratement of her office staff. These aspects of her character seem to be included in the film for no reason other than to eliminate any attraction audience members may feel for her lifestyle.

The film actually presents Marlene and Claire's relationship not as a paradigm of female friendship but rather as a juxtaposition of contrasting female life choices: Marlene the tough, rude, chain-smoking career woman who includes lasagna and blow jobs as part of the modern woman's role but never mentions children, and Claire, the perfect homemaker who gets in trouble just because she wants to grow flowers in her backyard. According to the film's logic, career and family are mutually exclusive, and the choice involves ending up a hard-nosed, driven career woman like Marlene or a sweet wife and mother like Claire. It really takes little effort to see which way this film guides its viewers.

Additionally, the friendship between Claire and Marlene is not nearly prominent enough in the film to serve, as Silver suggests it does, as a counterpoint to the negative female friendship that develops between Peyton and Claire. What the film really contrasts with Peyton's manipulative female friendship is the beatific vision of Claire's devotion to her family. At its center, *The Hand That Rocks the Cradle* does not pit a good female friendship against a bad one, as Silver proposes, but a good family against a bad female friendship. The film's ending, in fact, marginalizes Marlene's narrative importance significantly. Having realized Peyton's true identity, Marlene rushes to her friend's aid, but when she arrives at Claire's home, she dies at Peyton's hand in a trap originally set for Claire. When Claire returns home and discovers Marlene's body, she runs to the telephone to get help, but her shock provokes an acute asthma attack that not only prevents her from helping her friend but causes her to collapse and almost die herself.

Although Marlene demonstrates the qualities of a loyal female friend, Claire does not exactly reciprocate. She cannot overcome her physical infirmity to help her friend, but later, when it comes to protecting her family, she becomes a superwoman. The film, in fact, moves very quickly away from Marlene's death. Her loss is all too easily forgotten as *The Hand That Rocks the Cradle* rushes headlong to focus on Claire's final climactic battle to save her family from Peyton's evil designs. After Claire and Michael discover Peyton's true identity and relieve her of her duties, she sets out to murder them and kidnap their children. In her struggle to defeat Peyton, Claire again suffers an asthma attack. This time, however, she not only overcomes it, she even musters up enough strength to send Peyton hurtling through an attic window to her death. The spectator really cannot be expected to remember much about Marlene's loyalty to her friend after this rousing display of

Claire's motherly heroism. It is family, not friendship, that is exalted in this film and championed in its formulaic thriller conclusion.

The Hand That Rocks the Cradle's championing of family at the expense of female friendship does not prevent it from at the same time making a number of female-affirmative statements. The film's three major female characters, Claire, Peyton, and Marlene, all prove to be strong, intelligent, attractive women. Whether their intentions are malevolent or heroic, these are women who do not enact the role of the passive victim or the self-sacrificing martyr. Claire, who comes closest to the victim's role, manages in the end to overcome her physical infirmity and demonstrate great heroism in defense of her family. She is not saved by her husband or by any other man; instead, she saves herself and her children. All three women in the film, in fact, fight for what they want or believe, even to the death.

In addition, the film grants its female characters centrality in its plot structure, relegating men to peripheral roles. It also refuses overtly to promote male dominance or to advocate women's dependence on men. In contrast to the film's strong female characters, Claire's husband, Michael, its major male figure, is not at all presented as a powerful male presence. Characterized as the perfect husband, he is notable not as a dominant representative of male power, but as a supportive, sensitive, and caring spouse. At the same time, however, Michael never takes control of any situation throughout the film, is easily manipulated by Peyton, and at the opening of the film's climactic conclusion is quickly incapacitated by Peyton with a single blow that sends him tumbling down the basement stairs, breaks both his legs, and leaves Claire alone to protect her family.

The ending of *The Hand That Rocks the Cradle* can be interpreted as female affirmative and/or as advocating family values because the film is so plagued by "ideologically implicated ambiguities" that it can be read in a number of contradictory ways, none of which actually seems entirely satisfactory or capable of encompassing the entire text. Clearly, Claire's final heroic triumph over Peyton offers female viewers affirmation of women's agency and courage, yet this victory is restricted completely to the narrow confines of devotion to family. Evil in the person of the vengeful childless woman is purged by the good mother, but the symbolic significance attributed to Peyton's threat is never entirely clarified. For instance, the film can be interpreted as suggesting that the homemaker's fears of the career woman are misplaced and that the woman who is obsessively concerned with establishing the family ideal is the real danger. On the other hand, it can also be read as an affirmation of the American middle-class dream of the perfect family embodied in Claire and Michael's marriage and as an attack on a corrupt upper stratum of wealthy professionals like Peyton and her physician husband.

What is the significance after all of the fact that as Peyton falls to her death she breaks the white picket fence that Claire and Michael have had constructed around their home? Claire suggests when she has it built early in the film that this fence is partially intended to keep people in, but mostly to keep them out. Are we then to regard Peyton as an embodiment of the outside forces that broke into Claire and Michael's idyllic family life and have now been purged, or are we to see her as a representation of Claire's own inner fears that should be overcome so that she can herself break out of her isolation and interact with the outside world? Yet if Claire is to devote her energies entirely to her family, how exactly is she to get into the outside world? This woman, after all, cannot even go out into her backyard to build a greenhouse without getting into deadly trouble.

Added to this mix of seemingly irreconcilable thematic possibilities is the presence at the film's end of a character who has played only a marginal role in the film thus far, but who assumes major significance in its closing moments. Solomon (Ernie Hudson), a retarded African American handyman whom Claire and Michael had hired to do odd jobs around the house, turns out to be their most loyal family friend. As a result of Peyton's insinuations, Claire dismissed Solomon after accusing him of molesting her daughter, yet he returns at the film's end to help Claire defeat Peyton. The addition of this black character to the film's otherwise all-white social milieu is curious, and his presence at the end is particularly so.

Solomon's characterization throughout the film is plagued by racial stereotype. He is a faithful black servant in the Uncle Tom tradition who is totally in awe of and devoted to his white "masters." He is also completely isolated from other black characters, black family life, and black culture. His mental disability seems intended to make his stereotypical representation more acceptable. Because he is retarded, he can be presented as a simple soul without racial consciousness, a nonthreatening black male figure whose mental incapacity allows him to accept his "properly" subservient role willingly. By positioning Solomon as Claire's assistant in her struggle against Peyton, *The Hand*

That Rocks the Cradle attempts to exhibit at its conclusion an openness in regard to race and gender that throughout its narrative it has in every other way discouraged. When so much of the film supports isolation within the family and distrust of the outside world, it seems cynically manipulative for it to suggest at the very end, through its portrayal of Claire and Solomon's collaborative efforts against Peyton, a social message of greater trust and involvement between members of different races and genders.

Engaging the Female Spectator in an Anti-Female Friendship Portrayal

One thing that *The Hand That Rocks the Cradle* clearly demonstrates is that shifting women to the center of a narrative and incorporating a number of female-affirmative elements does not assure a progressive text. If these characteristics are aligned with a socially conservative thematic structure, they can act to support rather than challenge the patriarchal status quo, and the anti-female friendship film can become a particularly effective vehicle for drawing a female audience into acceptance of a conservative social stance. Because the anti-female friendship film utilizes the methods of engagement characteristic of other female friendship portrayals and then slowly dismantles them, the female spectator becomes engaged with the friendship that develops between the film's two female characters only to be forced eventually to repudiate this relationship.

Consider the portrayal in *The Hand That Rocks the Cradle* of the transference situations enacted between Claire and Peyton. The female spectator is drawn into the women's relationship as all three transference situations are enacted. Peyton pretends to act as a nurturing presence in Claire's household, engaging her in a mirroring transference situation. Under her disguise of helpfulness, she then proceeds to destroy Claire's self-confidence and to inhibit her personal growth. Finally, she even attempts to kill Claire. Peyton also pretends to form an idealizing transference with Claire, whom she appears to regard as a perfect model of womanhood, but she perverts the goal of merger with an ideal that characterizes the idealizing transference into a desire to eliminate Claire and assume her identity. The two women also enact a twinship transference by acting as alter egos, but their similarities result not in constructive shared commonality but instead in destructive jealousy and aggression. The film seems to use its enactments of these psychoanalytic transference situations to implicate the female spectator into the relationship between

Claire and Peyton only to have her experience all the more strongly this relationship's destructive potential.

In other ways as well, *The Hand That Rocks the Cradle* leads its female spectator in two mutually exclusive directions in terms of character involvement. First, the film promotes allegiance with Claire as the primary figure of spectator engagement. Through attachment to her, the viewer is led to identify with several perspectives. As noted above, by portraying the failure of all three of Claire's transference bonds with Peyton, the film promotes a deep distrust and even a paranoid fear of female involvement with other women. Second, the film cultivates a negative attitude in the female spectator in regard to female career ambitions and work outside the home. A career is presented as hardening a woman and endangering what should be her primary interest in her family.

Although the film strongly encourages attachment to Claire, it does not totally prevent engagement with Peyton as a figure of audience involvement. After all, she is initially presented as a victim of her husband's misdeeds, and the spectator is allowed some spatiotemporal attachment to her in a limited number of scenes. In fact, Peyton seems to represent a composite figure of the evil female double in earlier woman's films, the television soap opera villainess, and the film noir femme fatale, and as such she offers the female spectator an alternative to complete engagement with Claire's "good girl" character. Like these other powerful but evil female characters, Peyton can function for the resisting spectator as a safety valve, providing an opportunity for some female viewers to read the film against the grain, venting their frustrations against a society that judges women according to an unattainable ideal of domestic perfection. At the same time, however, Peyton's final punishment allows the female spectator to repudiate this subversive posture and return to a more socially acceptable position at the film's conclusion.

The Hand That Rocks the Cradle's attempts to hedge its bets are not confined to the figures of audience engagement it provides. The tension created by its thematic ambiguity, in fact, all but breaks the film apart. Joseph Natoli has succinctly summarized the nature of the film's ideological irresolution, noting that *The Hand That Rocks the Cradle* "has no scruples." On one side, it plays on conservative fears of the loss of family values, attacks feminism and the movement of women outside the home, establishes the man as the rightful breadwinner in the perfect family, cautions that women endanger their families if they relinquish their primary roles as wives and mothers to pursue interests outside the home, insists that there must be only one woman in a man's life, attacks female bonding, suggests children can be best cared for only by their mothers, and advocates family isolationism as protection from a corrupt outside world. It shamelessly proposes as well, however, quite to the contrary, that males are either molesting (the gynecologist) or self-absorbed (the husband), women have "all the guts and brains," male dominance of women and of their bodies is abhorrent, children know and recognize love when it is offered by others besides their parents, and the "rarifying [of] the family atmosphere so that any outside disturbance must be immediately removed is a sure way to make invalids out of people."[12]

What *The Hand That Rocks the Cradle* is really trying to say remains in the final analysis very uncertain. As an anti-female friendship film, it shares with other representatives of the female friendship film cycle the characteristic that I have been calling polysemy, an openness to various interpretations and reading possibilities. This quality works in the anti-female friendship film, as it does in the female friendship film cycle as a whole, to render many female friendship films incapable of making an unambiguous thematic statement. For the anti-female friendship film, however, which after all is centered on an attack on the notion of successful female bonding, this polysemy is a particular problem. The anti-female friendship film's attacks on female friendship are immersed in a text that seems determined to develop contradictory thematic possibilities, many of which are, in fact, female affirmative. In attempting to affirm women while at the same time attacking female bonding, the anti-female friendship film seems to self-destruct thematically.

Single White Female
The Deadly Roommate

As *The Hand That Rocks the Cradle* presents its audience with the nanny from hell, *Single White Female* centers its version of manipulative female friendship on a diabolical roommate. The film begins when an attractive young computer programming analyst, Allison Jones (Bridget Fonda), terminates her relationship with her fiancé, Sam (Steven Weber), after discovering that he has been cheating on her with his ex-wife. In an attempt to get over Sam's betrayal, Allison decides to seek companionship by advertising for a roommate to share her large rent-controlled New York apartment. She selects from among a number of unattractive applicants a shy, mousy young woman, Hedy Carlson (Jennifer Jason Leigh), who turns out to be a psychotic killer. Hedy determines to take over Allie's life. She begins by dressing like her friend and having her hair styled in exactly the same way. When Sam finally convinces Allie to take him back, Hedy attempts to seduce him. When he rebuffs her advances, she murders him. Although the film initially seems to concentrate on the creation of a bizarre psychological connection between the two roommates, it eventually succumbs entirely to the thriller format. Its formulaic conclusion involves a chase scene in which Hedy pursues Allie through the cavernous basement of the women's apartment building until Allie finally manages to kill her pursuer by stabbing Hedy in the back with a screwdriver.

Like *The Hand That Rocks the Cradle*, *Single White Female* is a manipulative female friendship film packaged within the thriller formula. Hedy and Allie's relationship, like Peyton and Claire's, is a mockery of sentimental female friendship portrayals. The intimacy so exalted in sentimental female friendship films develops in Allie and Hedy's case into a deadly connection when Hedy insanely demands that the relationship the two women share become total fusion. Like other manipulative female friendship films, *Single White Female* strongly conveys the message that women should beware of and fear other women. Allie turns to Hedy as a substitute companion when her heterosexual romance falls apart, and this type of substitution is shown to be highly dangerous, even potentially fatal.

Single White Female, however, is not just an anti-female friendship film but a virulent antilesbian film as well. It involves an attack not only on the sentimental qualities of female friendship portrayals but also on the erotic overtones overtly expressed in lesbian films and covertly manifest in many sentimental female friendship films. These erotic sentiments, as Lynda Hart suggests, are converted in anti-female friendship films such as *Single White Female* into "eroticized spectacles of mortal combat between two women, one of whom at first appears to be 'normal' but turns out to be pathological." Hart goes on to describe perfectly the scenario that ensues in *Single White Female*:

> The good women in such films assume the cultural function of eliminating their deviant counterparts. Thus they reinforce the division of

women through displacement of their aggression onto the woman whose sexuality is "deviant." The immense popularity of these films could be understood as a displacement of desire between women, which is, of course, enormously popular in heterosexual pornography. In mainstream cinema, the women can only be shown hacking each other to death.[13]

If *Single White Female* ends by associating Hedy's eroticization of her friendship with Allie with aggression, the majority of the film is spent associating it with perversion and insanity. This association is clearly manifest in the film's utilization of the female gaze, which becomes increasingly important as the voyeuristic aspects of Hedy and Allie's friendship develop. Rather than use the female gaze as it is employed in so many other female friendship films, to challenge the dominance of the male look, *Single White Female* employs it instead to delineate the normal woman from the insane one. Allie's gaze is associated initially with curiosity when Hedy first moves in, then with concern as Hedy's behavior becomes more unusual, and finally with terror as she becomes the victim of Hedy's aggression. Her looks at Hedy are never eroticized or connected with lesbianism. Hedy's looks at Allie, on the other hand, are eroticized, associated with insanity, aggression, and evil, and clearly marked as lesbian.

The film's use of the female gaze is illustrated in the repeated framing of the two women in frontal two shots, with their faces reflected in mirrors or mirroring surfaces. The mirror shots not only convey the sense of confinement, duplicity, and instability that characterizes their relationship, but also accentuate the crucial difference between Allie's and Hedy's looks. Allie is always portrayed looking straight ahead at the mirrored surface, while Hedy is often shown gazing at Allie with a mixture of desire, identification, and concealed malice. These mirror shots dichotomize the female gaze between Allie's "healthy" and Hedy's "unhealthy" ways of looking and as a result prevent it from functioning, as it does in many female friendship films, as a challenge to the male gaze.

In *Single White Female,* Allie's "appropriate" female gaze is associated with traits conventionally labeled feminine, such as narcissism, curiosity, and fear, whereas Hedy's more masculinely aggressive, erotically desiring "lesbian" gaze is connected with malice, danger, and insanity. The challenge that the female gaze, associated with mutual looking and shared affection between women, offers to the dominance/submission

The repeated use of mirror shots in Single White Female *(Schroeder, 1992) dichotomizes the female gaze into good and bad ways of female looking. Here, the good Allie (Bridget Fonda, left) narcissistically looks straight ahead at the mirrored surface, while the bad Hedy (Jennifer Jason Leigh) gazes at her friend with a mixture of desire, identification, and concealed malice.*

structure created by the male gaze is never enacted here; instead, the gaze structure divides the film's female characters into the "normal" passive Allie, whose looks are never eroticized, and the "deviant" active Hedy, whose gaze is associated with the same qualities of mastery and possessiveness that have been said to characterize the male gaze.

The female gaze is thus used as part of the film's overall thematic project to convince the female spectator that the only way she can avoid the dangers of association with other "deviant" women is to ally herself firmly with a man, even if that alliance entails forgiving his sexual transgressions in order to keep him. Like *The Hand That Rocks the Cradle, Single White Female* begins with a male betrayal, Allie's discovery of Sam's infidelity, which is then quickly displaced into a threatening female relationship. This relationship is called up, again as it is in the former film, by a woman's refusal to allow herself to be abused. Allie refuses to tolerate Sam's infidelity and breaks off their relationship. She literally summons Hedy as a replacement for Sam, someone to provide her with companionship so that she will not give in to Sam's continued requests for a reconciliation. As the film progresses, Sam's infidelity is minimized, forgiven, and forgotten in comparison to the deadly threat Hedy represents. In this respect, the film differs significantly from the novel upon which it is based. A comparison of the novel with the film demonstrates that the changes wrought by the film's male screenwriter and director not only maintained the patriarchally complicit aspects of the original text but even added to its misogynist and lesbophobic elements.

A Male Fantasy of Female Friendship Transferred from Novel to Film

As I have noted in regard to a number of female friendship films, female involvement in a project does not assure a progressive text. Female screenwriters and directors who have bought into patriarchal ideology can be as effective as male filmmakers in propagating misogynist notions. Often, however, female input, even when promoting sexist ideas, tends to produce a film that, like *The Hand That Rocks the Cradle,* works against itself, providing female-affirmative messages along with sexist ones. *Single White Female,* on the other hand, is entirely a product of the male imagination, and its message, although seemingly championing the victory of a strong female character, is really an unequivocal admonition to women to forgive their men rather than risk the dangers of female companionship. Based on John Lutz's 1990 pulp novel *SWF Seeks Same* and directed by Barbet Schroeder from a screenplay written by Don Roos, the film represents an unadulteratedly male vision of manipulative female friendship.

What Roos and Schroeder take from their novelistic source is the misogynist conception of an unhealthy female friendship that develops as a result of one woman's insanity and another's need for companionship. Lutz, however, develops this situation into a sensationalistic reworking of the already overworked theme of the dangers a single women faces in the big city. In the novel, Allie is betrayed by both Hedy and Sam, who, unlike his more saintly counterpart in the film, is easily seduced by Hedy's advances. After Hedy kills Sam, Allie is mistakenly accused of his murder, which Hedy committed while impersonating Allie. Reduced to living as a fugitive from the law, Allie is finally saved by a kindly old police officer, who is the only one who believes her story. After she is exonerated and Hedy is arrested, Allie flees the dangers of New York apartment life for the security of an isolated home in rural Illinois.

The film alters the story's focus significantly from the novel's presentation of the single woman's dangerous life in the big city to the problems that result when an unforgiving woman foolishly allows her man to slip away. The novel's philandering Sam is converted into the film's devoted male lover. Although he may have transgressed in a single instance, the film's Sam thereafter demonstrates complete fidelity to Allie. The film, in fact, goes to great lengths to demonstrate this fact, even adding a sexually explicit scene not found in the novel in order to provide Sam with the opportunity to rebuff Hedy's sexual advances in a particularly sensationalistic manner. Hedy, dressed as Allie, lets herself into Sam's hotel room and deceives him into allowing her to perform oral sex on him, which the film portrays as a virtual rape. Afterward, Hedy kills Sam when he expresses outrage at her behavior, declares his undying love for Allie, and threatens to tell Allie what has happened.

A Modern Female Double Film

Single White Female's accentuation of the sexually exploitative and sensationalistic thriller aspects of its pulp fiction source, combined with émigré director Barbet Schroeder's artistic pretensions, baffled many reviewers who sought deep symbolic significance and psychological complexity in the film's female friendship portrayal. Although a number of critics felt the film's opening sequences suggest interesting thematic possibilities, ranging from an examination of the duality of human nature to the instability of contemporary urban identity, they all agreed that none of these thematic directions is fully realized and that the film is left to conclude with a muddled explanation of Hedy's psychology and a crudely graphic thriller chase scene.[14]

The film's final explanation for Hedy's psychotic behavior is of particular interest because it suggests that the major cinematic predecessors of *Single White Female* are not the thrillers, such as *Vertigo* (Hitchcock, 1958) and *Rosemary's Baby* (Polanski, 1968), to which it at times alludes, but instead the female double film. If *Single White Female* refers successfully to any previous films and develops any coherent thematic perspective at all, it is to evil twin films from the 1940s such as *The Dark Mirror* and their thematic presentation of a dangerously divided female nature. *Single White Female*, in fact, can be seen in almost every respect as a faithful reincarnation of 1940s female double films. Like its predecessors, it sets out to illustrate male conceptions of socially acceptable female behavior by representing a clash between two women. Remarkably, the film demonstrates a view of approved female behavior that is little altered from the ideas expressed in films of the 1940s. Allie represents the acceptable woman, and like the heroines in earlier double films, she is sweet, essentially passive, emotional, and asexual.

Allie's traditionally feminine qualities are perhaps less obvious than those of her predecessors in 1940s films. She is depicted, for instance, as an intelligent career woman, which might appear to distinguish her sharply from earlier "good girl" characters. Significantly, however, although she may be accomplished in her field, she is notably unsuccessful in her pursuit of her career goals. Her attempts to get a start as a freelance computer analyst culminate only in her flight from a client's sexual harassment. One might also argue that, unlike the heroines in earlier double films, who are always rescued by a man, Allie develops into an active female hero who saves herself from Hedy's final attack. Yet it is important to note that it is not Allie's heroism that, according to the film's logic, renders her a good woman in contrast to Hedy's evil, nor is it her heroic behavior that the film argues will save her in the future. In fact, many of Allie's actions, such as throwing Sam out and acting so quickly to find a female roommate, get her into trouble. The film seems to suggest that if she had been more passively forgiving of Sam and less willing to act so impetuously, she might actually have prevented the tragedies that followed.

Allie also appears to differ from her 1940s predecessors in that she is not presented as totally asexual. The film even opens with a sex scene between Allie and Sam, yet Allie's sexuality, when contrasted with Hedy's, is extremely mild and decidedly nonthreatening. A comparison of Allie's desire for a monogamous relationship with Sam to his virtual rape by Hedy makes clear Allie's portrayal as the "normal," if not asexual at least less sexual, woman in contrast to Hedy's voracious female sexual urges. The film's division between the two women in terms of their sexuality is also manifest in the fact that it is Hedy, not Allie, who is repeatedly shown in the nude, even though Allie is presented as the more attractive woman.

In contrast to Allie, Hedy clearly represents unacceptable femininity. Underneath her facade of shyness, she is assertive, cunning, sexually aggressive, and feminist. As the film develops, all of these characteristics become associated with Hedy's misuse of female power, but her major characteristic, and the one that seems to be responsible for distorting all other aspects of her personality, is her inability to forgive. It is this quality that underlies the two seemingly contradictory explanations that are offered for her insanity. Near the film's conclusion, Hedy confesses that she resents Allie because she reminds Hedy of her twin sister, who died when the two girls were children. As Hedy describes her feelings for her sister, they involve only selfishness, jealousy, and hatred. She tells Allie: "Did you know that identical twins are never really identical? There's always one who's prettier, and the one who's not does all the work. She used me, and then she left me, just like you." Later, however, after Hedy's death, Allie explains Hedy's psychological problems not in terms of her resentment toward her sister but as the result of her love for her. According to Allie, "Hedy's parents said that for years they tried to explain to her that her sister's death wasn't her fault, but she never forgave herself for surviving."

This attempt to trace Hedy's dementia to an unhealthily close love/hate relationship with her sister is part of what Lynda Hart has called *Single White Female*'s attack on sameness, an attack that can also be found in 1940s female double films. As Hart points out, Allie is punished for her "segregationist impulse," which leads her to reject Sam's difference. This rejection renders her blind to the "terrors of 'sameness'" and results in her association with a "pathological 'lesbian'" whose distorted desire for exact similarity results in her attempts not only to become just like her friend but finally even to try to destroy and replace her.[15]

The film ends, like its 1940s predecessors, with Allie, the image of purified femininity purged of evil and realigned with goodness, forever cured of her desire for sameness. The final scenes show her alone in her apartment, trying to understand Hedy and mourning the loss of Sam. In voice-over, she tells the audience that although she "cried the whole week of Sam's funeral" she now realizes that this "won't bring him back" and that she must "start letting go." Over shots of Allie's hands as they shuffle through old pictures of Hedy and her sister, Allie's voice-over informs us that she knows now that it was the inability to forgive and to forget that destroyed Hedy: "So every day I try to forgive Hedy for Sam. Then I try to do what she couldn't, forgive myself. I know what can happen to someone who doesn't." Again the film drives home its central point that women's problems stem not from their treatment by men but instead from their failure to show men enough forgiveness and understanding. Blame for female discontent is placed entirely on women themselves and specifically on their failure to forgive their male lovers.

The film's final shot is a close-up of a composite photograph, half Allie and half Hedy. This shot suggests that the doubleness of female nature remains a persistent threat to socially acceptable femininity. Allie's forgiving, passive nature must constantly struggle against the temptation to succumb to Hedy's unforgiving, aggressive, and "unfeminine" tendencies. Allie must always be on guard against the constant threat of Hedy's evil within her. Not only does the film advocate passive forgiveness as the sign of true womanhood, it also seems to propose that women must police themselves constantly against any signs of regression to an underlying state of inner "evil."

Single White Female and the Female Spectator

As a female double film, *Single White Female* encourages its female spectator to form strong bonds of engagement with its "good" female character. Allie is offered as a figure with whom the female viewer is definitely expected to empathize. We follow her through the majority of the film, in terms of spatiotemporal attachment, and are given frequent access to her thoughts and feelings. Like Claire in *The Hand That Rocks the Cradle*, Allie is expressive and transparent in her subjectivity. The spectator not only knows what she is thinking but also understands why she acts as she does. Additionally, viewers are encouraged to ally themselves morally with Allie, who is not only the "good" woman but is also good-looking, intelligent, and strong.

Jeanine Basinger's argument that the female double film contains a subversive spectatorial effect must be considered in any discussion of the relationship of *Single White Female* to its female viewers. As I have noted in chapter 1, Basinger proposes that the double film offers its female spectator a potentially subversive engagement with the character of its villainess. This engagement is similar to what I have suggested may operate for some resisting viewers in *The Hand That Rocks the Cradle*. The spectator is afforded the opportunity to engage subversively with a female character who attacks accepted standards of femininity, yet this subversion is contained within a narrative structure that allows for a final rejection of the villainess's unconventional behavior and even for approval of her punishment and defeat. In this way the film has a safety valve effect that allows for the expression of female discontent and frustration while at the same time preventing these feelings from actually resulting in a socially critical stance.

This type of female spectatorial response seems as possible in *Single White Female* as it is in *The Hand That Rocks the Cradle*, which after all could also be seen as a female double film. In both films, however, as in their 1940s predecessors, adoption of the villainess's point of view is strongly discouraged by the narrative structure. Peyton in *The Hand That Rocks the Cradle* and Hedy in *Single White Female* are so thoroughly villainized as the films progress that any initial engagement with their perspectives, which might be encouraged in Peyton's case by her position as a victim of her husband's behavior and in Hedy's by her introduction as a painfully shy outcast, is entirely repudiated.

On close examination, *Single White Female* actually offers the female spectator little opportunity to adopt Hedy's position in the narrative. Because her psychology is not explained until the film's closing minutes, the viewer is denied access to her subjectivity for most of the film. We just do not understand her behavior enough to become attached to her point of view, especially given the easy access provided to Allie's transparent subjectivity. The spectator also is rarely aligned with Hedy in terms of spatiotemporal attachment. When alignment with Allie is broken and the camera remains with Hedy, it is only to show her engaging in psychologically unhealthy or socially reprehensible behavior, which actually works to minimize rather than increase spectatorial engagement with her perspective.

The minimal possibility that the film offers for engagement with Hedy's "bad girl" role and the attachment to Allie's "good girl" persona that it strongly encourages greatly influence *Single White Female*'s attempts to create an implied female spectatorial position. Although Allie is portrayed as a woman courageous and determined enough to take action to save herself when in danger, this is not the crucial aspect of her character to which the film repeatedly returns and that it emphasizes at the conclusion. Allie's final voice-over internal monologue, which acts to implicate the spectator strongly in her perspective, accentuates most emphatically the idea that the "good" woman is she who possesses an understanding and forgiving nature.

The film's concluding focus is on forgiveness, even on forgiveness between women, as Allie resolves "to forgive Hedy for Sam," yet Allie and Hedy's friendship has up to this point been portrayed so unrelentingly as unhealthy and destructive that a female spectatorial position that is not only anti-female friendship but even antiwoman seems to be created. In spite of its ending, what *Single White Female* really proposes is not understanding and forgiveness among women, but rather the notion that any female relationship is inevitably fraught with danger and hostility. It presents a perspective on female relationships that offers none of the "ideologically implicated ambiguities" and polysemous irresolution so often found in female friendship films. This male-authored anti-female friendship text, in fact, closes down meaning in a way that is very uncharacteristic of the female friendship film cycle as a whole. It makes the point strongly and repetitively that what women need is to form alliances with men and to beware of the dangers inherent in attachments to members of their own sex.

Poison Ivy

The Teenage Enemy

Another film released in 1992 that focuses on manipulative female friendship is Kat Shea Ruben's *Poison Ivy*. Like *The Hand That Rocks the Cradle, Poison Ivy*'s creative team was composed of both men and women. The screenplay was written by director Kat Shea Ruben and her husband Andy Ruben, who also produced the film, and the story was based on an idea by Peter Morgan and Melissa Goddard. The female creative influence on the project seems to have assured, as it did in *The Hand That Rocks the Cradle,* that the film's message would be a conflicted one. This female input, however, did not by any means guarantee that the film would represent a progressive text or that it would become a popular success with female audiences. In fact, *Poison Ivy* was a disastrous failure, both critically and financially. It was almost universally condemned by reviewers as sexually exploitative soft-core pornography. Female audiences at women's film festivals also walked out in protest against what they perceived to be the film's misogynist perspective. Interestingly, *Single White Female* received no such protests. It would appear that what was particularly appalling to female viewers of *Poison Ivy* was that a woman director could make such a sexually exploitative film and such an unrelentingly negative portrait of female friendship.

In Poison Ivy *(Ruben, 1992), two rebellious teenagers, Ivy (Drew Barrymore, right) and Sylvie (Sara Gilbert) enter into a troubled friendship that involves the adolescent reactivation of the female Oedipal crisis.*

Really Three Films

Poison Ivy actually represents a combination of what could be three different films. Much of it concerns the manipulative female friendship that develops between two teenage girls, Sylvie (Sara Gilbert) and Ivy (Drew Barrymore). Sylvie is the rebellious daughter in a wealthy and extremely dysfunctional Los Angeles family. Her father, Darryl (Tom Skerritt), is the station manager at a local television station and a conservative media pundit. His beautiful wife, Georgie (Cheryl Ladd), is an invalid, suffering from an advanced case of emphysema. Both apparently are distracted, self-indulgent parents who ignore their daughter. As a result, Sylvie has distanced herself from them and even at times responds to them with open hostility. Ivy, on the other hand, is an orphan living with an uncaring aunt. When she sees Sylvie's home, she is overwhelmed by the attraction of the family's wealth. She befriends the unpopular Sylvie and insinuates herself into her friend's household, first as a perpetual houseguest and then as Sylvie's father's lover.

Certainly, this portrait of adolescent friendship has all of the characteristics of an anti-female friendship film. The intimacy shared by Sylvie and Ivy becomes destructive and even deadly as the film shows their relationship to be plagued by underlying jealousy, envy, antagonism, and betrayal. *Poison Ivy* establishes itself, however, not only as a manipulative female friendship film, but also as a sexual exploitation film. It presents with soft-core pornographic explicitness the development of an intergenerational sexual relationship between Ivy and Darryl. With obvious allusions to *Lolita* (1962), Stanley Kubrick's earlier filmic portrayal of an older man's seduction by a teenage girl, *Poison Ivy* offers graphic scenes of a sexually titillating nature. Ivy first seduces Darryl in the same room and on the very bed where his dying wife sleeps in a drug-induced stupor, later they engage in spontaneous sex on the hood of his car, and finally Sylvie walks in on her nude father having sex with her best friend on the balcony of their home.

The film's determination to exploit these pornographic moments, as well as to vilify Ivy as a traitorous female friend, clashes with its much more interesting investigation of Ivy and Sylvie's turbulent adolescent Oedipal dramas. The troubled family lives of both girls appear to have prevented them from adequately resolving their childhood Oedipal dilemmas. As a result, they experience in their teenage years a problematic reactivation of their Oedipal desires. Sylvie's rebelliousness seems to reflect her conflicted relationship with both her parents, but most notably with her mother. As the comparatively unattractive daughter of an extremely beautiful, self-absorbed mother whom she admits to having perceived in her childhood years as omnipotent, Sylvie reacts by developing a jealous, competitive nature and a low sense of self-esteem.

Sylvie's Oedipal woes are paralleled by Ivy's, whose parents appear to have been even more inaccessible than Sylvie's. According to Ivy's account of her childhood, her mother, who died of a drug overdose, was so cold and distant that she even shrank from her daughter's touch, and her father ignored and eventually abandoned her. Whereas Sylvie expresses her unresolved Oedipal difficulties through animosity to her father and intermittent attempts to establish some sense of intimacy with her mother, Ivy expresses hers through a desire to usurp Georgie's maternal role. She initiates her sexual relationship with Darryl, it would appear, merely as a path to a desired merger with Georgie; she even seduces him in the same room and on the same bed where his wife lies sleeping. This desire for fusion with a maternal figure finally leads Ivy to murder Georgie in the hope that by replacing her completely she will finally resolve her Oedipal woes.

Admittedly, *Poison Ivy*'s portrayal of the adolescent girl's Oedipal crisis, the conclusion of which is played out to melodramatic effect on a stormy summer night, is considerably overwrought, yet the film is nevertheless effective in dramatizing several important aspects of female adolescent psychological development. Through the representation of the traumatic reactivation in adolescence of an unresolved childhood Oedipal crisis, the teenage girl's need for positive identification and an open relationship with a mother figure who provides both physical and emotional intimacy is dramatically enacted. Sylvie and Ivy's experiences also dramatize the difficult process of separation/individuation experienced during female adolescence and the formation of what psychoanalysts have called the female self-in-relation. This process ideally involves not a radical break with family ties, as theorists have claimed in regard to male development, but instead the formation of a female sense of identity experienced within the context of mutually empathic relational bonds with supportive parental figures. Neither Sylvie nor Ivy has this support.

The film's conclusion suggests that Sylvie at least, if not Ivy, finally does attain a troubled resolution of her Oedipal difficulties. By killing Georgie and attempting to replace her in Darryl's affections, Ivy has in a sense usurped the maternal role. She has established a melancholic connection with the figure of her dead mother by fusing with Georgie as a maternal image. In attempting to resolve her Oedipal woes through this melancholic pathway, however, Ivy fails really to come to terms with the loss of her mother; instead, she denies this loss by internalizing it and merging with Georgie as a representation of an encrypted mother figure. Sylvie, on the other hand, at the film's conclusion attempts an Oedipal resolution involving not the melancholic encryptment of her dead mother, but instead what psychoanalysts consider the more healthy path of Oedipal development, the mourning of maternal loss. By killing Ivy, even pushing her from the very balcony on which her mother was murdered, Sylvie acknowledges the painful loss of the maternal love object. She even gives this loss metaphorical expression through language in her final voice-over confession of her continuing love/hate relationship with Ivy. As Sylvie stands looking down from the balcony at Ivy's dead body on the pavement below, her voice-over declares: "I still think about her. I guess I still love her. She might have been even more alone than I was. I miss her." This statement, ostensibly referring to Ivy, could apply as well to Sylvie's feelings for her lost mother.

Poison Ivy and the Female Spectator

In one sense, Poison Ivy is an interesting attempt to dramatize the complex and problematic process of female Oedipal development in ways remarkably similar to recent psychoanalytic theories of female maturation. The film's complex investigation of the female adolescent Oedipal crisis is compromised, however, by its association with crassly exploitative sexual material and a simplistically manipulative female friendship plot. These elements obscure the film's portrayal of Sylvie's troubled Oedipal crisis to the extent that male reviewers entirely missed this aspect of the film and instead concentrated almost exclusively on its graphic portrayal of sexually titillating intergenerational sex.[16] Female viewers, however, would not necessarily approach the film in this way. A female spectator might as easily engage with the film's reactivation of her own traumatic Oedipal crisis as with its sexually explicit material or its portrayal of manipulative female friendship.

Poison Ivy, in fact, strongly encourages the female spectator to identify with Sylvie in her progression to Oedipal resolution. Spatiotemporal alignment is confined to Sylvie for most of the film, and her intermittent voice-over narration provides repeated access to her subjectivity. The spectator's moral allegiance and empathic attachment are also directed toward Sylvie. Although her rebellious personality and nonglamorous looks can have either an implicating or an alienating effect on spectatorial engagement, her honesty and courage in comparison to the duplicity and self-absorption that characterize all of the other major characters position her as the film's moral center.

A female spectator drawn into the film by its evocation of the twinship transference situation that develops between Ivy and Sylvie might be led initially to engage with both girls. As the film progresses, however, and the focus shifts more strongly to the Oedipal narrative, it is really Sylvie's, not Ivy's, Oedipal resolution that is most thoroughly worked out. Ivy can even be considered merely a symbolic representation of Sylvie's Oedipal desires to kill her mother and seduce her father, as well as of her seemingly contradictory needs to separate herself from, yet still maintain an affectional connection with, her mother and other women in her life. The film encourages this symbolic reading by portraying Ivy as a mysterious figure who suddenly appears in Sylvie's life as if she were called up as a phantom from her unconscious. She remains nameless, merely adopting the name that Sylvie assigns to her, and her manipulative nature makes it difficult even to know if what she reveals of her past experiences and current feelings is at all accurate.

Concluding Comments

Like *The Hand That Rocks the Cradle*, *Poison Ivy* is a text that in many ways acts to dismantle itself. Its attempts to involve its spectator in Sylvie's adolescent Oedipal crisis clash with its sensationalistic aspects, and the film is pulled in contradictory directions, achieving a polysemy that actually works to tear it apart. Its manipulative female friendship plot offers the typical anti-female friendship message that women should beware of other women, who are only out to destroy them. Its graphic scenes of intergenerational sex, on the other hand, offer the audience the tawdry sexual titillation and cheap sensationalism of softcore pornography, but below this surface, the film's dramatization of a troubled female Oedipal drama works against these other elements, suggesting the difficulty of healthy female development under patriarchy, the primacy and continuing significance of female relationships in women's lives, and the crucial importance of the mother-daughter bond in providing the relational framework that influences a girl's future connections with other women.

The confusion of themes that characterizes both *Poison Ivy* and *The Hand That Rocks the Cradle* may be tied to their attempts to attract a wide audience, male and female, conservative and progressive. It also seems to reflect the amount of female involvement in the films' screenwriting and directorial assignments. *Single White Female*, a film that is entirely a product of male creative talent, has no difficulty in presenting a message strongly supportive of the patriarchal status quo. It couples its anti-female friendship theme unhesitatingly with an admonition to women to dedicate themselves completely to men. Female screenwriters and directors, on the other hand, seem compelled to complicate simplistic reworkings of patriarchal ideology with thematic concepts that contradict basic tenets of male dominance. It is hardly surprising, therefore, that the manipulative female friendship film has not become a staple of the female friendship film cycle. It recounts a male fantasy of female friendship that begins to self-destruct as soon as it is exposed to the scrutiny of the contemporary female perspective.

Conclusion
The Future of the Female Friendship Film

The female friendship film clearly represents a major contemporary cycle in the history of women's cinema. Female friendship films are currently by far the most popular category of films directed to a female audience, and this trend shows little evidence of diminishing. Films that are centrally concerned with the issue of female bonding continue to be produced in large numbers by both Hollywood and independent filmmakers. Recent productions that demonstrate the continuing viability of the cycle include *Boys on the Side* (Ross, 1995), *Moonlight and Valentino* (Anspaugh, 1995), *How to Make an American Quilt* (Moorhouse, 1995), *Now and Then* (Glatter, 1995), *Waiting to Exhale* (Whitaker, 1995), *The Baby-Sitters Club* (Mayron, 1995), *The Incredibly True Adventures of Two Girls in Love* (Maggenti, 1995), and *Bar Girls* (Giovanni, 1995).

Although the popularity of the female friendship film is apparent, its nature and effect on its projected female audience is much more uncertain. My study of the cycle's development thus far indicates that the character of the films and the nature of their address to female viewers are areas of substantial complexity. It seems clear that the films represent mixtures of progressive and regressive elements. They affirm their female audience by presenting positive female characters who can serve as sympathetic figures of identification validating the self-worth of the female spectator. The female relationships portrayed also provide examples of female friendships that offer alternatives to women's com-

236

plete dependence on men and family for self-affirmation. On the other hand, these female-affirmative qualities are repeatedly harnessed to discourses that neutralize their potentially progressive effect on women viewers. The feminist ideas expressed by the films often seem appropriated merely to provide a basis for popularly entertaining narratives rather than to offer any serious confrontation with women's issues. Even when issues important to women are broached, their presentation is typically rendered on such a personal level or the solutions proposed are so simplistic and unrealistic that the significance of women's problems is minimized rather than accentuated.

Rather than taking a strong stand on any matter, what seems most notably to characterize the female friendship film cycle is its cultivation of varying and even contradictory viewer responses, ranging from the progressive to the conservative. The films' mixture of progressive and regressive elements makes them particularly open to multiple reading possibilities, a characteristic that can be labeled polysemy, "ideologically implicated ambiguities," or simply wide audience address. In any case, this quality renders the female friendship film a highly negotiated cinematic form that represents neither a progressive challenge to the patriarchical status quo nor a reactionary prop of dominant ideology; instead, the individual films should be seen as complex instances of an intricate process of negotiation involving the intersection of the competing ideological frameworks of both the films' creators and their audiences. The complexity of the films and the multiplicity of their address does not mean, however, that they should not be examined individually and categorically for the thematic positions they assume in regard to contemporary issues, nor does it mean that their textual construction should be ignored in favor of simply studying what their audiences make of the films.

In fact, in spite of their polysemy the different types of female friendship films do attempt to speak to their female viewers in specific ways and to place these viewers in certain subject positions in regard to the texts. Sentimental female friendship films, for instance, with their focus on close, emotionally effusive ties among women and their emphasis on the nurturing and psychologically enriching qualities of these relationships offer female friendship not as a route to political action and social change but largely as a means of female social integration. The dominance of this category of female friendship films throughout the period places sentimental female friendship portrayals and their essentially conservative social message at the forefront of the cycle. The sentimental female friendship film began with an emphasis on dyadic friendships, but it moved in the late 1980s firmly into the category of group friendship portrayals, and this trend seems a particularly strong one at the current moment. In fact, the recent release of a large number of sentimental group female friendship portrayals indicates strongly that these films have come to dominate the cycle. Of the female friendship films released in 1995, all—with the exception of the openly lesbian films—were group friendship portrayals.

Group female friendship films contain one outstanding attribute of sentimental female friendship portrayals that has remained consistent throughout the period of the cycle's development. Except for early representatives of the category, such as *Julia* and *Girl Friends,* the sentimental female friendship film has consistently demonstrated a tendency to move from an initial emotionally engaging portrayal of sentimental female friendship into the realm of the social female friendship film. As the films' narratives develop, they go beyond the friends' personal psychological growth and present female friendship as a means of women's integration into the existing social structure.

Increasingly, as the cycle develops the sentimental female friendship film becomes a vehicle for the propagation of a conservative social message of female accommodation to a reformed patriarchy. Women's relationships come to represent a nurturing tie that not only binds women to each other but also leads them back from a state of alienation to renewed social involvement. This socially conforming message represents the most prominent feature of the female friendship film at the present time, and group female friendship portrayals have provided the privileged format for its expression. The current wave of sentimental group female friendship films, which include *Moonlight and Valentino, How to Make an American Quilt,* and *Boys on the Side,* all show alienated young women aided in their return to societal accommodation by the advice and consolation of a group of female friends.

The sentimental female friendship film's movement into the realm of group female friendship has not in any way diminished its sentimental qualities or the emotionality of the response it seeks to provoke in its spectator. Over the period, the movement to group female friendship films has been accompanied by a parallel progression to a heightened sentimentality that seems to have reached its peak in the late 1980s with the release of *Beaches* and *Steel Magnolias* but is still represented in such recent films as *Moonlight and Valentino* and *Boys on the Side*. In these films, as in their 1980s predecessors, a heightened emotional effect is produced not so much by the increased sentimentality of the female friendship portrayal as by its amalgamation with earlier woman's film plot formulas associated with maternal melodramas and medical discourse films. By opening up female subject positions in regard to the texts that are antithetical to progressive readings, these older woman's film forms facilitate the female friendship film's propagation of an increasingly conservative message.

In contrast to the sentimental/social female friendship film that seems currently to dominate the cycle and at the same time to contain its most regressive qualities, female friendship films that focus on female maturation and psychological development seem to offer more progressive possibilities. Represented most recently by *Now and Then* and *The Baby-Sitters Club,* these films, like their sentimental counterparts, also have moved into the realm of group friendship portrayals. The films' strong association with recent feminist theories of female psychological development, however, leads them to concentrate in ways that sentimental female friendship films do not on women's needs not only for relatedness but also for autonomy in their formation of a sense of identity. Unfortunately, these recent films still resemble earlier dyadic maturational female friendship films in that they have difficulty envisioning exactly where the female quest for autonomy might lead. Like *Desperately Seeking Susan, Housekeeping,* and *Mystic Pizza* before them, *Now and Then* and *The Baby-Sitters Club* leave their female audience with the image of women's autonomous self-determination but with few practical suggestions for where this autonomy might fruitfully find expression.

While the sentimental female friendship film has established itself as the dominant branch of the cycle, the less emotionally intense but much more patriarchically challenging political female friendship film seems to have all but disappeared. The rarity of mainstream political female friendship portrayals clearly demonstrates how limited the radical potential of the cycle really is. In fact, *Thelma & Louise* stands alone as the only contemporary female friendship film that can be read as unrecuperatedly political. Even *Thelma & Louise,* this most politically "radical" of popular female friendship films, does not provide an incisive political analysis of women's issues, but rather represents a popular culture attempt at political critique contained within a comedic female buddy road movie formula that can work to undercut the film's political message.

If *Thelma & Louise* represents the high point in the development of the political female friendship film, it also seems to have initiated the demise of this branch of the cycle. As long as the political female friendship film was strongly associated with the comedic format, the cartoonish representation of female revenge scenarios, and a fantasy happy ending as in *Nine to Five* and *Outrageous Fortune*, it continued to find limited representation. Once it became associated with female violence presented in a more serious context, as it is in *Thelma & Louise* and *Mortal Thoughts*, a movement that demonstrates a heightened level of women's political desperation, the political female friendship film seems to have become too politically challenging for mainstream cinematic representation. At the present time, political female friendship portrayals have all but completely disappeared and no longer really seem to represent a prominent branch of the cycle.

This does not mean, however, that female friendship films with political implications have not been produced since *Thelma & Louise* and *Mortal Thoughts* in 1991. Lesbian films and female friendship films that deal with race and ethnicity, such as *Go Fish* and *Mi Vida Loca,* continue to develop politically challenging thematic possibilities. Erotic female friendship portrayals, in fact, have been and continue to be a prominent branch of the cycle, represented by both ambiguously and openly lesbian representations. The progress of lesbian films throughout the period is one of the cycle's most dramatic and progressive developments. A clear movement can be seen from heterosexually conceived, male-authored representations aimed at heterosexual viewers to lesbian-authored, lesbian-directed, and lesbian-affirmative films made for lesbian audiences. The lesbian film also seems to have progressed from the simplistic "positive images approach" that merely seeks to portray gay characters in a favorable light to representations that originate within the lesbian community itself and try to portray the diversity of lesbian lifestyles with greater verisimilitude. Finally, lesbian representations throughout the period also demonstrate a movement from an earlier tradition of somber coming-out stories that focus on a woman's often painful coming to terms with her lesbianism to lighter-toned portrayals of lesbian romance and the lesbian community that reject notions of doomed lesbian love and document instead the formation of lesbian relationships that end happily.

Optimism about the progress of lesbian portrayals must be tempered, however, by recognition of the limitations to this development. The movement to lighter-toned lesbian films, for instance, seems to have resulted in a trend toward lesbian comedies, such as the recent *Bar Girls* and *The Incredibly True Adventures of Two Girls in Love,* that lack the political edge of more ambitious issue-oriented films like *Go Fish.* The lesbian film can be said in these cases to have moved to comedic affirmations of lesbian romance that fail to engage with other significant social issues. The progressive changes in the development of lesbian films also largely reflect the movement of independent films into mainstream distribution rather than substantive changes in Hollywood representational strategies, and, of course, it is Hollywood films that receive the widest theatrical distribution.

The most recent Hollywood lesbian portrayal is Whoopi Goldberg's openly lesbian character in *Boys on the Side,* a very problematic film in terms of its representation of both sexual preference and race. Although Goldberg's character is presented as openly gay, she remains throughout the film decidedly asexual. She is allowed to engage only in an ambiguously lesbian romance with a dying AIDS victim, who proclaims herself resolutely heterosexual until she is on the brink of death. Only then does she declare her love, which is never specified as either sexual or platonic, for Goldberg's character. Even in presenting an openly lesbian character, Hollyood refuses to construct an unambiguously positive representation of a lesbian relationship that ends happily. As *Boys on the Side* demonstrates, lesbians in Hollywood films are still being presented as unhappy or dying, albeit now in highly sympathetic contexts, and their relationships are shown to be plagued by ambiguity, doomed to failure, and associated with sadness, death, and disease.

If lesbian portrayals have made significant advances throughout the period at least in the independent sector, female friendship films dealing with issues of race and ethnicity have unfortunately made very little progress. Interracial, intraracial, interethnic, and intraethnic films are both rare and highly problematic in their attempts to deal with racial and minority issues. The rarity and inadequacy of these representations reflects not only the paucity of women of color involved in the film industry but also what appears to be a reluctance on the part of both Hollywood and independent filmmakers to take their films openly into the political realm that a discussion of race and ethnicity necessitates. Regrettably, the segregated nature of the industry and its apolitical tendencies have prevented female friendship films from even laying a foundation for a serious consideration of this very important issue.

Manipulative or anti-female friendship films continue surprisingly in these conservative times to be a rarity in the female friendship film cycle. Given the dominance of group sentimental/social female friendship portrayals that thematically support women's acclimation to the existing social structure, this lack of overt attacks on female friendship seems easily explained. The anti-female friendship film represents a short-lived response to the politically challenging association of female friendship and violence found in such films as *Thelma & Louise* and *Mortal Thoughts*. This branch of the cycle shows no signs of reappearance, and as long as the female friendship film continues to move in the direction of social rather than political female friendship portrayals, there appears to be no need for the anti-female friendship film's rejuvenation. In fact, the anti-female friendship film represents a very problematic division of the female friendship film cycle. Its overt attacks on female friendship risk alienating a substantial segment of its female audience, and within a cycle that attempts to achieve a wide address this quality is particularly damaging. Group sentimental/social female friendship films work much more subtly and effectively than overt anti-female friendship portrayals to subvert the radical potential inherent in representations of female bonding, yet they can still remain female affirmative on a personal level. Given this situation, the anti-female friendship film is rendered superfluous.

The Female Friendship Film and Its Female Audience

A close study of the mainstream female friendship film demonstrates that it has never really been employed as a means of overt political intervention in women's struggle against patriarchy; instead, it works subtly as a seemingly apolitical influence on women's psychological and social development. Rather than offering female friendship as the basis for the formation of a feminist collectivity that could initiate political action against a patriarchal social structure, female friendship films serve instead as explorations of female relationships and their impacts on women's personal lives. This seemingly apolitical quality masks a more conservative dimension to the films that emerges in spite of their polysemous openness to varied reading possibilities. Overwhelmingly, the portraits of female friendship and women's development offered by female friendship films serve in the end to integrate women all the more comfortably into the existing social order. This is especially true of what has come to be the dominant branch of the cycle, the sentimental/social group female friendship film. The conservative qualities of these films should not be allowed, however, to obscure their female-affirmative elements, which seem, if only indirectly, to have progressive political implications. To affirm women is to strengthen them for political action and feminist community. Inevitably, as feminist theorists have always pointed out, the personal and the political cannot be separated, and the female friendship film's effects on its female audience remain a complex mixture of conflicting influences.

Where does the female friendship film fit, for instance, with theories of female spectatorship? In the tradition of the woman's film of which it is a subgenre, the female friendship film can be said to contrast with the majority of mainstream films in that it offers its female spectator a female rather than a male spectatorial position. In viewing the female friendship film, the woman viewer can be said to avoid the necessity of oscillating or double identifying with male and female poles of spectator positioning; instead, the film overtly addresses a female audience and seems to carve out a spectatorial position that a female viewer can comfortably occupy. In spite of the female friendship film's clear address to a female spectator, however, the subject position it offers does not appear to be radically different from the one that theorists have suggested other mainstream films offer to women. Many female friendship films involve Oedipal dramas or developmental scenarios that are resolved, as Teresa de Lauretis has suggested of all mainstream films, in ways that are beneficial to patriarchy.[1] Also employed are traditional woman's film formulas taken from maternal melodramas and medical discourse films, plot conventions that Mary Ann Doane has identified as constructing a female subject position associated with masochism and overidentification with the screen image.[2]

If female friendship films possess any one decidedly progressive characteristic in regard to spectator positioning, it is a quality that Linda Williams has suggested is commonly found in female-oriented genres. Like many other films addressed to a female audience, the female friendship film's polysemous nature offers its spectator multiple entry points into the text and a number of different characters and perspectives with which to identify. Although Williams suggests that this characteristic facilitates a dialectical viewing experience in which the film is experienced from a variety of different, even contradictory, viewpoints,[3] the female friendship film clearly demonstrates that multiply proffered potential subject positions do not necessarily have this effect. Just because a viewer is offered different ways of approaching a text does not by any means guarantee that she or he will accept all these different positions. In the female friendship film, the multiplicity of subject positions offered seems to work instead merely to allow the text to avoid taking a stand on any issue and to afford viewers from different ends of the ideological spectrum the opportunity to select one of the subject positions offered and engage with the film as they choose.

If female friendship films do not radically alter the subject position offered to the female spectator in any substantial way, they do change the female spectator-text relationship in one important respect. The films' reactivation of the female developmental scenario and the early mother-daughter relationship through the portrayal of female transference situations indicates that the intrapsychic effects they may have on their female viewers can be profound. Female friendship films not only dramatize their female characters' shaping or reshaping of their sense of self, but, as Judith Kegan Gardiner has suggested about fictional portrayals of women's relationships, they reach out to their audience to implicate them in the female quest for self-development.[4] As such, they set out to form not only the self-images of their female characters but also the sense of identity of their female viewers as well.

One way that female friendship films manage this profound effect is by offering their female audience viewing pleasure that can be identified as specifically female. Part of this pleasure involves, as Jackie Stacey has suggested, an eroticized identification with the female characters presented on the screen triggered by the conflation of desire and identification found in the film's portrayal of their friendship.[5] Although this component is particularly notable in sentimental and erotic female friendship films, it does not seem to be essential to all female friendship representations. The recognition of the existence of this component in some female friendship portrayals does not necessarily result, however, as Teresa de Lauretis has suggested it might, in the blurring of female friendship and lesbian films;[6] instead, it can actually help to facilitate an understanding of the relationship between the two types of portrayals. Rather than delineating a strong break between female friendship and lesbian representations, the two types of films can perhaps best be described as existing on a continuum, with the female friendship film privileging identification and the lesbian film foregrounding desire between women.[7] In between, intermingling desire and identification, lie erotically implicated female friendship films and ambiguous lesbian films.

Much of the pleasure for female audiences in the female friendship film can be found not just in identification with and/or desire for the female characters on the screen, but in the female affirmation these portrayals afford. In fact, in addition to their polysemy, the female-affirmative nature of female friendship films seems to be their most prominent quality. The danger of this strong emphasis on female affirmation, of course, is that the films can easily fall into the category of idealized female friendship portrayals, glorifying female relationships so extravagantly that they become in essence the equivalents of what Pat O'Connor has described as mental constructs of perfect friendships created by women as replacements for imperfect real-life female bonds.[8]

Idealized female friendship portrayals, like mental constructs of women's relationships, contain a number of potentially harmful effects on female viewers. For instance, they can have a "palliative coping effect" on the female audience, providing them with emotional uplift and empty affirmation that serves as a substitute for real action to bring about needed sociopolitical change. This depoliticizing tendency is complemented by a privatizing influence that reinforces rather than challenges women's traditional confinement to the domestic sphere and discourages them from venturing into the outside world. In other words, idealized female friendship portrayals as prepackaged mental constructs of perfect female relationships can provide the female viewer with a fantasy substitute for real-life female bonding and for activity in the public sphere of work and achievement.

In analyzing the female friendship film's always mixed nature, one should not dismiss the positive effects on female audiences of the female affirmation that these films offer simply because these qualities are combined with potential dangers. The affirmation of female self-worth found in the female friendship film cannot but have a strengthening effect on women's characters. Female friendship films validate their female audience, instilling in them the self-confidence they need to interact more productively with other women and to cultivate more involvement in both private and public spheres.

Female Friendship Films: A New Direction in Women's Cinema?

Are female friendship films, as the most prominent contemporary representatives of women's cinema, merely a rehashing of old woman's film conventions or do they mark a new direction in the genre? Is their effect on female viewers substantially different from that of older woman's films of the 1930s and 1940s? The answers to these questions are neither simple nor unequivocal. These "new woman's films" are both similar to and significantly different from their predecessors. Like earlier woman's films, the female friendship film cycle represents a mixed bag of progressive and regressive films as well as films that contain both progressive and regressive elements. The films also at times reach back to adopt older woman's film formulas that position female viewers in masochistic subject positions and associate female viewing pleasure with women's victimization and with a "respeaking" of legitimate women's concerns in a way that allows the feminist message to be lost in the translation.

Female friendship films are crucially dissimilar to their predecessors, however, in one important way. I have argued that in 1930s and 1940s woman's films, contrary to Jeanine Basinger's contentions, female viewers were not offered double-voiced discourses that both empowered them and at the same time engineered their accommodation to the patriarchical status quo. What these films really offered was a decidedly conservative perspective; it was only inadvertently that they opened themselves up to alternative progressive reading possibilities. Only the resisting female viewer who interpreted the films against the grain could deconstruct their overt ideological projects and construct a liberating reading of the gaps and flaws in their textual construction. The primary function of 1930s and 1940s woman's films was overwhelmingly to convince women of the crucial importance of men in their lives and to persuade them to devote themselves all the more fully to heterosexual romance and family life.

Female friendship films offer substantially greater potential to the female audience for liberatory readings that challenge rather than support the patriarchal status quo. Whereas progressive readings of earlier woman's films necessitate "against the grain" interpretation, contemporary female friendship films offer much more polysemy and as a result allow much more room for variant reading possibilities. Because they are such complex mixtures of progressive and regressive elements, the viewer is largely left to construct the meanings she prefers, hence the films' remarkable popularity with wide and diverse female audiences. Additionally, female friendship films are substantially more female affirmative than their predecessors. They are much less likely than earlier woman's films to champion unequivocally women's total devotion to men, to denigrate female career ambitions, or to use female friendship merely as a backdrop for male-female relationships.

From a feminist perspective, what we see in the development of the contemporary female friendship film cycle is progress on a limited and equivocal basis, with some steps forward and some steps back. What is even more apparent from a study of these films is that the female friendship film is at the current time an extremely popular representative of women's cinema, one that is currently at the height of its popularity and that shows every sign of moving ahead unabated. As a result of its remarkable success and in spite of its mixed nature, the female friendship film is not a cinematic form that feminist critics can afford to ignore.

Notes

Introduction

1. For examinations of the male buddy film, see, for example, Cynthia Fuchs, "The Buddy Politic," in *Screening the Male: Exploring Masculinities in Hollywood Cinema,* ed. Steven Cohan and Ina Rae Hark (New York: Routledge, 1993), 194–212; Ed Guerrero, "The Black Image in Protective Custody: Hollywood's Biracial Buddy Films of the Eighties," in *Black American Cinema,* ed. Manthia Diawara (New York: Routledge, 1993), 237–46; Arthur Nolletti Jr., "Male Companionship Movies and the Great American Cool," *Jump Cut* 12–13 (December 1976): 35–36; Yvonne Tasker, "Black Buddies and White Heroes: Racial Discourse in the Action Cinema," in *Spectacular Bodies: Gender, Genre, and the Action Cinema* (New York: Routledge, 1993), 35–53.

2. Mary Ann Doane, *The Desire to Desire: The Woman's Film of the 1940s* (Bloomington: Indiana University Press, 1987), 3.

3. Ibid., 36.

4. Family melodramas of the 1950s that attempted to appeal to both male and female viewers include, for example, *Written on the Wind* (Sirk, 1956), *East of Eden* (Kazan, 1955), and *Giant* (Stevens, 1956).

5. Annette Kuhn, "Hollywood and New Women's Cinema," in *Films for Women,* ed. Charlotte Brunsdon (London: BFI, 1986), 126.

6. Lorraine Gamman and Margaret Marshment, "Introduction," in *The Female Gaze: Women as Viewers of Popular Culture* (Seattle: Real Comet, 1989), 3.

7. Claudette Charbonneau and Lucy Winer, "Lesbians in Nice Films," *Jump Cut* 24–25 (March 1981): 25–26.

8. Kuhn, "Hollywood and New Women's Cinema," 125–30; Julia Lesage, "The Hegemonic Female Fantasy in *An Unmarried Woman* and *Craig's Wife,*" *Film Reader 5* (1982): 83–94; Christine Gledhill, "Pleasurable Negotiations," in *Female Spectators: Looking at Film and Television,* ed. E. Deidre Pribram (London: Verso, 1988), 64–89.

9. Lesage, "The Hegemonic Female Fantasy," 91.

10. For a thorough examination of this process of negotiation, see Gledhill, "Pleasurable Negotiations."

11. Janet M. Todd, *Women's Friendship in Literature* (New York: Columbia University Press, 1980), 3–4.

12. Paulina Palmer, *Contemporary Women's Fiction: Narrative Practice and Feminist Theory* (Jackson: University Press of Mississippi, 1989), 130–1.

13. Ibid., 131.

14. Ibid.

15. Sigmund Freud, "Femininity," in *Freud and Women: A Reader,* ed. Elisabeth Young-Bruehl (New York: W. W. Norton, 1990), 362.

16. Sigmund Freud, "The Dissolution of the Oedipus Complex," in *Freud and Women: A Reader,* ed. Elisabeth Young-Bruehl (New York: W. W. Norton, 1990), 299–300.

17. See, for example, Nancy Chodorow, *The Reproduction of Mothering: Psychoanalysis and the Sociology of Gender* (Berkeley: University of California Press, 1978); Jessica Benjamin, *The Bonds of Love: Psychoanalysis, Feminism, and the Problem of Domination* (New York: Pantheon, 1988); Carol Gilligan, *In a Different Voice: Psychological Theory and Women's Development* (Cambridge: Harvard University Press, 1982); Dorothy Dinnerstein, *The Mermaid and the Minotaur: Sexual Arrangements and Human Malaise* (New York: Harper & Row, 1976).

18. Chodorow, *The Reproduction of Mothering*, 110.

19. Ibid., 125–26, 127.

20. Ibid., 206–7.

21. For a summary of the major criticisms of Dinnerstein's and Chodorow's theories, see Rosemarie Tong, *Feminist Thought: A Comprehensive Introduction* (Boulder, Colo.: Westview, 1989), especially chapter 5.

22. Jane Flax, "The Conflict between Nurturance and Autonomy in Mother-Daughter Relationships and within Feminism," *Feminist Studies* 4, no. 2 (1978): 171–89; Jane Flax, "Forgotten Forms of Close Combat: Mothers and Daughters Revisited," in *Disputed Subjects: Essays on Psychoanalysis, Politics and Philosophy* (New York: Routledge, 1993), 59–71.

23. Flax, "The Conflict between Nurturance and Autonomy," 175–76.

24. Ibid., 174–75.

25. Ibid., 177, 179.

26. Ibid., 179–80.

27. Ibid., 186.

28. Elizabeth Abel, "(E)Merging Identities: The Dynamics of Female Friendship in Contemporary Fiction by Women," *Signs* 6, no. 3 (1981): 413–35; Judith Kegan Gardiner, "The (US)es of (I)dentity: A Response to Abel on '(E)Merging Identities,'" *Signs* 6, no. 3 (1981): 442–44; Judith Kegan Gardiner, "The Heroine as Her Author's Daughter," in *Feminist Criticism,* ed. Cheryl Brown and Karen Olson (Metuchen, N.J.: Scarecrow, 1978), 244–53; Judith Kegan Gardiner, *Rhys, Stead, Lessing, and the Politics of Empathy* (Bloomington: Indiana University Press, 1989).

29. Abel, "(E)Merging Identities," 419.

30. Ibid., 421.

31. Ibid., 421, 423.

32. Gardiner, "The (US)es of (I)dentity," 442.

33. Gardiner, *Rhys, Stead, Lessing,* 164.

34. Ibid., 169, 170.

35. Laura Mulvey, "Visual Pleasure and Narrative Cinema," in *Feminism and Film Theory,* ed. Constance Penley (New York: Routledge, 1988), 57–68.

36. Ibid., 64.

37. Mary Ann Doane, untitled contribution to "The Spectatrix" (special issue), *Camera Obscura* 20–21 (1989): 142–43.

38. Giuliana Bruno, untitled contribution to "The Spectatrix" (special issue), *Camera Obscura* 20–21 (1989): 105.

39. Laura Mulvey, "Afterthoughts on 'Visual Pleasure and Narrative Cinema' Inspired by *Duel in the Sun*," in *Feminism and Film Theory*, ed. Constance Penley (New York: Routledge, 1988), 69–79.

40. Ibid., 79.

41. Mulvey, "Visual Pleasure," 62.

42. Teresa de Lauretis, *Alice Doesn't: Feminism, Semiotics, Cinema* (Bloomington: Indiana University Press, 1984), 144.

43. Ibid., 121.

44. Ibid., 134.

45. Mary Ann Doane, *Femmes Fatales: Feminism, Film Theory, Psychoanalysis* (New York: Routledge, 1991), 22.

46. Ibid., 25.

47. Linda Williams, "'Something Else besides a Mother': *Stella Dallas* and the Maternal Melodrama," *Cinema Journal* 24, no. 1 (1984): 8.

48. Ibid., 20.

49. Gaylin Studlar, *In the Realm of Pleasure: Von Sternberg, Dietrich, and the Masochistic Aesthetic* (Urbana: University of Illinois Press, 1988).

50. Miriam Hansen, "Pleasure, Ambivalence, Identification: Valentino and Female Spectatorship," *Cinema Journal* 25, no. 4 (1986): 6–32; David Rodowick, *The Difficulty of Difference* (New York: Routledge, 1991); Elizabeth Cowie, "Fantasia," *m/f* 9 (1984): 70–105.

51. Murray Smith, *Engaging Characters: Fiction, Emotion, and the Cinema* (New York: Oxford University Press, 1995), 82.

52. Ibid., 143, 188.

53. Ibid., 76–77.

54. Ibid., 97, 99.

55. Jackie Stacey, *Star Gazing: Hollywood Cinema and Female Spectatorship* (New York: Routledge, 1994), 230–31.

56. Ibid., 173.

57. Teresa de Lauretis, "Film and the Visible," in *How Do I Look? Queer Film and Video*, ed. Bad Object-Choices (Seattle: Bay, 1991), 259–62; Teresa de Lauretis, *The Practice of Love: Lesbian Sexuality and Perverse Desire* (Bloomington: Indiana University Press, 1994), 116–22. De Lauretis's objections are echoed by Judith Mayne, who sees Stacey as "wishing lesbian desire onto the screen in ways that make [her] uneasy." Judith Mayne, "Lesbian Looks: Dorothy Arzner and Female Authorship," also in *How Do I Look?* 139.

58. De Lauretis, "Film and the Visible," 250.

59. Stacey, *Star Gazing*, 29.

60. De Lauretis, "Film and the Visible," 258.

61. Flax, "Forgotten Forms of Close Combat," 59.

62. Ibid., 65, 66–67.

63. Pat O'Connor, *Friendships between Women: A Critical Review* (New York: Guilford, 1992), x.

64. Janice G. Raymond, *A Passion for Friends: Toward a Philosophy of Female Affection* (Boston: Beacon, 1986), 21; Lillian Faderman, *Surpassing the Love of Men: Romantic Friendship and Love between Women from the Renaissance to the Present* (New

York: William Morrow, 1981); Lillian Faderman, *Odd Girls and Twilight Lovers* (New York: Columbia University Press, 1991).

65. O'Connor, *Friendships between Women*, 12.

66. For a summary of this debate, see Robert A. Strikwerda and Larry May, "Male Friendship and Intimacy," in *Rethinking Masculinity: Philosophical Explorations in Light of Feminism*, ed. Larry May, Robert A. Strikwerda, and Patrick Hopkins (Lanham, Md.: Rowman & Littlefield, 1992), 95–110.

67. O'Connor, *Friendship between Women*, 31.

68. Ibid., 24, 57.

69. Ibid., 182.

1. Woman's Film Precedents

1. Molly Haskell, *From Reverence to Rape: The Treatment of Women in the Movies* (New York: Holt, Rinehart & Winston, 1974), 154.

2. Ibid., 160–61.

3. Ibid., 154.

4. Ibid., 168.

5. Mary Ann Doane, *The Desire to Desire: The Woman's Film of the 1940s* (Bloomington: Indiana University Press, 1987).

6. For a more extensive discussion of the images of women approach and its limitations, see Suzanna Danuta Walters, *Material Girls: Making Sense of Feminist Cultural Theory* (Berkeley: University of California Press, 1995), 32–47.

7. Doane, *The Desire to Desire*, 7.

8. Ibid., 19.

9. Ibid., 180.

10. Ibid.

11. Jeanine Basinger, *A Woman's View: How Hollywood Spoke to Women, 1930–1960* (New York: Knopf, 1993), 23.

12. Ibid., 13.

13. Lucy Fischer, *Shot/Countershot: Film Tradition and Women's Cinema* (Princeton, N.J.: Princeton University Press, 1989), 180–81.

14. Ibid., 184.

15. Ibid., 184–85.

16. Basinger, *A Woman's View*, 105.

17. Lucy Fischer, "Two-Faced Women: The 'Double' in Woman's Melodrama of the 1940s," *Cinema Journal* 23, no. 1 (1983): 37.

18. Basinger, *A Woman's View*, 111.

19. *A Letter to Three Wives* did not initiate this tradition of presenting women's relationships as plagued by jealousy, cattiness, and competition for men. It followed a long tradition of negative group female friendship portrayals that include, for example, such notable films as *The Women* (Cukor, 1939) and *Stage Door* (La Cava, 1937).

20. Fredric Jameson, "Reification and Utopia in Mass Culture" (1979), in *Signatures of the Visible* (New York: Routledge, 1990), 29.

2. The Sentimental Female Friendship Film

1. Janet M. Todd, *Women's Friendship in Literature* (New York: Columbia University Press, 1980), 318–19.

2. Carolyn G. Heilbrun, *Writing a Woman's Life* (New York: Ballantine, 1988), 100.

3. Joan Mellen, "The Return of Women to Seventies Film," *Quarterly Review of Film Studies* 3, no. 4 (1978): 527.

4. Charlotte Brunsdon, for instance, describes the film as one in which "a competent, political woman is mainly off-screen and progressively physically mutilated as the film progresses." Charlotte Brunsdon, "A Subject for the Seventies," *Screen* 23, nos. 3–4 (1982): 24 n. 15.

5. Mellen, "The Return of Women," 539.

6. See, for example, Janet Todd's description of Lovelace's opposition to Clarissa's friendship with Anna in Samuel Richardson's *Clarissa*, in *Women's Friendship in Literature*, 59–63. See also Pat O'Connor, *Friendships between Women: A Critical Review* (New York: Guilford, 1992), 56.

7. Mellen, "The Return of Women," 537.

8. Annette Kuhn, "Hollywood and New Women's Cinema," in *Films for Women*, ed. Charlotte Brunsdon (London: BFI, 1986), 128.

9. Claudette Charbonneau and Lucy Winer, "Lesbians in Nice Films," *Jump Cut* 24–25 (March 1981): 25.

10. Mellen, "The Return of Women," 532–33.

11. Kuhn, "Hollywood and New Women's Cinema," 128.

12. Teresa de Lauretis, *The Practice of Love: Lesbian Sexuality and Perverse Desire* (Bloomington: Indiana University Press, 1994), 121.

13. Jackie Stacey, *Star Gazing: Hollywood Cinema and Female Spectatorship* (New York: Routledge, 1994).

14. Lucy Fischer, *Shot/Countershot: Film Tradition and Women's Cinema* (Princeton, N.J.: Princeton University Press, 1989), 218.

15. Kuhn, "Hollywood and New Women's Cinema," 127.

16. Fischer, *Shot/Countershot*, 225.

17. The first screen adaptation of the play was the 1943 film of the same name starring Bette Davis and Miriam Hopkins and directed by Vincent Sherman.

18. Fischer, *Shot/Countershot*, 229.

19. John van Druten, *Old Acquaintance* (New York: Random House, 1940), 181.

20. *Rich and Famous*'s concentration on Liz's sexuality was actually praised by some reviewers as a forthright examination of female heterosexual desire. Critics especially lauded the film's presentation of sex scenes from the female point of view; see, for example, Carrie Rickey, review of *Rich and Famous, Village Voice*, October 14, 1981, 50. The most notable instance of this presentation occurs when Liz engages in anonymous sex with a young man she has picked up in the street. The camera gazes with her as she becomes sexually aroused when he seductively removes his clothes. As Lucy Fischer describes the scene: "In her room, she [Liz] drinks and watches him slowly undress, clearly lusting for his flesh. A rear-angle shot (from behind) shows him pulling down his pants, as she sits (at his pelvis level) on the bed. They make love." *Shot/Countershot*, 228. Although this scene does associate the camera's perspective with the female sexual gaze, it connects this gaze with Liz's sexual aberrance, her use of surrogate lovers, and her penchant for anonymous sex. The incident seems to evoke female sexual desire only to associate it with psychological illness rather than with healthy sexuality.

21. Fischer, *Shot/Countershot*, 232. Given Cukor's reputed homosexuality, the film can also be read as a disguised portrayal of gay male sexuality.

22. Caryn James, "Are Feminist Heroines an Endangered Species?" *New York Times*, July 19, 1989, sec. 2, p. 15.

23. Mary Ann Doane, *The Desire to Desire: The Woman's Film of the 1940s* (Bloomington: Indiana University Press, 1987), 67, 86.

24. Quoted in Lizzie Francke, *Script Girls: Women Screenwriters in Hollywood* (London: BFI, 1994), 104.

25. Iris Rainer Dart, *Beaches* (New York: Bantam, 1985), 308.

26. Carroll Smith-Rosenberg, "The Female World of Love and Ritual: Relations between Women in Nineteenth-Century America," in *Disorderly Conduct: Visions of Gender in Victorian America* (New York: Oxford University Press, 1985), 53–76 (reprinted from *Signs: Journal of Women in Culture and Society* 1, no. 1 [1975]: 1–29). Cited in Lisa Tyler, "Mother-Daughter Myth and the Marriage of Death in *Steel Magnolias*," *Film/Literature Quarterly* 22, no. 2 (1994).

27. Tyler, "Mother-Daughter Myth," 101.

28. Ibid., 102.

3. The Female Friendship Film and Women's Development

1. Nona P. Lyons, "Listening to Voices We Have Not Heard," in *Making Connections: The Relational Worlds of Adolescent Girls at Emma Willard School,* ed. Carol Gilligan, Nona P. Lyons, and Trudy J. Hammer (Cambridge: Harvard University Press, 1990), 32.

2. Recent studies of female development include Carol Gilligan, Nona P. Lyons, and Trudy J. Hammer, eds., *Making Connections: The Relational Worlds of Adolescent Girls at Emma Willard School* (Cambridge: Harvard University Press, 1990); Carol Gilligan, Janie Victoria Ward, and Jill McLean Taylor, with Betty Bardige, eds., *Mapping the Moral Domain* (Cambridge: Harvard University Press, 1988); Judith V. Jordan, Alexandra G. Kaplan, Jean Baker Miller, Irene P. Stiver, and Janet L. Surrey, eds., *Women's Growth in Connection* (New York: Guilford, 1991).

3. See Jane Root, "Celine and Julie, Susan and Susan," *Monthly Film Bulletin* 52 (October 1985): 328.

4. Lisa A. Lewis, *Gender Politics and MTV: Voicing the Difference* (Philadelphia: Temple University Press, 1990), 186.

5. Quoted in Dan Yakir, "Celine and Julie Golightly: Side-by-Side-by-Seidelman," *Film Comment* 21 (May–June 1985): 21.

6. Lewis, *Gender Politics,* 186.

7. Quoted in Yakir, "Celine and Julie Golightly," 19.

8. Quoted in ibid., 21.

9. Quoted in ibid., 20.

10. Susan Morrison, "Girls on Film: Fantasy, Desire, and Desperation," *Cineaction* 2 (Fall 1985): 3.

11. Karen Hollinger, "The Female Oedipal Drama of *Rebecca* from Novel to Film," *Quarterly Review of Film and Video* 14, no. 4 (1993): 17–30.

12. Lewis, *Gender Politics,* 185.

13. For a fuller discussion of the film's use of the good/bad girl split, see Lucy Fischer, "The Desire to Desire: *Desperately Seeking Susan*," in *Close Viewings: An Anthology of New Film Criticism,* ed. Peter Lehman (Tallahassee: Florida State University Press, 1990), 200–214.

14. Ibid., 204.

15. Quoted in Yakir, "Celine and Julie Golightly," 19.

16. Barish's screenplay, annotated as the revised second draft and dated September 5, 1984, is housed in the Academy of Motion Picture Arts and Sciences Library in Los Angeles.

17. David Edelstein, "Cheerfully Grilling Susan: The Straight Life and Wiggy Times of an Aspiring Auteur," *Village Voice,* April 2, 1985, 47.

18. Jackie Stacey, "Desperately Seeking Difference," in *The Female Gaze: Women as Viewers of Popular Culture*, ed. Lorraine Gamman and Margaret Marshment (Seattle: Real Comet, 1989), 115, 127.

19. Not all feminist critics agree with Stacey that the film expresses female homoerotic desire. Both Judith Mayne and Teresa de Lauretis, for instance, argue that Stacey is infusing erotic desire into relationships where it does not exist. Mayne sees Stacey as "wishing lesbian desire onto the screen in ways that make [her] uneasy," and de Lauretis attacks Stacey's interpretation by calling upon Freud's distinction between narcissistic or ego-libido and object-libido, between identification and desire. Judith Mayne, "Lesbian Looks: Dorothy Arzner and Female Authorship," in *How Do I Look? Queer Film and Video*, ed. Bad Object-Choices (Seattle: Bay, 1991), 139; Teresa de Lauretis, "Film and the Visible," also in *How Do I Look?* 259–62.

20. My discussion of this film is based in part on a conference paper titled "Co-parenting the Text: Forsyth's Adaptation of *Housekeeping*," which I cowrote with AnnLouise Keating, presented at the annual meeting of the South Central Modern Language Association, Memphis, Tenn., October 1992.

21. Bill Forsyth, "Houseproud," *Films and Filming* 399 (December 1987): 7.

22. Ibid., 6–7.

23. Ibid., 7.

24. Marilynne Robinson, *Housekeeping* (New York: Bantam, 1980), 180.

25. Judith Butler, *Gender Trouble: Feminism and the Subversion of Identity* (New York: Routledge, 1990), 57–72.

26. Robinson, *Housekeeping*, 214.

27. Ibid., 219.

4. The Political Female Friendship Film

1. Christine Holmlund first proposed that the late 1980s and early 1990s witnessed the rise of a group of films that she labels "deadly doll films" in "A Decade of Deadly Dolls: Hollywood and the Woman Killer," in *Moving Targets: Women, Murder, and Representation*, ed. Helen Birch (Berkeley: University of California Press, 1994).

2. See, for example, Pauline Kael, *Nine to Five* (film review), *New Yorker*, March 9, 1981, 112; Martin A. Jackson, *Nine to Five* (film review), *USA Today* magazine, March 1981, 88; Stanley Kaufman, *Nine to Five* (film review), *New Republic*, January 31, 1981, 21.

3. James R. Baron, "*9 to 5* as Aristophanic Comedy," in *Classics and Cinema*, ed. Martin M. Winkler (Lewisburg, Pa.: Bucknell University Press, 1991), 232–50.

4. Quoted in David Ansen with Peter McAlevey, "Some Down and Dirty Zingers," *Newsweek*, January 26, 1987, 76.

5. Arthur Nolletti Jr., "Male Companionship Movies and the Great American Cool," *Jump Cut* 12–13 (December 1976): 35–36.

6. Holmlund, "A Decade of Deadly Dolls," 127.

7. Ibid., 131. Both Holmlund and Birch also point out that real-life female killers are in almost every respect, including their rarity, completely unlike their screen counterparts. In contrast to the plethora of female killers that hit the screen in the late 1980s and early 1990s, statistics indicate that the percentage of women killers over history has remained at a consistently low figure. Cinematic presentations of female killers also focus on erotic or sexualized violence, whereas the vast majority of real murders by women are domestic homicides involving the killing of a husband, lover, or children, and many of them are victim precipitated, occurring in response to a history of repeated spousal abuse.

See Helen Birch, "Introduction," in *Moving Targets: Women, Murder, and Representation,* ed. Helen Birch (Berkeley: University of California Press, 1994).

    In deadly doll films, female killers are also overwhelmingly white, sexy, and beautiful, and even their violent acts are eroticized. Additionally, female murderers are rarely allowed to be as unpleasant as male killers. Typically, their actions are not brutal, mindless, or deranged. In fact, deadly doll films are much more concerned with why women would kill than with the actual killing itself. As a result, much more film time is spent investigating the motives for female killers' actions than in portraying the actions themselves. See Holmlund, "A Decade of Deadly Dolls," 128–30. Finally, female killers are not only eroticized on the screen, they are either explicitly or implicitly identified with lesbianism to a degree that is not at all representative of actual murder statistics. See Lynda Hart, *Fatal Women: Lesbian Sexuality and the Mark of Aggression* (Princeton, N.J.: Princeton University Press, 1994), x.

    8. Birch, "Introduction," 2.

    9. See Lizzie Francke, *Script Girls: Women Screenwriters in Hollywood* (London: BFI, 1994), 132.

    10. Quoted in ibid., 130.

    11. Quoted in ibid., 127.

    12. Quoted in Holmlund, "A Decade of Deadly Dolls," 281–82, n. 26.

    13. Richard Schickel, "Gender Bender," *Time,* June 24, 1991, 52.

    14. The first quote is from Bill Cosford, *Miami Herald* movie reviewer, cited in ibid.; the second is from Stuart Klawans, "Films," *The Nation,* June 24, 1991, 836. See Holmlund, "A Decade of Deadly Dolls," as well for a comprehensive overview of initial critical responses to the film.

    15. Sheila Benson, *Los Angeles Times* film critic, quoted in Schickel, "Gender Bender," 52.

    16. Pat Dowell, "The Importance of Women," in "Should We Go Along for the Ride? A Critical Symposium on *Thelma and Louise,*" *Cineaste* 18, no. 4 (1991): 28–36; Margaret Carlson, "Is This What Feminism Is All About?" *Time,* June 24, 1991, 57.

    17. Carlson, "Is This What Feminism Is All About?" 57.

    18. Quoted in Holmlund, "A Decade of Deadly Dolls," 146.

    19. Quoted in Francke, *Script Girls,* 129–30.

    20. Marsha Kinder, "*Thelma and Louise* and *Messidor* as Feminist Road Movies," in "The Many Faces of *Thelma and Louise,*" ed. Ann Martin, *Film Quarterly* 45, no. 2 (1991–92): 30.

    21. Tom Prasch, "Women Outlaws: The Sexual Politics of *Thelma and Louise,*" *Ryder Magazine,* July 17–30, 1991, 26.

    22. Harvey R. Greenberg, "*Thelma and Louise*'s Exuberant Polysemy," in "The Many Faces of *Thelma and Louise,*" ed. Ann Martin, *Film Quarterly* 45, no. 2 (1991–92): 20.

    23. Although Khouri has stated that Scott cut much of the intimate relating between the two women that was in her screenplay (see Janice C. Simpson, "Moving into the Driver's Seat," *Time,* June 24, 1991, 55), a reading of Khouri's final shooting script suggests that there was not that much to cut. The script contains only one scene in which the two women tell each other of their feelings. They discuss their fears of old age and their concerns about what they envision would happen to them in prison much more extensively than they do in the film. *Thelma & Louise* final shooting script, dated June 5, 1990 (housed in the Academy of Motion Picture Arts and Sciences Library, Los Angeles), 92–93.

    24. In the screenplay, after the two women blow up the tanker of the truck driver who sexually harassed them, Thelma asks Louise where she learned to shoot so well, and

Louise tells her, "Texas—You were right about what happened to me there." Earlier, Thelma had suggested that Louise had been raped years ago when she lived in Texas. Louise at that point tells Thelma in both screenplay and film that she never wants to talk about that again, and in the film she never does. Khouri, *Thelma & Louise* final shooting script, 116. Curiously, the version of the screenplay contained in *Thelma and Louise and Something to Talk About: Screenplays by Callie Khouri* (New York: Grove, 1996) follows the film and omits Louise's confession that she was raped in Texas.

25. Francke, *Script Girls*, 132.

26. Alice Cross, "The Bimbo and the Mystery Woman," in "Should We Go Along for the Ride? A Critical Symposium on *Thelma and Louise*," *Cineaste* 18, no. 4 (1991): 33.

27. Ibid., 34.

28. Hart, *Fatal Women*, 70.

29. Sarah Kofman, *The Enigma of Woman: Woman in Freud's Writings*, trans. Catherine Porter (Ithaca, N.Y.: Cornell University Press, 1985), 66; cited in Hart, *Fatal Women*.

30. Hart, *Fatal Women*, 70.

31. Kinder, "*Thelma and Louise*," 30.

32. Elayne Rapping, "Feminism Gets the Hollywood Treatment," in "Should We Go Along for the Ride? A Critical Symposium on *Thelma and Louise*," *Cineaste* 18, no. 4 (1991): 31, 30.

33. In spite of the film's attempts to foreground its heroines' heterosexuality, its polysemic qualities are too strong to prevent lesbian readings of the women's relationship. Lesbian interpretations of the film have, in fact, been proposed by Cathy Griggers, "*Thelma and Louise* and the Cultural Generation of the New Butch-Femme," in *Film Theory Goes to the Movies*, ed. Jim Collins, Hilary Radner, and Ava Preacher Collins (New York: Routledge, 1993), 129–41; and by Hart, *Fatal Women*, 65–80.

34. Carol J. Clover, "High and Low: The Transformation of the Rape-Revenge Movie," in *Women and Film: A Sight and Sound Reader*, ed. Pam Cook and Philip Dodd (Philadelphia: Temple University Press, 1993), 84; Peter Lehman, "'Don't Blame This on a Girl': Female Rape-Revenge Films," in *Screening the Male: Exploring Masculinities in Hollywood Cinema*, ed. Steven Cohan and Ina Rae Hark (New York: Routledge, 1993), 106.

35. Lehman, "'Don't Blame This on a Girl,'" 107, 113.

36. Ibid., 108.

37. Harlan's appearance is changed significantly from Khouri's screenplay, which describes him as a heavyset man in his late forties.

38. This is another change that Scott made from the screenplay, which has Louise shoot Harlan in the face. Khouri, *Thelma & Louise* final shooting script, 27.

39. Clover, "High and Low," 84.

40. Ibid., 81.

41. Many critics praised the film for the acting performances of its stars, Demi Moore, Glenne Headly, and Bruce Willis, its successful mixture of black comedy and suspense, director Alan Rudolph's stylized visuals, and its avoidance of the cheap shock tactics reviewers associate with the Hollywood thriller formula. Positive reviews of the film include those by Jay Carr, *Boston Globe*, April 19, 1991, Arts and Film sec., p. 44; and Dave Kerr, *Chicago Tribune*, April 19, 1991, Friday: Take 2 sec., p. C. Others summarily dismissed the film, criticizing especially its classist stance in regard to its working-class characters, Rudolph's "artsy" visuals, and Willis's "overblown, sweaty, naturalistic" performance. The film's ending easily took the heaviest beating, seen as so tricky that it left viewers feeling deceived and annoyed. Negative reviews include those by Mike Clark, *USA Today*, April 19, 1991, Life sec., p. 2D; Vincent Canby, *New York Times*, April 19, 1991, C1; and Peter Rainer, *Los Angeles Times*, April 19, 1991, F1.

42. Jonathan Romney, "*Mortal Thoughts*," *Sight and Sound* 1, no. 7 (1991): 49.

43. Hart, *Fatal Women*, x.

44. This reduction of female friendship to mere sympathetic commiseration is even more literally and sentimentally presented in an earlier version of the film's screenplay. In that version, Cynthia tells only one story, and it is the final account that in the film she experiences only later as a flashback in her car. After having confessed, she meets Joyce in the hallway, where Joyce is waiting to give her own statement. Joyce sits next to Cynthia and asks if she said anything. Cynthia leans forward and begins to cry as Joyce puts her arm around her friend's shoulder. The screenplay ends with the two women weeping together, a perfect image of social female friendship. (The revised shooting script for *Mortal Thoughts,* dated February 18, 1990, is housed in the Academy of Motion Picture Arts and Sciences Library, Los Angeles.)

45. Kofman, *The Enigma of Woman*, 65.

46. Catherine Clément and Hélène Cixous, *The Newly Born Woman*, trans. Betsy Wing (Minneapolis: University of Minnesota Press, 1986), 5.

47. Martine Debaisieux, "From Criminality to Hysteria: Translating the Marquise de Merteuil," *Romantic Review* 78, no. 4 (1987): 468.

48. Lynda Hart sees Cynthia as a rebellious hysteric using her feigned desire to cooperate with the detective as a ruse to lead him astray. *Fatal Women*, 81–82. What Hart does not recognize is that Cynthia's hysteria in the end works not to deceive the detective but to facilitate her submission to his authority.

49. Ibid., 87.

50. For a full treatment of the use of voice-over in narrative film, see Sarah Kozloff, *Invisible Storytellers: Voice-Over Narration in American Fiction Film* (Berkeley: University of California Press, 1988).

51. For an extended treatment of the use of voice-over narration in these two genres, see Karen Hollinger, "*Embattled Voices: The Narrator and the Woman in Film Noir and the Woman's Film*" (Ph.D. diss., University of Illinois, Chicago, 1990); and for its use in selected film noir texts of the 1940s, see Hollinger, "Film Noir, Voice-Over, and the Femme Fatale," in *Film Noir Reader,* ed. Alain Silver and James Ursini (New York: Limelight Editions, 1996), 243–59.

52. For an extended discussion of the use of a confessing narrator in film noir, see my "Film Noir, Voice-Over, and the Femme Fatale."

53. Jackie Stacey, *Star Gazing: Hollywood Cinema and Female Spectatorship* (New York: Routledge, 1994), 229–32.

54. Tania Modleski, *Loving with a Vengeance: Mass-Produced Fantasies for Women* (New York: Methuen, 1982), 97–98.

55. Stacey, *Star Gazing*, 120–21.

56. Jay Carr, "*Leaving Normal* Slips into Sitcom," *Boston Globe*, April 29, 1992, Arts and Film sec., p. 44.

57. *Leaving Normal* was, in fact, in production at the same time as *Thelma & Louise* and was originally scheduled to open in 1991; see Mike Clark, "Road Movie 'Normal': Driving without a Map," *USA Today,* April 29, 1992, Life sec., p. 5D. One is therefore forced to conclude that it was not a deliberate conservative reworking of the earlier film's plot, although it certainly reads like one.

58. The quote that heads this section is from Steve Murray, "This Muddled Buddy Movie Is Far from Normal," *Atlanta Constitution,* May 1, 1992, H7.

59. The backlash in the industry against the film is also indicated by the fact that after having written this blockbuster hit, Khouri did not get another screenplay produced until 1995, when *Something to Talk About* (Hallstrom), a much less politically challenging film than *Thelma & Louise,* was released.

5. The Erotic Female Friendship Film

1. For a history of lesbian representations in film, see Andrea Weiss, *Vampires and Violets: Lesbians in Film* (New York: Penguin, 1992), especially chapter 6, which provides an overview of lesbian independent cinema.

2. The contemporary film that initiated the cycle of ambiguously lesbian films is *Entre Nous* (Kurys, 1983), a French feature that deals with the friendship/love affair between two married women. It found limited art house distribution in the United States at the time of its release.

3. Towne's prior screenwriting credits include such popular successes as *Bonnie and Clyde* (Penn, 1967), *Chinatown* (Polanski, 1974), and *Shampoo* (Ashby, 1975).

4. Elizabeth Ellsworth, "Illicit Pleasures: Feminist Spectators and *Personal Best*," *Wide Angle* 8, no. 2 (1986): 49.

5. Quoted in Christine Holmlund, "When Is a Lesbian Not a Lesbian? The Lesbian Continuum and the Mainstream Femme Film," *Camera Obscura* 25–26 (January–May 1991): 150.

6. Quoted in ibid., 154.

7. Chris Straayer, "*Personal Best*: Lesbian/Feminist Audience," *Jump Cut* 29 (February 1984): 41–42.

8. Linda Williams, "*Personal Best*: Women in Love," in *Films for Women*, ed. Charlotte Brunsdon (London: BFI, 1986), 146.

9. Straayer, "*Personal Best*," 43.

10. Williams, "*Personal Best*," 150.

11. Richard Dyer, "Stereotyping," in *Gays in Film*, rev. ed., ed. Richard Dyer (New York: New York Zoetrope, 1984), 34.

12. Ibid.

13. Holmlund, "When Is a Lesbian Not a Lesbian?" 155.

14. Williams, "*Personal Best*," 151.

15. Ibid.

16. Chris Straayer, "The Hypothetical Lesbian Heroine," *Jump Cut* 35 (1990): 50.

17. Ibid.

18. Sue Ellen Case, "Towards a Butch-Femme Aesthetic," *Making a Spectacle: Feminist Essays on Contemporary Women's Theater*, ed. Lynda Hart (Ann Arbor: University of Michigan Press, 1989), 282–89.

19. Straayer, "*Personal Best*," 42.

20. Ellsworth, "Illicit Pleasures," 53.

21. Ibid., 55.

22. Robert Towne, screenplay for *Personal Best*, dated February 22, 1980, revised February 27, 1980 (housed in the Academy of Motion Picture Arts and Sciences Library, Los Angeles), 168.

23. Williams, "*Personal Best*," 154.

24. *Lianna* has been given substantial attention by feminist critics disproportionate to its actual mainstream theatrical distribution. Feminist critical analyses of the film include those by Mandy Merck, "'Lianna' and the Lesbians of Art Cinema," in *Films for Women*, ed. Charlotte Brunsdon (London: BFI, 1986), 166–75; and Lucy Fischer, *Shot/Countershot: Film Tradition and Women's Cinema* (Princeton, N.J.: Princeton University Press, 1989), 260–68.

25. Jackie Stacey indicates that *Desert Hearts* was voted most popular lesbian feature in a 1992 survey of British lesbian audiences. Jackie Stacey, "'If You Don't Play, You Can't Win': *Desert Hearts* and the Lesbian Romance Film," in *Immortal Invisible:*

Lesbians and the Moving Image, ed. Tamsin Wilton (New York: Routledge, 1995), 94. Deitch describes the film's initial reception as follows: *"Desert Hearts* . . . is still one of the highest-grossing independent features right now. When we opened in New York, we came within tickets of breaking the house record for the cinema—and that was previously held by *Rocky III."* Quoted in Stacey, 94.

26. Teresa de Lauretis, for example, criticizes *Desert Hearts* for making its lesbian romance "in every other respect the same as any other" and therefore neglecting to represent the specificity of lesbian experience. Teresa de Lauretis, "Film and the Visible," in *How Do I Look? Queer Film and Video,* ed. Bad Object-Choices (Seattle: Bay, 1991), 256. Christine Holmlund categorizes the film with other lesbian films of the early 1980s, like *Personal Best* and *Lianna,* and criticizes them all for presenting "a standardized and homogenized view of lesbianism" that denies difference "through a relatively asexual definition of lesbian love." "When Is a Lesbian Not a Lesbian?" 166. Mandy Merck, on the other hand, sees the appeal of the film's "standard plot line" of popular romance as enhanced by the uniqueness of the lesbian element, yet she still condemns the film for divesting its novelistic source of its social and political implications in order to reduce it entirely to a personal love story. Mandy Merck, *"Desert Hearts," Independent,* July 1987, 16. Similarly, Cindy Patton criticizes the film's narrative structure as "'too male,' not different enough from the traditional boy-gets-girl plot to amount to more than the insertion of lesbians into someone else's story." Cindy Patton, "The Cum Shot: Three Takes on Lesbian and Gay Sexuality," *Outlook* 3 (Fall 1988): 73. Martha Gever sees the film not as a replication of popular romance conventions but as "faithfully repeat[ing] conventions of 'art' cinema that use 'the figure of the woman to signify sexual pleasure, sexual problems, sex itself,' and thus hardly depart from gendered codes so dear and central to patriarchical institutions." Martha Gever, "Girl Crazy: Lesbian Narratives in *She Must Be Seeing Things* and *Damned If You Don't," Independent,* July 1988, 15. Even Jackie Stacey, who recognizes the film's obvious popularity with lesbian audiences, still labels it a failure, lacking in emotional intensity. For her, the whole idea of a popular lesbian romance film is a "contradiction in terms," if, as she suggests, popular indicates using "recognizable Hollywood conventions." Stacey, "'If You Don't Play,'" 112.

27. De Lauretis, "Film and the Visible," 256.

28. Stacey, "'If You Don't Play,'" 111.

29. In a letter to Deitch (contained in the clippings file for the film, housed in the Academy of Motion Picture Arts and Sciences Library in Los Angeles), Rule expressed her confidence in Deitch's production and her belief that the film would not crudely exploit its lesbian content.

30. Stacey, "'If You Don't Play,'" 94.

31. As Deitch indicates in the film's press packet, "We redid one car-mount shot, but other than that, if we didn't get it, we didn't get it." *Desert Hearts* production notes (housed in the Academy of Motion Picture Arts and Sciences Library, Los Angeles), 3.

32. Several scenes substantiate this interpretation. Early in the film, Cay and Vivian meet in the ranch kitchen as Cay attempts to make herself a midnight snack without waking Frances. Her attempt is unsuccessful, and Frances awakens and asks Cay to bring her a bottle of soda. As Jackie Stacey points out, the subsequent meeting between Frances and Cay in Frances's bedroom is filmed using conventions associated with love scenes. Frances pulls the half-unclothed Cay into bed next to her, and Deitch cuts to an overhead medium close-up of the two women's faces next to each other on a pillow as they touch and talk intimately (Stacey, "'If You Don't Play,'" 100–101). Later, Frances dances with Cay at Silver's engagement party, and when she and Cay embrace and declare their love for each other after Silver's wedding, Frances breaks from the embrace, insisting, "Look at us . . . standing in the middle of the street . . . next thing you know they'll be talking about me."

33. De Lauretis, "Film and the Visible," 256 n. 30.

34. Jane Rule, *Desert of the Heart* (Tallahassee, Fla.: Nyad, 1985), 9.

35. Marilyn R. Farwell, "Heterosexual Plots and Lesbian Subtexts: Toward a Theory of Lesbian Narrative Space," in *Lesbian Texts and Contexts: Radical Revisions,* ed. Karla Jay and Joanne Glasgow (New York: New York University Press, 1990), 102.

36. Merck, "*Desert Hearts,*" 16.

37. Teresa de Lauretis, *The Practice of Love: Lesbian Sexuality and Perverse Desire* (Bloomington: Indiana University Press, 1994), 88.

38. Stacey, "'If You Don't Play,'" 107.

39. Holmlund, "When Is a Lesbian Not a Lesbian?" 153.

40. Ibid., 160.

41. Stacey, "'If You Don't Play,'" 107.

42. Holmlund, "When Is a Lesbian Not a Lesbian?" 153.

43. *Desert Hearts* production notes, 1.

44. De Lauretis, *The Practice of Love,* 265.

45. Ibid., 263.

46. For another reading of the film that also argues for its reduction of the novel's lesbian and racial dimensions, but regards the film's revisions in a somewhat more positive light than I do, see Jenifer Ross Church, "The Balancing Act of *Fried Green Tomatoes,*" in *Vision/Revision: Adapting Contemporary Fiction by Women to Film,* ed. Barbara Tepa Lupack (Bowling Green, Ohio: Bowling Green State University Popular Press, 1996), 193–209.

47. Lisa M. Walker, "How to Recognize a Lesbian: The Cultural Politics of Looking Like What You Are," *Signs* 18, no. 4 (1993): 875.

48. Judy Grahn, *Another Mother Tongue: Gay Words, Gay Worlds* (Boston: Beacon, 1984), 85; quoted in ibid., 881–82.

49. Clare Whatling, "Reading Awry: Joan Nestle and the Recontextualization of Heterosexuality," in *Sexual Sameness: Textual Differences in Lesbian and Gay Writing,* ed. Joseph Bristow (New York: Routledge, 1992), 217.

50. Quoted in ibid., 219.

51. Quoted in David Ehrenstein, "*Fried Green Tomatoes* Caps a Banner Year for Delesbianization," *Advocate,* February 11, 1992, 67.

52. Ibid., 57.

53. Christine Holmlund, "Cruisin' for a Bruisin': Hollywood's Deadly (Lesbian) Dolls," *Cinema Journal* 34, no. 1 (1994): 36.

54. Ibid., 40.

55. Ibid., 41.

56. Ibid., 40.

57. Ibid.

58. Ehrenstein, "*Fried Green Tomatoes,*" 67.

59. Adrienne Rich, "Compulsory Heterosexuality and Lesbian Existence," *Signs* 5, no. 4 (1980): 631–60.

60. For a sampling of responses to the film, see Elliot, "Review: *Claire of the Moon,*" *Off Our Backs* 23, no. 6 (1993): 16; Thyme S. Siegel, "In Defense of *Claire,*" *Off Our Backs* 23, no. 9 (1993): 26, 34; Nicole Conn, "What Price, Entertainment," *Off Our Backs* 23, no. 11 (1993): 20.

61. For extended descriptions of their production difficulties and distribution successes, see Rose Troche's and Guinevere Turner's forewords to the film's published screenplay, *Go Fish* (Woodstock, N.Y.: Overlook, 1995), 11–32.

62. See, for instance, Emanuel Levy, "Girl Meets Girl," *Advocate,* June 14, 1994, 93–94.

63. Quoted in David Ansen with Abigail Kuflik, "No Angst, Just a Happy Romance," *Newsweek*, June 27, 1994: 53–54.

64. Quoted in ibid., 54.

65. Michele Kort, "Gone Fishing," *Advocate*, February 8, 1994, 59.

66. Jonathan Romney, "Angling for Controversy," *New Statesman and Society*, July 15, 1994, 33.

67. Ibid.

68. Ibid.

69. Ansen, "No Angst," 54.

70. Kort, "Gone Fishing," 59.

71. Quoted in Ansen, "No Angst," 54.

72. Martha Baer, "Go Figure," *Village Voice*, June 27, 1994, 69.

6. The Female Friendship Film and Women of Color

1. This scene with the black bicyclist is not found in Callie Khouri's final shooting script for *Thelma & Louise*. Lizzie Francke suggests in *Script Girls: Women Screenwriters in Hollywood* (London: BFI, 1994) that Scott added the scene during shooting to lighten the film's mood as it moved toward its dramatic conclusion (134).

2. Yvonne Tasker, *Spectacular Bodies: Gender, Genre, and the Action Cinema* (New York: Routledge, 1993), 32.

3. Quoted in Jacqueline Bobo, *Black Women as Cultural Readers* (New York: Columbia University Press, 1995), 74.

4. Quoted in ibid., 75.

5. See, for instance, James A. Miller, "From Sweetback to Celie: Blacks on Film into the 80s," in *The Year Left 2*, ed. Mike Davis, Manning Marable, Fred Pfeil, and Michael Sprinkler (London: Verso, 1987), 139–59; Andrea Stuart, "*The Color Purple:* In Defense of Happy Endings," in *The Female Gaze: Women as Viewers of Popular Culture* (Seattle: Real Comet, 1989), 60–75; Ed Guerrero, "The Slavery Motif in Recent Popular Cinema," *Jump Cut* 33 (February 1988): 52–59; Sara Halprin, "*The Color Purple:* Community of Women," *Jump Cut* 31 (March 1986): 1, 28; Manthia Diawara, "Black Spectatorship: Problems of Identification and Resistance," in *Black American Cinema*, ed. Manthia Diawara (New York: Routledge, 1993), 211–20; Michelle Wallace, "Blues for Mr. Spielberg," *Village Voice*, March 18, 1986, 21–26.

6. Jacqueline Bobo, "Reading through the Text: The Black Woman as Audience," in *Black American Cinema*, ed. Manthia Diawara (New York: Routledge, 1993), 279.

7. For an analysis of the differences in the treatment of white racism in the novel and the film, see Stuart, "*The Color Purple.*"

8. Ibid., 69–70.

9. Cheryl B. Butler, "*The Color Purple* Controversy: Black Woman Spectatorship," *Wide Angle* 13, nos. 3–4 (1991): 63.

10. Bobo, *Black Women as Cultural Readers*, 68.

11. Bobo, "Reading through the Text," 275.

12. Stuart, "*The Color Purple*," 71–72.

13. Jacqueline Bobo, "Black Women in Fiction and Nonfiction: Images of Power and Powerlessness," *Wide Angle* 13, nos. 3–4 (1991): 78; SDiane A. Bogus, "The 'Queen B' Figure in Black Literature," in *Lesbian Texts and Contexts: Radical Revisions*, eds. Karla Jay and Joanne Glasgow (New York: New York University Press, 1990), 275–90.

14. Michelle Wallace even suggests in "Blues for Mr. Spielberg" that Shug's reconciliation with her father represents the film's climax (24).

15. Bobo, *Black Women as Cultural Readers,* 29.

16. See, for instance, Marcia Pally, "When the Gaze Is Gay: Women in Love," *Film Comment* 22, pt. 2 (1987): 36; Wallace, "Blues for Mr. Spielberg," 24.

17. Pally, "When the Gaze Is Gay," 36.

18. Bobo, *Black Women as Cultural Readers,* 115.

19. Wallace, "Blues for Mr. Spielberg," 24.

20. Ibid., 25.

21. According to Jacqueline Bobo, the film earned $95 million in its first year of release, with production costs amounting to only $15 million. It also drew a substantial audience when broadcast on network TV and is at the top of the list of black-themed video rentals. *Black Women as Cultural Readers,* 61–62.

22. Ibid., 3.

23. bell hooks, "The Oppositional Gaze: Black Female Spectators," in *Black American Cinema,* ed. Manthia Diawara (New York: Routledge, 1993), 288–302.

24. Jacqueline Bobo even goes so far as to propose that Spielberg replaces Celie with Albert as the film's protagonist. According to Bobo, the film is transformed under Spielberg's direction into "a chronicle of an abusive black man's journey to self-understanding" and ultimate redemption. *Black Women as Cultural Readers,* 69.

25. Alice Walker did, in fact, express her support for and approval of the film. When *The Color Purple* was released, Spielberg announced in interviews that Walker not only thought highly of the film but was even on the set during shooting 50 percent of the time. Quoted in Pally, "When the Gaze Is Gay," 36; see also Donald Chase, "Spielberg Speaks Out," *Millimeter* 14 (February 1986): 57. Walker herself is quoted as having said the following in regard to Spielberg's direction: "What impressed me was Steven's absolute grasp of the essentials of the book, the feeling, the spirit. We may miss our favorite part, but what is there will be its own gift . . ." (Quoted in Wallace, "Blues for Mr. Spielberg," 26.

26. Butler, "*The Color Purple,*" 68.

27. Jane Shattuc, "Having a Good Cry over *The Color Purple*: The Problem of Affect and Imperialism in Feminist Theory," in *Melodrama: Stage, Picture, Screen,* ed. Jacky Bratton, Jim Cook, and Christine Gledhill (London: BFI, 1994), 150.

28. It was not until 1995 that another Hollywood intraracial female friendship film, *Waiting to Exhale,* found mainstream release. See my discussion of this film in the concluding section of this chapter.

29. Maitland McDonagh, "Sad Girls," *Film Comment* 30, no. 5 (1994): 76.

30. Rosa Linda Fregoso, "Hanging Out with the Homegirls? Allison Anders's *Mi Vida Loca,*" *Cineaste* 21, no. 3 (1995): 37.

31. Tim Car, "Gangsta Love," *Houston Post,* August 7, 1994, G1.

32. Fregoso, "Hanging Out with the Homegirls?" 36.

33. Ibid., 37.

34. Candice Russell, "Lopez Lends Mousie Her Moxie in 'Vida Loca,'" *Sun-Sentinel* (Fort Lauderdale, Fla.), October 30, 1994, 1F; Car, "Gangsta Love," G1.

35. Quoted in Car, "Gangsta Love," G1.

36. In "Hanging Out with the Homegirls?" Fregoso mentions, for instance, Kevin Thomas, "The Road to 'Mi Vida Loca' Paved with Good Intentions," *Los Angeles Times,* July 22, 1994; Pat Dowell, "Poor Creatures," *In These Times,* August 8, 1994; and Susan Gerhard, "True Colors," *San Francisco Bay Guardian,* August 3, 1994 (37).

37. Car, "Gangsta Love," G1; Fregoso, "Hanging Out with the Homegirls?" 37.

38. Fregoso, "Hanging Out with the Homegirls?" 37.

39. Ibid.

40. Car, "Gangsta Love," G1.

41. See, for example, Fregoso, "Hanging Out with the Homegirls?" 36.

42. Anders has been quoted as saying that she tried to avoid making judgments about her characters' actions: "I felt like it was inappropriate. The film basically is a melodrama, not a social drama. Because of that, it isn't really involved with the criminality of these characters. It's more involved with their inner lives." Car, "Gangsta Love," G1.

43. Quoted in McDonagh, "Sad Girls," 75.

44. Quoted in Fregoso, "Hanging Out with the Homegirls?" 37.

45. Sheila McLaughlin's independent feature *She Must Be Seeing Things* (1987) presents an interracial lesbian couple, but the film did not find mainstream distribution and was shown only on the film festival circuit. For an extensive analysis of *She Must Be Seeing Things,* see Teresa de Lauretis's essay "Film and the Visible," in *How Do I Look? Queer Film and Video,* ed. Bad Object-Choices (Seattle: Bay, 1991), 223–63, which is also included as chapter 3 of de Lauretis's *The Practice of Love: Lesbian Sexuality and Perverse Desire* (Bloomington: Indiana University Press, 1994). Of note as well is the discussion of the film that follows "Film and the Visible" in *How Do I Look?* (264–76) and concerns in part the film's failure to deal with the racial issues raised by its focus on a biracial lesbian couple.

46. See Elizabeth Schultz, "Out of the Woods and into the World: A Study of Interracial Friendships between Women in American Novels," in *Conjuring: Black Women, Fiction and Literary Tradition,* ed. Marjorie Pryse and Hortense Spillers (Bloomington: Indiana University Press, 1985), 67–85.

47. Ibid., 74.

48. Ed Guerrero, *Framing Blackness: The African American Image in Film* (Philadelphia: Temple University Press, 1993), 131–32.

7. Backlash

1. Lucy Fischer, in fact, views *The Hand That Rocks the Cradle* not as an anti-female friendship film at all, but rather as a "maternal thriller." For her analysis of the film, see *Cinematernity: Film, Motherhood, Genre* (Princeton, N.J.: Princeton University Press, 1996), 135–44.

2. One might add to the anti-female friendship category other thrillers that contain elements of female friendship as part of the backgrounds of their plots. Recent examples would include *Black Widow* (Rafelson, 1987) and *Diabolique* (Chechik, 1996), films that seem to stand on the periphery of the female friendship cycle.

3. Susan Faludi, quoted in Markie Robson-Scott, "Hitting Parents Where It Hurts," *Guardian,* March 11, 1992: 20; cited in Lizzie Francke, *Script Girls: Women Screenwriters in Hollywood* (London: BFI, 1994), 134. See Faludi's *Backlash: The Undeclared War against American Women* (New York: Crown, 1991).

4. Quoted in Francke, *Script Girls,* 134–35.

5. Quoted in ibid., 135, 134.

6. Quoted in ibid., 135.

7. Quoted in ibid.

8. Quoted in ibid., 134.

9. Quoted in ibid., 135.

10. Quoted in ibid.

11. Ibid., 134.

12. Joseph Natoli, *Hauntings: Popular Film and American Culture, 1990–1992* (Albany: State University of New York Press, 1994), 69-70.

13. Lynda Hart, *Fatal Women: Lesbian Sexuality and the Mark of Aggression* (Princeton, N.J.: Princeton University Press, 1994), 173 n. 40.

14. A sampling of reviewers who tried to find something more in the film than a sexually explicit thriller includes Michael Rechtshaffen, "Thriller Combines the Carnal with Carnage," *Financial Post,* August 17, 1992, sec. 5, p. S7; Janet Maslin, "Whose Life Is It, Anyway?" *New York Times,* August 16, 1992, sec. 2, p. 12; Jay Carr, *"Single White Female* Skims the Surface of Evil," *Boston Globe,* August 14, 1992, Living sec., p. 41; Dave Kehr, "Roommate with a View," *Chicago Tribune,* August 14, 1992, Friday sec., p. C; Eleanor Ringel, "Single, White, Screwy *Female* Packs Some Singularly Chilling Thrills," *Atlanta Journal and Constitution,* August 14, 1992, E1; Peter Rainer, *"SWF* Finds Roomie Who Splits More Than Rent," *Los Angeles Times,* August 14, 1992, F1.

15. Hart, *Fatal Women,* 114–15.

16. For a sampling of reviews that focus on the film's sexual content, see Jay Carr, *"Poison Ivy,"* *Boston Globe,* June 26, 1992, Arts and Film sec., p. 29; Stephen Hunter, *"Poison Ivy:* A Work of Terminal Murk," *Toronto Star,* June 26, 1992, C5; Malcolm Johnson, *"Poison Ivy* Suffers from Bad Case of Predictability," *Hartford Courant,* May 30, 1992, B6.

Conclusion

1. Teresa de Lauretis, *Alice Doesn't: Feminism, Semiotics, Cinema* (Bloomington: Indiana University Press, 1984), 134.

2. Mary Ann Doane, *The Desire to Desire: The Woman's Film of the 1940s* (Bloomington: Indiana University Press, 1987), 7.

3. Linda Williams, "'Something Else besides a Mother': *Stella Dallas* and the Maternal Melodrama," *Cinema Journal* 24, no. 1 (1984): 20.

4. Judith Kegan Gardiner, "The (US)es of (I)dentity: A Response to Abel on '(E)Merging Identities,'" *Signs* 6, no. 3 (1981): 442.

5. Jackie Stacey, "Desperately Seeking Difference," in *The Female Gaze: Women Viewers of Popular Culture,* ed. Lorraine Gamman and Margaret Marshment (Seattle: Real Comet, 1989), 129.

6. Teresa de Lauretis, "Film and the Visible," in *How Do I Look? Queer Film and Video,* ed. Bad Object-Choices (Seattle: Bay, 1991), 258.

7. See Christine Holmlund's "When Is a Lesbian Not a Lesbian? The Lesbian Continuum and the Mainstream Femme Film," *Camera Obscura* 25–26 (January–May 1991): 146–47, for a discussion of the use of Rich's idea of a lesbian continuum in regard to ambiguous lesbian films.

8. Pat O'Connor, *Friendships between Women: A Critical Review* (New York: Guilford, 1992), 57.

Index

Karen Hollinger is associate professor of film and literature at Armstrong Atlantic State University. She is coeditor, with Virginia Wright Wexman, of *Letter from an Unknown Woman* and has published numerous articles on representations of women in film.